HEALTH CARE FOR STUDENTS WITH DISABILITIES

HEALTH CARE FOR STUDENTS WITH DISABILITIES

An Illustrated Medical Guide for the Classroom

by

J. CAROLYN GRAFF, R.N., M.N.
University Affiliated Program
The University of Kansas Medical Center

MARILYN MULLIGAN AULT, Ph.D.
Department of Special Education
The University of Kansas

DOUG GUESS, Ed.D.
Department of Special Education
The University of Kansas

MARIANNE TAYLOR, R.N., M.S.
Children's Development and Rehabilitation Unit
The Oregon Health Sciences University

and

BARBARA THOMPSON, Ph.D.
Department of Special Education
The University of Kansas

Illustrations by ALVIN HOWELL

·P A U L·H·
BROOKES
PUBLISHING C⁰

Baltimore • London • Toronto • Sydney

Paul H. Brookes Publishing Co.
P.O. Box 10624
Baltimore, Maryland 21285-0624

Copyright © 1990 by The University of Kansas.
All rights reserved.

Funding for preparation of this material was provided by the U.S.
Department of Education, Contract No. G008630168-88. The opin-
ions expressed herein do not necessarily reflect the opinion or
policy of the U.S. Department of Education, and no official en-
dorsement by the department should be inferred.

Typeset by Brushwood Graphics, Inc., Baltimore, Maryland.
Manufactured in the United States of America by
The Maple Press Company, York, Pennsylvania.

Illustrations by Alvin Howell.

Library of Congress Cataloging-in-Publication Data

Health care for students with disabilities: an illustrated medical
  guide for the classroom / J. Carolyn Graff . . . [et al.] ; illustrations by Alvin Howell.
      p.   cm.
  Includes bibliographical references.
  ISBN 1-55766-037-9 :
  1. Physically handicapped children—Medical care.   2. Pediatric emergencies.   3. Teachers of handicapped children.   I.
Graff, J. Carolyn.
RJ138.H4   1990
362.4'048–dc20   89-23864
                                                     CIP

CONTENTS

FOREWORD

The purpose of modern education is to assist families in preparing their children for adult roles in contemporary society. Academic and technical skills are relevant to the extent that they prepare students for future vocational, recreational, and social roles, but these technical skills are only part of the total curriculum. Schools function in a dual manner. They prepare students for the roles they will fill in society in the future, but they are also an important part of society in the present. Current and future social functions must be supported consistently for education to effectively take place. Schooling that fails to provide relevant contemporary social experiences cannot prepare students for subsequent participation in society. Only through education that provides for immersion in society can the skills critical for social adjustment be successfully identified and taught. Although the specific content and the methods of education used may differ, the purpose of education remains the same regardless of the abilities or disabilities of the students involved in the process. This educational process of social integration is particularly critical for persons with disabilities because they have traditionally been isolated from the mainstream of society.

For the first two-thirds of the twentieth century, persons with severe disabilities were increasingly clustered into large institutions. These settings not only excluded persons with disabilities from society, but also provided them with few opportunities to participate in normal experiences that might help teach the skills required for eventual return to society. However, during the last 2 decades this trend toward isolation has been reversed. Many individuals who formerly would have lived their lives in institutions are now integrated into community home, school, work, and recreational environments. Integrated schooling, as close as possible to the mainstream experiences of student peers, is a key factor in community living for persons with disabilities. Nevertheless, meeting the requirements of students with intensive health care needs is a challenge for most schools, as well as for a variety of other community agencies.

The Education for All Handicapped Children Act of 1975, PL 94-142, requires schools to provide the *related services* that students need for an appropriate education. Many issues regarding the provision of these services still need to be resolved: *Who should carry out various procedures? What kind of training and clinical supervision should be provided? How should these procedures be coordinated with educational programming?* While the specific responsibility for carrying out these procedures varies across jurisdictions, depending on law, administrative policy, and service delivery models, the need for involvement of various educational and other nonmedical staff is a key factor to successful community integration. Unless students who require these procedures can be served successfully in school environments, they and their families will be forced to choose between restrictive placements equipped to meet their health-care needs or inferior health care in more socially appropriate educational settings.

This book provides nonmedical team members with some essential information about many of the procedures that will be required by their students with intensive and complex health-care needs. This book is not intended to replace the consultation provided between medical and nonmedical team members; it is designed to facilitate the communication between them. Such coordinated efforts are necessary to meet the holistic needs of the child, combining educational, medical, and other related services into a single unified system of service delivery. It is past the time for us to leave the age when students and their families have to choose between having either their educational needs or their medical needs met; we must enter the age in which they can expect a unified program to meet both of these needs.

Health Care for Students with Disabilities: An Illustrated Medical Guide for the Classroom helps us move toward this new age. The collaborative efforts of the authors of this book, who have diverse professional backgrounds, provide us with a model for collaboration in implementing these procedures. This book provides a wealth of practical information on how to carry out procedures and on how to recognize and record many of their intended and unintended effects. Enhanced understanding of the health-care procedures described will help to make integrated education a reality for students with intensive and complex health-care needs, bringing them closer to the mainstream and preparing them for future adult roles in society.

Dick Sobsey, R.N., Ed.D
Severe Disabilities Program
University of Alberta
Edmonton
Canada

ACKNOWLEDGMENTS

The authors wish to thank a number of professionals who contributed greatly to the quality and content of this book through their thorough and thoughtful evaluation of earlier versions. These persons include both professional school and community nurses, as well as teachers of students with severe and multiple disabilities.

We wish to first thank Joyce Markendorf, R.N., M.N., School Nurse Consultant, Department of Health and Environment, State of Kansas, for her competent review of the book as well as for her assistance in identifying a group of community and school nurses to serve as additional reviewers. These professional nurses include Susan Boos, R.N., B.S.N., School Nurse, USD 489, Hays; Vesta Cheatham, R.N., B.S.N., M.A., School Nurse, USD 229, Blue Valley; Beverly J. Gaines, R.N., M.S., Administrator/ Health Officer, Butler-Greenwood Bi-County Health Department, El Dorado; Janet Klosing, R.N., M.S., Home Health Nursing Supervisor, Butler-Greenwood Bi-County Health Department, El Dorado; Kathleen Tucker, R.N., M.Ed., School Nurse, USD 259, Wichita; and Janice Watson, R.N., USD 501, Topeka.

A number of professional teachers who have years of experience in dealing with students with medically fragile or complex conditions also contributed greatly to the book's responsiveness to the needs of the classroom teacher. These Kansas professionals include Susan Oshe, M.S., Phyllis Schmidt, M.S., and Nancy Stabb, M.S., Special Purpose School, Topeka; Eileen Cronan, M.S., Katherine Carpenter School, Shawnee Mission; Pam Amott, M.S., Levy School, Wichita; Aida Ayala, M.S., and Renni Judd, M.S., Developmental Learning Center, Olathe; Mary Lou Reardon, M.S., Elreka Grade School, Hutchinson; and Barbara Guy, doctoral student, University of Kansas. Significant comments also were contributed by Joan Houghton, M.S. (a Kansas transplant), TASH Technical Assistance Project, University of Pittsburgh, Pennsylvania.

Special thanks also go to Toni Adams for her continued and ever patient revisions of the manuscript.

HEALTH CARE FOR STUDENTS WITH DISABILITIES

INTRODUCTION

Teachers of students with severe disabilities and medically fragile or medically complex needs have shown a willingness to do what is needed to maintain these students in the classroom (Mulligan Ault, Guess, Struth, & Thompson, 1988; Thompson & Guess, 1989). Often this means that teachers must participate in implementing procedures that are not educational in nature but that must be completed during the school day. These may include health-related procedures such as gastrostomy feedings, oxygen supplementation, changing tracheostomy tubes and ties, catheterization, and so forth. Local school districts differ in the identification of who should be responsible for the implementation of the procedures, how much training is required, and what support personnel are needed. Regardless of whether the teachers are identified as the individuals responsible for implementing the procedures, they should have a working knowledge of what is involved in order to act as informed members of the team that designs a comprehensive plan for students.

This book provides the teacher with a description of what is involved for 16 health-related procedures likely to be ongoing in classrooms for students with severe disabilities. The order of the chapters reflects the prevalence of these procedures in classrooms for students with severe impairments. Chapter 1, Seizure Monitoring, is the most commonly implemented health-related procedure, and Chapter 16, Tracheostomy Care, is the least often health-related procedure per-

1

formed in classrooms for students with severe impairments (Mulligan Ault et al., 1988).

A teacher may use this book to obtain general knowledge about health-related procedures, or to seek specific information about a particular procedure for a student with a medically complex condition. In the first instance, the teacher may find information that suggests that a student may require additional health related services. Based on the information in this book the teacher may, with the assistance of the health personnel in the district, seek to refer the student to, for example, a nutritionist, skin specialist, or inhalation therapist. If the teacher is seeking information specifically for the needs of a particular student, then the book will present the teacher with the information necessary to understand the reason for, and protocol surrounding, the implementation of a procedure.

This book does *NOT* do two important things. It does not identify the professional who should be responsible for the routine implementation of the health-related procedures in the classroom. This decision should be made at the local level, with the application of the local guidelines, made on a case by case basis by the district or school.

This book also does *NOT* train teachers in the implementation of any health related procedure. This training should be received through the appropriate professional health personnel in the local district or community and documented and updated routinely. The book does, however, present sufficient information about the implementation of the procedure to familiarize the teacher with what is involved. Each chapter includes a brief description of the purpose of the procedure; an overview of why the procedure is usually used; what specifically is involved in the preparation, implementation, and follow up of the procedure; the identification of warning signs; what to do in an emergency; and suggestions for sources of training.

The development of this book came about in response to concerned teachers and therapists who wanted to know more about conditions affecting students in the classroom and who wanted to do everything they could to keep students in school. This book is intended to inform. It is hoped that it will also support these professionals in their efforts.

REFERENCES

Mulligan Ault, M., Guess, D., Struth, L., & Thompson, B. (1988). The implementation of health related procedures in classrooms for students with severe multiple impairments. *The Journal of The Association for Persons with Severe Handicaps, 13*(2), 100–109.

Thompson, B., & Guess, D. (1989). Students who experience the most profound disabilities: Teacher perspectives. In Brown, F. & Lehr, D. (Eds.), *Persons with profound disabilities: Issues and practices* (pp. 3–42). Baltimore: Paul H. Brookes Publishing Co.

SEIZURE MONITORING

$\mathbf{A}$ number of students with disabilities experience seizures. The monitoring of students' seizures has been identified as one of the major health-related procedures performed by the classroom teacher (Mulligan-Ault, Guess, Struth, & Thompson, 1988). It is, therefore, highly likely that a student with a seizure disorder will be present in a classroom and may experience seizures during the school day. The purpose of seizure monitoring is to protect the child from injury during a seizure, to carefully observe the seizure in order to provide information for management of the seizure disorder, and to distinguish between behaviors related to the seizure and behaviors not related to the seizure.

OVERVIEW OF SEIZURES AND EPILEPSY

Epilepsy is a disorder of the nervous system in which there is a tendency toward recurrence of seizures. From 5%–7% of all persons will have at least one seizure in their lifetime (Low, 1982). The prevalence of seizures (not including seizures associated with fever) ranges from 5.2 to 7.3 per 1000 school children (Baumann, 1982). Children having repeated seizures, or epilepsy, generally have normal intelligence, and their seizures are effectively controlled with anticonvulsant medications. A small number of these children have seizure disorders as part of a multi-disabling condition, such as cerebral palsy or mental retardation. These children have more severe seizures that are more difficult to control (Batshaw & Perret, 1981).

Definition and Types of Seizures and Epilepsy

A seizure is a temporary change in behavior resulting from sudden, abnormal bursts of electrical activity in the brain. This change in electrical activity may be limited to one area of the brain or may begin in one area and spread to other areas of the brain. If the electrical disturbance is limited to only part of the brain, then the result is a *partial seizure.* For example, the child may experience stiffening or jerking of one arm or leg. If the electrical disturbance affects the entire brain, the result is a *generalized seizure* (Dreifuss, Gallagher, Leppik, & Rothner, 1983).

Generalized Seizures   Types of generalized seizures include the grand mal or tonic-clonic seizure and the petit mal or absence seizure. The grand mal or tonic-clonic seizure is the most common type of seizure and is usually referred to as epilepsy (Batshaw & Perret, 1981). Before such a seizure, the student often has an aura or warning that it is about to begin. The eyes roll upward and the student looses consciousness, falls to the ground, and becomes rigid, that is, tonic, as the muscles tighten. This is followed by jerking movements of the entire body as muscles undergo rhythmic tightening and relaxation, the clonic phase. During this phase, the student may lose urine and stool as muscles controlling these areas relax. The entire seizure usually lasts less than 5 minutes. The jerking movements are followed by drowsiness or deep sleep, lasting up to 2 hours (Batshaw & Perret, 1981; Low, 1982; Whaley & Wong, 1987).

Petit mal or absence seizures (sometimes called "staring spells") can be mistaken for daydreaming or inattentiveness. The student may simply stare blankly for 5–10 seconds; may drop objects because of loss of muscle tone; and may have minor movements such as lip-smacking, twitching of eyelids or face, or slight hand movements. The student will be unable to recall what happened during these brief periods. If untreated, absence seizures can occur many times a day. Most often students between 4 and 15 years of age experience these seizures (Batshaw & Perret, 1981; Whaley & Wong, 1987).

Partial Seizures   The two types of partial seizures are focal, or simple partial seizures, and psychomotor, or complex partial seizures.

During a focal, or simple partial seizure the student's eyes or eyes and head turn to one side and the arm on that side may be extended with fingers clenched. The student seems to be looking toward the closed fist and may be conscious or unconscious during this movement. The simple partial seizure lasts usually less than 30 seconds (Whaley & Wong, 1987).

During a psychomotor, or complex partial seizure the student experiences an aura that is most commonly described as a strange feeling in the pit of the stomach that rises toward the throat. This is often accompanied by odd or unpleasant odors or tastes, auditory or visual hallucinations, or feelings of elation or strangeness. The student may cry or run for help. During this time, the student is unaware of the environment and unable to respond to the environment. After the aura, the student may suddenly cease activity, appear dazed, stare into space, become confused and apathetic, or become limp or stiff. The most obvious behaviors may be lip smacking, chewing, drooling, swallowing, and nausea or abdominal pain followed by stiffness, a fall, and sleep. The seizure lasts from 5 to 15 minutes and occurs from 3 years of age to adolescence (Batshaw & Perret, 1981; Low, 1982; Whaley & Wong, 1987). Partial seizures may spread to become generalized seizures, grand mal type (Low, 1982).

Minor Motor Seizures   Minor motor seizures refer to a group of seizures that have certain characteristic features in common. One feature is myoclonus, or sudden, involuntary jerks of muscles. Myoclonic jerks can occur under normal conditions in light sleep. Minor motor seizures are frequently associated with mental retardation and are difficult to control (Low, 1982).

The most common seizure pattern in children with disabilities is grand mal seizure plus minor motor seizures (Batshaw & Perret, 1981). School staff often will be involved in administering medications to students with this seizure pattern, as well as reporting to parents and/or caregivers, health care workers, or physicians the effects of the medication on the student. Commonly administered anticonvulsants and their possible side effects are listed in Table 1.1.

Diagnosis and Treatment of Seizures

Diagnosis of the student with a seizure disorder is generally made according to the behaviors exhibited by the student during the seizure, the electroencephalogram (EEG), and the underlying cause. The EEG is a procedure that helps in identifying the presence and location of electri-

Table 1.1.   Common anticonvulsant medications for children

Trade Name	Generic name	Possible side effects
Klonopin	Clonazepam	Drowsiness, ataxia, behavior problems, appetite loss
Depakene	Valproic acid	Nausea, vomiting, indigestion, diarrhea, constipation, appetite loss, sedation, tremor, hair loss, weakness, liver impairment
Depakote	Dival proex sodium (Sodium valproate and valproic acid)	Nausea, vomiting, indigestion, diarrhea, constipation, appetite loss, sedation, tremor, hair loss, weakness, liver impairment
Dilantin	Phenytoin	Nystagmus, ataxia, slurred speech, confusion, dizziness, insomnia, nausea, vomiting, constipation, rash, gum overgrowth, body hair increase
Phenobarbital	Phenobarbital	Drowsiness, irritability, hyperactivity, ataxia, sleep difficulties, rash
Tegretol	Carbamazepine	Dizziness, drowsiness, unsteadiness, nausea, vomiting, rash, blurred vision, nystagmus, anemia, liver impairment
Zarontin	Ethosuximide	Drowsiness, headache, dizziness, irritability, hyperactivity, fatigue, appetite loss, nausea, vomiting, hiccups, liver impairment

Adapted from *Physicians' Desk Reference* (43rd ed.). (1989). Oradell, New Jersey: Medical Economics Company.

cal activity in the brain. During a seizure the electrodes placed on the scalp are used to record abnormal electrical brain impulses (Mac-Dougall, 1982). Computerized axial tomography (CAT scan) may also be used to find abnormalities in the structure of the student's brain. During a CAT scan the student's head rests inside a donut shaped machine, and X-rays of the brain are taken 1 degree at a time in a 180 degree scan.

Once the type of seizure has been identified, an appropriate medication may be prescribed to attempt to reduce the number of seizures. The major goal of the physician should not be achieving total control of the seizures, but rather achieving a level of control that will allow the student to do as well as possible in school. Side effects of certain medications can result in undesirable effects such as drowsiness, decreased alertness, or hyperactivity. Although the physician hopes to eliminate seizures completely with a limited amount of medication, it may be preferable for a student to have an occasional absence seizure or focal seizure and be alert, than to be seizure-free but drugged and unable to participate in activities and learn (Prensky & Palkes, 1982). Most students with seizure disorders receive anticonvulsants daily and often several times a day. One medication is adequate to control seizures in about half of the students with seizures. Students having more than one type of seizure are the most likely to receive more than one anticonvulsant.

PROCEDURES

Preparation for Assisting a Student with a Seizure Disorder

Adequate preparation for meeting the needs of all students with seizure disorders requires information on the type of seizure generally apparent as well as typical behaviors seen before, during, and after the seizure. It is also appropriate for school staff to be aware of any changes in behavior due to medication, particularly if the physician is in the process of evaluating the student's prescription and dosage. Communication with the student's parents and/or physician can provide this important information.

After obtaining the above information, the staff can prepare the school areas accordingly. For example, the student producing large amounts of secretions during the seizure will need a suction machine or bulb syringe available in the classroom to remove secretions from the mouth. A student may also become somewhat drowsy approximately 2 hours after administration of the medication or generally around 9:30 A.M. In this instance, the teacher needs to plan for activities requiring less interaction and response from the student around 9:30 A.M.

Awareness of the potential for injury to the student during a seizure is a concern for all school staff. Students whose seizures are not well-controlled can experience a head injury resulting from a seizure-related fall. Often these students wear a lightweight helmet to protect the head. The student must *never* be restrained during a seizure because of the possibility of breaking bones, or tearing muscles or ligaments (of the child or the school staff) while the student is held or restrained (Yard, 1980).

Additionally, the school environment must be adapted to be as safe as possible for students who experience seizures. Objects (e.g., furniture, equipment, or toys) that could injure the student if the student fell or hit the object should be portable enough to be removed during a student's seizure. Pathways and environments of instruction should be wide and free of unnecessary objects (e.g., unused wheelchairs, storage boxes) to minimize the chance of injury during a fall.

What to Do During a Seizure

1. All individuals must remain calm. It is helpful to remember that no one can stop a seizure once it has started.
2. An adult needs to stay with the student to monitor the student's progress through the seizure.
3. Events happening before the seizure should be recorded on an appropriate form.
   a. Did the student cry out?
   b. Did the student yell?
   c. Did the student recognize the onset of the seizure?
   d. Who noticed a change in the student's behavior?
4. During the seizure, the student should be placed on the side or stomach so the tongue does not block the airway and the student does not choke on secretions.
5. *NOTHING* (e.g., fingers, objects) is to be placed into the student's mouth. The student could be injured or begin vomiting.
6. Tight clothing should be loosened, especially around the neck.
7. If the student is standing or sitting at the beginning of the seizure, the student should be eased down to avoid a fall. This should be done even if the student is secured in adaptive equipment, for example, a wheelchair, standing frame, or prone board. When possible, a cushion or blanket can be placed under the student's head to prevent injury during jerking movements.

8. The student should *not* be given medications or anything to drink during the seizure.
9. The student's activity during the seizure should be recorded on a moment by moment basis:
   a. When did the seizure begin?
   b. In what area of the body did the seizure begin?
   c. Did the seizure begin in one area of the body and move to another area?
   d. What were movements of the head, face, eyes, arms, and legs?
   e. Was the student's body limp or rigid?
   f. Were the student's eyes rolled back, to the right or to the left?
   g. Did the student stop breathing?
   h. Did the student bite his or her tongue?
   i. Was the student's skin pale, blue, or reddened in color?
   j. When did the seizure end?

What to Do After a Seizure

1. After the seizure has ended, secretions should be cleared from the mouth with a suction machine or bulb syringe.
2. The student's breathing should be monitored. *If breathing is absent, the emergency medical system must be notified immediately and resuscitation efforts begun* (see Chapter 8, Cardiopulmonary Resuscitation) (Dreifuss et al., 1983; Low, 1982; O'Neill, 1984; Percy & Percy, 1986; Prensky & Palkes, 1982; Rich, 1986; Whaley & Wong, 1987; Yard, 1980).
3. The teacher should immediately talk or otherwise interact with the student to determine the student's level of awareness (i.e., alert, drowsy, confused, unable to respond) and record this information.
4. The teacher should determine whether the student is able to move his or her arms and legs or if there is any change in the student's ability to move.
5. The teacher should check for loss of control of urine and stool (this can be embarrassing for the student) and determine if the student sustained any injuries (e.g., bleeding from the mouth).
6. Efforts should be made to make the student comfortable and quiet, allowing opportunity to sleep if it seems needed (a student may sleep up to 2 hours after a seizure).
7. The length of the seizure (in seconds or minutes) and what hap-

pened during the seizure are recorded in writing. An Anecdotal Record for the Student with Epilepsy has also been recommended by Prensky and Palkes (1982) for use by teachers in a classroom.

Warning Signs

An increase in the number of seizures per day or per week may indicate that the student is not receiving medication as prescribed, or that the student is in need of a change in medication as a result of a change in the student's metabolism or altered utilization of the medication (Low, 1982). Careful, accurate reporting of seizure activity to parents and/or health care workers hopefully will result in improved seizure management. As a result of information provided through careful seizure monitoring, the student's physician may decide to run a blood test to determine the level of medication in the student's blood and whether the present dosage is appropriate.

Anticonvulsant medications occasionally may be harmful or toxic. Some signs indicating possible toxicity to the student include rash, nausea and vomiting, and changes in the student's behavior (e.g., increased drowsiness, irritability). Reliable documentation of any of these signs should be reported immediately to parents, health care workers, or the student's physician to avoid additional harmful side effects (see Table 1.1).

SIGNS OF AN EMERGENCY

A series of consecutive seizures during which the student does not regain consciousness is called status epilepticus. This is a true medical emergency, requiring immediate medical care. This is particularly true if the seizure is the grand mal or tonic-clonic type (Low, 1982). Seizures lasting longer than 10–15 minutes require immediate hospitalization of the student (Dreifuss et al., 1983). Seizures lasting longer than 20–30 minutes can lead to brain damage (Menkes, 1985). Status epilepticus can also lead to exhaustion, respiratory failure, and death. Death occurs in 5%–15% of persons experiencing status epilepticus (Low, 1982).

Careful observation and timing of the student's seizure is crucial in identifying status epilepticus. The most common causes of status epilepticus are changes in medications, stopping medications, and infections (Low, 1982; Menkes, 1985). Because abruptly stopping medication can result in status epilepticus, anticonvulsants should be tapered off and never stopped suddenly.

ADDITIONAL RESOURCES

Preparation for monitoring seizures may be accomplished by following the recommendations described in the sections on "Preparation for Assisting a Student with a Seizure Disorder" and "What to do During a Seizure" in this chapter. Additionally, the student's parent(s) or caregivers should provide clear, descriptive information on the type of seizure the student experiences and what is done at home when the student has a seizure.

The Epilepsy Foundation of America sponsors a wide variety of programs and activities for persons with epilepsy, as well as workshops and training for staff, and kits developed for educators working with students with epilepsy. Local affiliates can be located in local telephone directories. Information from the national organization is available from:

Epilepsy Foundation of America
4351 Garden City Drive, Suite 406
Landover, Maryland 20785
(301) 459-3700 or (toll free) 1-800-332-1000

The list of Literature Cited in this chapter provides more detailed information on monitoring seizure disorders in students. Careful communication between school staff and parents, and between school staff and the student's physician, is the key to providing optimal educational and health services for the student.

LITERATURE CITED

Batshaw, M.L., & Perret, Y.M. (1981). *Children with handicaps: A medical primer.* Baltimore: Paul H. Brookes Publishing Company.

Baumann, R.J. (1982). Classification and population studies of epilepsy. In V.E. Anderson, W.A. Hauser, J.K. Penry, C.F. Sing (Eds.), *Genetic bases of the epilepsies* (pp. 11–20). New York: Raven Press.

Dreifuss, F.E., Gallagher, B.B., Leppik, I.E., & Rothner, D. (1983). Keeping epilepsy under control. *Patient Care, 17,* 107–149.

Dreisbach, M., Ballard, M., Russo, D.C., & Schain, R.J. (1982). Educational intervention for children with epilepsy: A challenge for collaborative service delivery. *The Journal of Special Education, 16*(1), 111–121.

Low, N.L. (1982). Seizure disorders in children. In J.A. Downey & N.L. Low (Eds.), *The child with disabling illness: Principles of rehabilitation* (pp. 121–144). New York: Raven Press.

MacDougall, V. (1982). Teaching children and families about seizures. *The Canadian Nurse, 78*(4), 30–35.

Menkes, J.H. (1985). *Textbook of child neurology.* Philadelphia: Lea & Febiger.

Mulligan-Ault, M., Guess, D., Struth, L., & Thompson, B. (1988). The implementation of health related procedures in classrooms for students with severe impairments. *The Journal of The Association for Persons with Severe Handicaps, 13*(2), 100–109.

O'Neill, S. (1984). Dealing with seizures. *RN, 47*(8), 39–41.

Percy, A.K., & Percy, P.D. (1986). Acute management of seizures in children. *Nurse Practitioner, 11*(2), 15–28.

Prensky, A.L., & Palkes, H.S. (1982). *Care of the neurologically handicapped child.* New York: Oxford University Press.

Rich, J. (1986). Action stat! Generalized motor seizure. *Nursing '86, 16*(4), 33.

Whaley, L.F., & Wong, D.L. (1987). *Nursing care of infants and children.* St. Louis: C.V. Mosby.

Yard, G.J. (1980). Managing seizures in mainstream education. *The Journal for Special Educators, 17*(1), 52–56.

2

TEETH AND GUM CARE

The health and appearance of the mouth, teeth, and gums greatly affect an individual's overall health, as well as his or her ability to use oral speech and interact in society. Proper attention to the care of teeth and gums, or teaching the student to perform his or her own teeth and periodontal care, will significantly affect a student's quality of life. There are, therefore, three major purposes to the development of a routine of oral hygiene, independent or assisted, that is ongoing and consistent between home and school. They are: 1) preventing periodontal (or gum) disease by maintaining healthy teeth and gums, 2) promoting good eating habits in terms of what is eaten and how it is eaten, and 3) promoting good speech habits and a positive body image (Mott, Fazekas, & James, 1985).

OVERVIEW

Dental problems are very evident among all children and adolescents (Luce & Sande, 1983). Tooth decay is present in 40% –55% of all 3- and 4-year-olds. Ninety percent of 12-year-olds have one or more cavities, with the average having five decayed teeth (Nizel, 1977). A study comparing dental health in school age persons identified that there were few differences in the occurrence of cavities between children with and without disabilities (Shaw, Maclaurin, & Foster, 1986). Treatment for decay, however, was more likely to result in the removal of the tooth in the child with a disability than the restoration of the tooth, as in the child without a disability. Overall, children with disabilities had poorer levels of oral hygiene compared to children without disabilities. When distinguishing between the types of disabling conditions, the study found that children with mental retardation were least likely to have good oral hygiene and most likely needed periodontal treatment. This group included students with the most severe disabilities, some with physical impairments, and those who had difficulty manipulating a toothbrush (Shaw et al., 1986). Unfortunately for persons with disabilities, dental care is not perceived as a priority by their families, the dental profession (Schuman, 1983), or their teachers.

COMPONENTS OF TEETH AND GUM CARE

The major components of teeth and gum care include oral hygiene, nutrition and eating habits, and dental care. Some of these components may be addressed instructionally during the school day and some require cooperation between the school and home.

Oral Hygiene

The purpose of oral hygiene is to prevent cavities by the removal of food debris and plaque from the teeth. Cavities result from the breaking down of enamel and dentin of the teeth. Enamel is the hard, white covering of the teeth, and dentin is the tissue of the tooth that surrounds the pulp, or the inner part of the tooth. Bacteria developing from food debris make use of sugar in the mouth to produce plaque, which adheres to tooth enamel. Plaque, or these bacterial deposits, continues to use sugars to produce acids that break down the enamel and dentin, eventually allowing bacteria to invade and decay the tooth (Luce & Sande, 1983).

The most effective methods for preventing plaque buildup are brushing and flossing. Routine oral hygiene should begin as soon as teeth appear during infancy; generally this means toothbrushing should begin around 18 months of age. Because a child at this age does not have the cognitive or motor ability to brush the teeth, parent(s) or other caretakers must brush the teeth. As new skills and abilities are acquired, the child eventually learns to perform toothbrushing independently (Luce & Sande, 1983). According to Boraz (1981), most dentists believe that the majority of children do not possess motor skills to brush their teeth properly until they are able to write script and suggest that most children are not able to floss properly until about 8 or 9 years of age.

Serious tooth decay may occur in children who are put to bed with a bottle containing milk or juice. The liquid from the bottle bathes the teeth, resulting in severe decay of the upper front teeth and some decay of the lower teeth. Since toothbrushing generally does not occur for the rest of the night, the fluid remains on the teeth, allowing bacterial buildup. This is called nursing bottle mouth syndrome or nursing bottle cavities (Wilkins, 1976).

Students are again particularly prone to tooth decay during ages 4–8 years and 12–18 years. These are considered the cavity prone years, when new teeth do not yet have adequate surface minerals to resist decay (Nizel, 1977). Proper oral hygiene as well as appropriate diet are particularly crucial during this period.

Nutrition

In addition to careful brushing and flossing, proper nutrition and fluoride applications protect healthy teeth and prevent cavities. A diet providing optimal levels of protein, calcium, phosphorus, and vitamins A, D, and C foster the development of healthy teeth (Chow, Durand, Feldman, & Mills, 1984). Milk provides protein, calcium, phosphorus, vitamins A and D; meats, fish, poultry, and dry beans or peas provide protein in the diet; fruits and vegetables provide vitamins A and C (Mott et al., 1985). Foods high in refined sugars and foods that are sticky and cling to the teeth (e.g., candy, raisins, caramels, sugared gum, peanut butter, and jelly) promote the development of cavities (Luce & Sande, 1983).

Fluoride should also be considered when evaluating a student's nutrition (see Chapter 6, Nutrition Monitoring and Supplementation). When adequate amounts of fluoride are taken in, the enamel is more resistant to decay or more resistant to the breaking down effects of acids. Fluoridation of community water supplies, fluoride toothpastes, and applications of fluoride by the dentist have been shown to reduce cavities 50%–70% (Horowitz, 1981). Fluoride mouth rinses are available without a prescription and, in additon to brushing and flossing, can help prevent tooth decay (American Dental Association, 1984).

Dental Care

Regular visits to the dentist may begin as early as 18 months of age, and should begin by around 3 years of age. Dental care, or its absence, can affect any child's health and development. Many factors, such as improperly formed jaws and teeth, lack of stimulation from chewing, inadequate cleaning of the teeth and gums, infrequent dental care, and the side effects of medications, can result in unhealthy and malformed teeth and gums. In addition, the unattractive mouth affects not only the student's physical well-being, but also the child's acceptance by others (Woelk, 1986).

Locating dentists who agree to work with and can work effectively with students who have disabilities may not be easy. The dental profession has been reluctant to work with persons with disabilities (Braff, 1985; Miller, 1965; Nowak, 1976; Schuman, 1983). Pedodontists (dentists caring for children's teeth) can be a source for parents searching for a dentist. Parents or caregivers may successfully locate a dentist by contacting other parents of children and youth with disabilities. Preparation of both the dentist and the student may affect the success of a dental program. Training in the school as well as practice visits to the dental office may help reduce fears and increase the student's ability to cooperate with the examination.

Before any oral hygiene program is begun, the teacher or nurse must determine how teeth and gum care is performed in the home. If there is no dental care being performed at home, the school staff should initiate an oral hygiene procedure and serve as models for the parents.

PROCEDURES

Preparation for Teeth and Gum Care

Equipment required for teeth and gum care includes a toothbrush, toothpaste, water, cup or syringe, emesis basin (receptacle for fluid removed from the mouth) or sink, towel (King, Wieck, & Dyer, 1983) and dental floss. Each student requires a toothbrush, toothpaste, and emesis basin at school. A sink that is not used for food preparation must be available. Identical items are to be kept at home for use there. Toothbrushing is performed after meals and snacks, flossing is performed at least once a day. School staff should determine whether gloves should also be used when completing any oral hygiene procedure.

The time required to complete teeth and gum care must be included when planning for the student's individual program. Initially the student with a disability may require complete assistance with toothbrushing and flossing. With instruction, hopefully, the student will acquire new skills, and toothbrushing and flossing may then be performed with assistance from the staff. The goal of instruction is for the student to be able to brush his or her teeth independently or with minimal assistance from staff.

Oral Hygiene   In order to facilitate adequate oral hygiene, the student must be positioned to facilitate toothbrushing and flossing. If unable to sit up, the student can be on his or her back (Figure 2.1a) or turned onto the side with the face along the edge of a pillow, and a towel and basin placed under the chin. If the student can sit, several positions are suggested. The student can sit on the floor while the adult sits behind him or her on a chair, with the student's head straddled by the adult's thighs. The adult can reach around with one hand supporting the student's chin and brush the teeth with the other hand. A second position may be with the student sitting in a wheelchair; the adult can stand or sit behind the student and reach around with one hand supporting the student's chin and opening the student's mouth. The teeth can then be brushed using the other hand (Figure 2.1b).

If biting is a problem when cleaning the teeth, a padded tongue blade or a new, clean rubber door stopper can be placed between the biting surfaces of the upper and lower jaw (Woelk, 1986). Toothbrushing can then be carried out with this device holding the mouth slightly open. If at all possible, brushing should be accomplished in the bathroom in front of a sink with both the student and teacher looking in the mirror.

Toothbrushing   The following procedure for toothbrushing has been suggested by the American Dental Association:

1. Place the head of the toothbrush beside the teeth, with the bristle tips at a 45 degree angle against the gumline.
2. Move the brush back and forth in short (half-a-tooth-wide) strokes several times, using a gentle "scrubbing" motion.
3. Brush the outer surfaces of each tooth, upper and lower, keeping the bristles angled against the gumline.
4. Use the same method on the inside surfaces of all the teeth, still using short back-and-forth strokes.
5. Scrub the chewing surfaces of the teeth.
6. To clean the inside surfaces of the front teeth, tilt the brush vertically and make several gentle up-and-down strokes with the "toe" (the front part) of the brush.

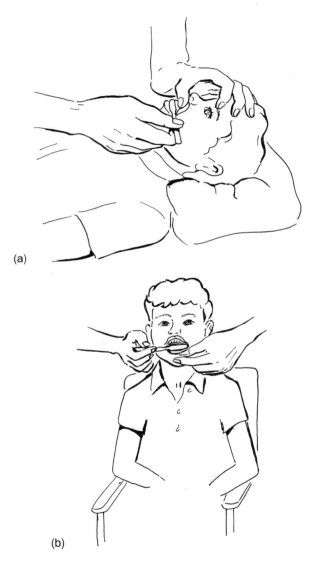

(a)

(b)

Figure 2.1.   Alternate positions appropriate for toothbrushing. The student
may be lying down (a); the person assisting in brushing may be positioned
behind the student (b).

7. Brushing the tongue will help freshen the breath and clean the mouth by removing bacteria (American Dental Association, 1984, p. 8)

Flossing The American Dental Association has recommended the following procedure for flossing the student's teeth (Figure 2.2):

1. Break off about 18 inches of floss, and wind most of it around one of your middle fingers.
2. Wind the remaining floss around the same finger of the opposite hand. This finger will "take up" the floss as it becomes soiled.
3. Hold the floss tightly between the thumbs and forefingers, with about an inch of floss between them. There should be no slack. Using a gentle sawing motion, guide the floss between the teeth. Never "snap" the floss into the gums.
4. When the floss reaches the gumline, curve it into a C-shape against one tooth. Gently slide it into the space between the gum and the tooth until resistance is felt.
5. Hold the floss tightly against the tooth. Gently scrape the side of the tooth, moving the floss away from the gum.
6. Repeat this method on the rest of the teeth. Don't forget the back side of the last tooth. (American Dental Association, 1984, p. 6)

After brushing and flossing, the student's mouth is rinsed with cool water. The student takes water from a cup or a syringe, if possible. If the student is unable to control the movement of water in the mouth, the student's head can be tilted forward allowing the water to flow from the mouth into the emesis basin. Irrigating devices, such as a Water Pik, can be used to remove loose bits of food and other materials from around the teeth. These devices are not effective as a substitute for brushing or flossing, since they cannot effectively remove plaque (American Dental Association, 1984).

Procedures Following Oral Hygiene

Careful observations are made of the student's teeth, gums, tongue, and lips during oral hygiene. Any abnormal appearance of the teeth, gums, lips, or tongue (see the next section "Warning signs") should be reported to the school nurse and the family and/or caregivers. Assistance from the health care worker in the school may be necessary when making observations and determining whether or not the mouth is healthy.

The toothbrush is thoroughly rinsed in cool water and placed in a clean area to air dry. The student's cup or syringe is washed and dried thoroughly. The equipment is placed in a clean area designated for this equipment. The toothbrush is discarded as soon as the bristles become frayed or bent.

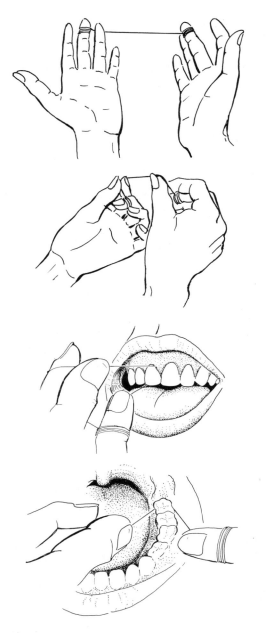

Figure 2.2. Steps for flossing recommended by the American Dental Association.

Warning Signs

Many warning signs indicating potential problems can be observed while assisting the student with or providing oral hygiene. These include the condition of teeth, tongue, and gums and the positioning of the teeth and jaw. Any observations should be confirmed with the health care worker in the school or the parent or caregiver. Many times the parent or caregiver may be aware of certain conditions (e.g., malocclusions); other times the conditions may be first identified during classroom procedures.

It must be recognized that the provision of teeth and gum care have not traditionallly been a high priority for students with disabilities. Since treatment of some structural problems of the teeth and jaw may be expensive and involved, the teacher must make a strong case for pursuing treatment. A number of conditions may occur that require immediate response and there may be some conditions requiring cooperation across disciplines. Following is a list of conditions indicating the presence of problems:

Whitish Coating and Brown Spots   The presence of a *whitish coating on the teeth* (plaque) is a sign of poor oral hygiene. Brown spots on or between the teeth may indicate cavities. Liquid iron supplements taken through the mouth can result in a greenish black stain on the teeth, which will disappear when the iron supplement is stopped (Luce & Sande, 1983). The presence of cavities and/or the continued presence of plaque indicate that a rigorous oral hygiene program needs to be implemented.

Red, Swollen Gums that Bleed Easily   Red, swollen gums that bleed easily indicate the presence of gingivitis (inflammation of the gums) (Figure 2.3a). If untreated, gingivitis can progress to pyorrhea (periodontitis). In this condition, the gums may pull back exposing the neck of the tooth, resulting in a loosened tooth (Bates, 1983) (Figure 2.3b). The neck of a tooth is the area of the tooth connecting the crown to the root of the tooth. Some students with pyorrhea or periodontitis may have normal appearing gums with the only sign of pyorrhea being the increased mobility of the teeth (i.e., loose teeth).

The student with gingivitis or with pyorrhea may also have a sore mouth. This soreness may be relieved by using warm salt water rinses, a Water Pik to irrigate the mouth, and a specially constructed toothbrush. Strict attention is recommended to improving toothbrushing and flossing at school and at home. The parents and/or caregiver and health care worker in the school must be notified when gingivitis or pyorrhea is

(a)

(b)

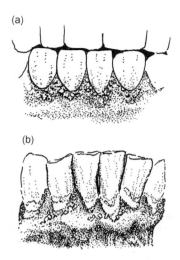

Figure 2.3.   Swollen gums indicating the presence of gingivitis (a), and the progression of the disorder to pyorrhea (b).

suspected, and a referral to a dentist is usually recommended (Chow et al., 1984).

Hyperplasia (Enlargement) of the Gums   Hyperplasia or enlargement of the gums refers to growth of the gums over the teeth. This is cosmetically unpleasant and promotes decay. Hyperplasia of the gums can result from a variety of causes, such as receiving Dilantin, mouth breathing, or vitamin deficiency. Dilantin is a seizure control medication (review Chapter 1, Seizure Monitoring). Hyperplasia of the gums usually appears 2–3 months after Dilantin is begun. This overgrowth of the gums can be reduced by strict toothbrushing and flossing, daily massaging of the gums with the fingers, and cutting away of the enlarged gum tissue by the dentist (Menkes, 1985). Note that the gums may bleed after toothbrushing and appear tender. Discussions among school staff, parents or caregiver, and health care worker should take place to outline the procedures for an intensive oral hygiene program.

Malocclusions   Malocclusions are improper alignment of the teeth and the improper fitting together of the teeth when chewing. Malocclusion can occur as a result of midline abnormalities or by lip biting, mouth breathing, tongue thrusting, teeth grinding, and thumb sucking (Chow et al., 1984). Malocclusion results in an unpleasant appearance, difficulty in chewing food properly, and difficulty in speaking (Figure 2.4). These results may or may not be obvious to the caregiver so any

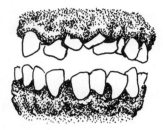

Figure 2.4. An example of extreme malocclussions, that is, improper alignment of the teeth.

observations made by the school staff should be reviewed with the parent and dentist to identify causes and methods of treatment.

Tongue Thrusting   Tongue thrusting normally occurs in infancy and disappears around 6 months of age (Mott et al., 1985). Persistent tongue thrusting can also hinder eating and speaking. Some consider that a tongue thrust may not be preventable (Luce & Sande, 1983). Other dentists suggest the use of prosthetics to facilitate proper tongue positioning during swallowing.

White Coating on the Tongue   A white coating on the tongue can indicate thrush, a contagious fungal infection. White, milky, or cheesy patches can also occur on the tongue and/or sides of the mouth. If thrush is suspected, the parents must be notified and the student referred to a physician for treatment. If a diaper rash appears along with thrush, a fungal diaper infection is suspected (Chow et al., 1984).

Injured Tongue   If the tongue is injured (e.g., by accidental biting, injuries by sharp objects), it may appear red and swollen or have blisters that disappear in a few days. Ice may be used for the swelling and an antiseptic mouthwash may help prevent infection. A cool liquid may also be used to reduce discomfort. Depending on the seriousness of the injury, the student may need to be referred to a physician (Chow et al., 1984). A red or swollen tongue could also indicate the presence of an infection that has spread throughout the body (Luce & Sande, 1983). The health care worker in the school should assist in evaluating the student to determine the need for referral to a physician (Luce & Sande, 1983).

SIGNS OF AN EMERGENCY

For the student with poor muscle control and poor coordination, the potential for aspiration is present. Fluid from the mouth may be pulled (aspirated) into the lungs. This can result in the student beginning to choke, having difficulty breathing, or turning blue. If one of these problems occurs, a call for assistance is required (see Chapter 8, Cardiopulmonary Resuscitation). It may be helpful if the student is placed with the head down and on the side, allowing gravity to help liquid and secretions to flow from the mouth. Trained staff may use the suction machine to remove secretions, taking care not to stimulate the student's gag reflex. The teeth may be brushed without toothpaste, resulting in less liquid in the mouth.

Because drooling may occur during toothbrushing and flossing, it may be necessary to position the student to facilitate the flow of secretions from the mouth. This may mean that the student will need to sit forward with the head slightly flexed. The student with poor muscle control and coordination may collect secretions in the back of the mouth and throat and be unable to swallow or spit out secretions. Suctioning of these secretions with a suction machine or bulb syringe can help avoid choking and aspiration. School staff removing secretions from the mouth must perform careful handwashing before and after suctioning.

School staff must also wash hands before and after providing care to the teeth and gums. Special attention must be given to handwashing when working with a student having an infection in the mouth. Standing behind the student when toothbrushing and flossing may help protect the school staff from secretions that the student coughs or spits out. Handwashing should be done whether the student does or does not have an infection. Care must be taken to prevent the spread of infection among the student, school staff, and other students.

ADDITIONAL RESOURCES

The American Dental Association provides information on care of the teeth and gums. Information can be obtained from local dentists or from:

Bureau of Health Education and Audiovisual Services
211 East Chicago Avenue
Chicago, IL 60611.

Information and assistance may be available from the local health department. Protocols have been developed for dentists and dental hygientists working with persons having herpes (McMechen & Wright,

1985) and with persons having AIDS (aquired immune deficiency syndrome) (Evans, 1986).

The student's parents can be an invaluable resource to school staff in planning the most effective method of providing dental care. The student's dentist and/or physician can provide guidance and assistance to the school staff. A dentist or dental hygientist should be encouraged to visit the classroom to demonstrate brushing and flossing techniques and analyze techniques being used by school staff and parents. An evaluation can be made by a nutritionist to determine the effectiveness of the student's diet in preventing tooth decay and gum problems (see Chapter 6, Nutrition Monitoring and Supplementation).

LITERATURE CITED

American Dental Association. (1984). *Cleaning your teeth and gums.* Chicago: Bureau of Health Education and Audiovisual Services.

Bates, B. (1983). *A guide to physical examination.* Philadelphia: J. P. Lippincott.

Boraz, R.A. (1981). Preventive dentistry for the pediatric patient. *Issues in Comprehensive Pediatric Nursing, 5,* 89–97.

Braff, M.H. (1985). Dental treatment for developmentally disabled patients. *Special Care in Dentistry, 5*(3), 109–111.

Chow, M.P., Durand, B.A., Feldman, M.N., & Mills, M.A. (1984). *Handbook of pediatric primary care.* New York: John Wiley & Sons.

Evans, B.E. (1986). AIDS-dental considerations: A 1986 update. *New York State Dental Journal, 52*(9), 40–48.

Horowitz, H.S. (1981). Community water fluoridation. In D.J. Forrester, M.L. Wagner, & J. Fleming (Eds.), *Pediatric dental medicine* (pp. 301–311). Philadelphia: Lea & Febiger.

King, E.M., Wieck, L., & Dyer, M. (1983). *Pediatric nursing procedures.* Philadelphia: J. B. Lippincott.

Luce, M., & Sande, D. (1983). Oral health in children: Prevention of dental cavities. *Nurse Practitioner, 8*(3), 43–53.

McMechen, D.L., & Wright, J.M. (1985). A protocol for the management of patients with herpetic infections. *Dental Hygiene, 59*(12), 546–548.

Menkes, J.H. (1985). *Textbook of child neurology.* Philadelphia: Lea & Febiger.

Miller, S.L. (1965). Dental care for the mentally retarded: Challenge to the profession. *Journal of Public Health Dentistry, 25*(3), 111–115.

Mott, S.R., Fazekas, N.F., & James, S.R. (1985). *Nursing care of children and families.* Menlo Park, CA.: Addison-Wesley Publishing Co.

Nizel, A. (1977). Preventing dental caries: The nutritional factors. *Pediatric Clinics of North America 24*(1), 141–154.

Nowak, A.J. (1976). *Dentistry for the handicapped patient.* St. Louis: C.V. Mosby.

Schuman, N.J. (1983). Dentistry and the handicapped: A persistent dilemma. *Annals of Dentistry, 42*(1), 25–26.

Shaw, L., Maclaurin, E.T., & Foster, T.D. (1986). Dental study of handicapped children attending special schools in Birmingham, UK. *Community Dentistry and Oral Epidemiology, 14*(1), 24–27.

Wilkins, E.M. (1976). *Clinical practice of the dental hygienist.* Philadelphia: Lea & Febiger.

Woelk, C.G. (1986). The mentally retarded child and his family. In G.M. Scipien, M.U. Barnard, M.A. Chard, J. Howe, & P.J. Phillips (Eds.), *Comprehensive pediatric nursing* (pp. 639–666). New York: McGraw-Hill.

3

MEDICATION ADMINISTRATION

It is not unusual for elementary or secondary school students to receive medications during the school day. Earlier studies have indicated that 1%–2% of all elementary age students received medications for behavior (primarily hyperactivity) or seizure disorders, and the numbers rose to between 9% and 20% for students in self-contained special education classrooms (Gadow, 1979; Gadow & Kane, 1983). Students with severe impairments are very likely to require medications during the school day, particularly if the students have medically fragile or complicated conditions (Trahms, Affleck, Lowenbraum, & Scranton, 1977).

Persons currently administering medication in the school generally include the teacher, school nurse, student, teacher aide, and secretary. In almost half of the cases surveyed, the child's classroom teacher was in charge of administering medication (Gadow & Kane, 1983). In a more recent study of classrooms for students with severe impairments, medications were administered in 85% of the classrooms surveyed, with the teacher responsible 47% of the time (Mulligan-Ault, Guess, Struth, & Thompson, 1988).

OVERVIEW

The general purpose of administration of medication is to relieve symptoms, to treat an existing disease, or to promote health and prevent disease. Since many medications require administration throughout the day, many students would be unable to attend school unless administration of their medication could be provided there. Some of the variables surrounding medication administration include when and how the medications are given and factors affecting the body's absorption of the medication.

When Medications May Be Given

Medication may be given to the student as prescribed by the student's physician, or as requested by the parents or caregiver in over-the-counter medications (OTC medications). A related issue is the ability of parents or caregivers to authorize the school to give nonprescription or OTC medications. Some districts or schools accept the responsibility to give these medications; others do not.

Medication may be given to the student for either an acute or chronic illness with the length of time a student takes a medication depending on the reasons the student is receiving it. A student with an infection (an acute condition) may take antibiotics for 7, 10, or 14 days. The antibiotic may need to be given every 6 hours, requiring that a dose be given when the student is in school. The student with a seizure disorder (a chronic condition) may take medication for several years. The medication may need to be given four times a day at intervals that would necessitate a dose also being given during school hours. In both these instances, school staff would be responsible for administering medication under the supervision of a registered nurse.

How Medications May Be Given

Medications may be given to students using various routes or methods. These include: oral (through the mouth or using an in-place nasogastric or gastrostomy tube), rectal (placed in the student's rectum), intravenous (through a vein), intramuscular (into a muscle), subcutaneous (into subcutaneous tissue, i.e., tissue between the skin and muscle), topical (placed on the student's skin), otic (placed in the student's ear), ophthalmologic (placed in the student's eye), and nasal (placed in the student's nose). Although the school nurse or other qualified health professional may be giving medications by several of the above routes or methods, the information presented here will focus on the oral (through the mouth) method.

Absorption of Medication

Medication administration to a child differs from administration to an adult. A child differs from an adult in the ability to absorb, distribute, use, and eliminate medication. There are no standardized ranges for doses of medications for children, as there are for adults. Many medications are prepared in adult dose strength. For a child, formulas using the child's age, weight, and surface area of the body determine the medication dose (Whaley & Wong, 1987).

Some students have been referred to as "rapid metabolizers," which means that they may metabolize or utilize medications faster than other children. Such a student may weigh the same as another, but still not benefit from a similar drug dose. Conversely, one student may develop a tolerance to a certain level of drug that is toxic (harmful) to another student (Dickey, 1987).

During periods of rapid growth and development, such as the toddler years and puberty, the student may have increased sensitivity to the side effects of medications. It is difficult to recognize adverse effects of medications in the preverbal or nonverbal student, since the student is unable to report sensations. Common reactions that may be difficult to report are ringing in the ears or pain (Dickey, 1987). Teachers, therefore, must be specifically aware of changes in the student's posture, mood, temperament, attention, and skin color as signs of reactions to medications. Suspected reactions should be reported to the school health care worker and parents and/or caregiver.

PROCEDURES

Preparation for Administering Medication

Before administering any medication, the policies of the school district related to approval or consent for medication administration must be reviewed. These should include: parental request or authorization to give medication, physician's written approval or request for administration of medication (the prescription on the medication container may be an example), and secure storage for the medication (Gadow & Kane,

1983). The requirement of a physician's written approval may also apply for OTC medications.

If a medication is to be given during the school day it must generally be made available at the school. The medication container must be labeled with the student's name, dosage, frequency of administration, and the prescribing physician's name. A system for recording and documenting when the medication was administered to the student must be established.

Routine Procedures   Some prior discussion with the student's parent or caregiver about the most effective techniques for administration of the medication can be helpful and time-saving to the staff as well as beneficial to the student. For example, a student may prefer that a tablet be crushed and mixed with jelly, that liquid be given before or after the administration, or that administration be done when the student is alone with the person administering the medication.

When the medication is taken from the storage area, hospital procedures usually require that the label on the medication container must be read three times (i.e., when removing it from the cabinet or storage area, when pouring out the medication, and when returning the medication to the storage area). In addition to reading the label three times, the written record of administration of the medication to be given is compared with what is written on the label. Liquid medication is placed in a cup or pulled up in a syringe. A tablet or capsule is placed in a cup to hold it until given to the student. The remaining medication is placed in the designated locked storage area. The person carrying out the above steps should also be the person giving the medication to the student (Wagner, 1983). This procedure is also recommended for school staff administering medication to ensure that the correct medication is given to the correct student.

An additional precaution must be taken to be sure that the student has experience with the medication prior to receiving it at school. School staff, therefore, must never administer the *first dosage* of any medication. The staff must have a guarantee of prior exposure to the medication with administration having been carried out by the parent, caregiver, or a qualified health professional.

The medication may be prepared in a number of ways to make it palatable to the student. Crushed tablets and the contents of capsules can be mixed with food. It is wise to avoid mixing essential food items such as milk, formula, cereal, or orange juice, since the student may become adversely conditioned against these foods and refuse to take them. When medication is mixed with liquid or food, only a small amount of liquid or food is used because the student may refuse to take the entire amount and receive only a partial dose of medication (Whaley & Wong, 1987). Sometimes oral medications are more readily swallowed if they are followed by a "chaser" of water, juice, carbonated beverage, or a popsicle or frozen juice bar. This may help reduce a slightly unpleasant aftertaste (Whaley & Wong, 1987).

Most liquid medications are prescribed in teaspoonsful. Unfortunately, household teaspoons vary greatly in size, and persons using the same household teaspoon will pour different amounts into the spoon. A medication prescribed to be given in teaspoons should be given in milliliters; the established standard is 1 teaspoon equals 5 milliliters. Medicine spoons with measurements are available at drug stores. The most accurate means for measuring small amounts of medication is the use of a plastic, disposable (not glass) syringe or plastic dropper. A small plastic cup can be used to administer the medication to the student who is able to drink from a cup (Whaley & Wong, 1987). See Figure 3.1 for examples of containers used for administering medications.

Crushed tablets and contents of capsules can be dissolved in small amounts of water or mixed with syrup, jelly, or fruit and given by spoon (Chard & Scipien, 1986). If a tablet is to be crushed before being given to a student, it can be crushed between two spoons. It is important to

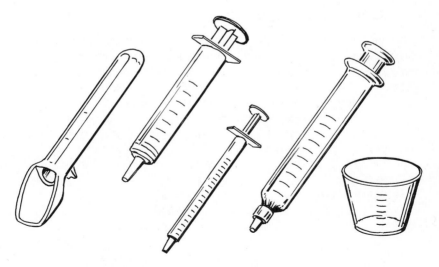

Figure 3.1.   Containers used for administering medications.

make certain that the bits of crushed medication do not cling to the sides of the spoon (Whaley & Wong, 1987). Parents or school staff may need to check with the school health worker, pharmacist, or physician to determine if the effectiveness of the medication is lost when it is crushed (Wagner, 1983).

Before preparing and administering any medication, the person administering the medication must thoroughly wash his or her hands (in sinks *not* related to toileting). The medication may actually have to be placed into the student's mouth if the student is unable to accomplish this task unassisted. Therefore, careful handwashing by school staff before preparing and administering medication can help prevent inadvertent contamination of the medication.

The "Five Rights" of Medication Administration   Before giving the medication, the "Five Rights" (Dickey, 1987) or the "universal precautions" (Wong & Whaley, 1986) should be used to ensure correct administration. The person administering the medication makes certain that the *right dose* of the *right medication* is given to the *right patient* at the *right time* by the *right route* (Wagner, 1983). These guidelines are used every time a medication is given. A few minutes of double-checking a medication or writing down routine procedure can prevent a serious error that may result in regretful and painful experiences for the school staff, the student, and the family.

Administering Medications

The method of administration of medication depends on the developmental age of the student and the student's ability to chew and swallow. For students whose level of development is that of an infant or for those who have difficulty retaining food or fluid in the mouth, the student is usually held in a semireclining position. The smaller student can be held (Figure 3.2), while the larger student can remain in a wheelchair or chair (Whaley & Wong, 1987). When holding or supporting a student it is important to be sure that he or she is in a relaxed position to decrease the chances of choking. This may be achieved by making sure that the student's neck is flexed, the shoulders are rounded, and the student is in a slightly forward, or flexed, position.

The medication is placed in the student's mouth from a spoon, plastic dropper, or plastic syringe (of course, without a needle on the syringe). The dropper or syringe is placed along the side of the student's tongue. The medication is given slowly to ease swallowing and avoid

Figure 3.2.   Administering medication through a syringe (without the nee-dle) to a smaller student held on the teacher's lap.

causing the student to choke. For the student with tongue thrust, med-ications may need to be rescued from the student's lips or chin and re-administered. If the student uses a suck to take in liquid, a nipple may be used as in Figure 3.3. The medication can also be slowly pushed into the nipple while the student is sucking (Whaley & Wong, 1987).

   If the student is able to swallow a tablet, the medication may be placed on the middle of the tongue. The student can then swallow it

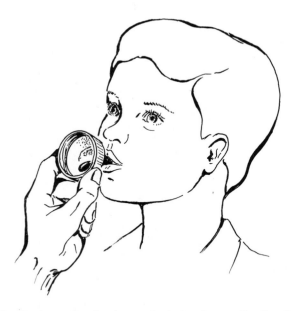

Figure 3.3.   An example of using a nipple to give medication to a student who uses a suck when taking in liquid.

with juice or water (Wagner, 1983). Because of the possibility of aspiration (pulling the tablet and/or secretions into the lungs), a whole tablet should not be given until the student is about 5 years old.

Procedures Following Medication Administration

Equipment used to dispense the medication must be washed thoroughly, dried, and placed in the storage area for the student. Documentation needs to be made in the student's health record and medication log of the dosage of medication and the time it was given. If the medication was not given, this too needs to be documented in the health record and medication log, reported to the school health worker, *and* recorded in a written note or log to the student's parents and/or caregivers. The reason for not giving the medication must be given.

Potential Problems

Several problems may arise around the practice of administering medications in the schools. These include the possibility that a student will not take the medication or receives only a portion of the dosage, takes the wrong medication, has an unusual response to the medication, or chokes during administration of the medication. Each situation presents a different problem to the teacher and health care worker. Each situation must be documented in writing in the student's health record and reported to the parent and/or caregiver.

Incomplete Dosage   For various reasons, the student may not receive some or all of the required dosage of the medication. The student may refuse to take the medication, spit out a portion, or vomit shortly after the medication is given.

If the student resists taking the medication, it is recommended that school staff not try to force the dosage. If a resistant student is forced to take medication, the medication could be aspirated. A crying student can easily aspirate a medication, particularly if the student is lying on his or her back. Rather, efforts need to be made to determine why the student resists taking the medication. Possible problems may be with the taste, texture, or size of the dosage. Combining the medication with foods and breaking the dosage into smaller units may be appropriate alternative strategies. If the student continues to refuse the medication, the teacher may wait for 20–30 minutes and offer the medication again (Whaley & Wong, 1987). If the problem continues, the teacher may skip the administration. It may be necessary to arrange for a parent, caregiver, or health care worker to come to the school to assist the school staff in administering the medication. Any missed medication administration must be reported to the health care worker and the parent or caregiver.

If the student spits out or vomits the medication, repeating administration is recommended (King, Wieck, & Dyer, 1983). The teacher may need to investigate why these reactions occurred and develop alternative procedures. These procedures may include mixing the medication with food, using smaller dosages, altering the student's position to be more upright, and so forth. The teacher may wish to wait 20–30 minutes and offer the medication again.

Incorrect Medication   If the wrong medication is given, the school staff need to notify the health care worker in the school immediately. It is important to know the name of the medication and the approximate dosage that was given to the student. The student's physician must be informed as soon as possible so that the student may be observed for reactions, so that an antidote may be given, or in case the student needs to be compelled to vomit the medication.

The following protocol is suggested to prevent administration of the wrong medication: The medication should be in its original container with the student's name, name of medication, dose, time, and route (method) of administration listed. A designated space for each student's medication should be specified in the locked cabinet. Staff should prepare and administer medication to one student at a time, rather than setting out medication for two or more students at the same time. In order to avoid the opportunity for a student to reach the medication and accidentally take it, medication should *never* be left on a counter or other easily accessible place. Adults should not take medications in front of students. Medications should never be called candy (Wagner, 1983).

Responses to Medications   After a medication is administered, the teacher may need to be aware of possible responses to the medication. These may include a reaction, a side-effect, or an allergic reaction. It is not unusual for students to experience reactions to medications that are the opposite of the reactions expected. These reactions describe chemical responses in the body producing other than anticipated results. For example, Ritalin, given in an attempt to regulate hyperactivity, can result in a state of excitement rather than calming the student (Dickey, 1987).

Side effects are additional results that may occur after taking a medication. Side effects are any effect the medication has in addition to what was intended to be therapeutic or healing. Side effects may be tolerated because the medication's healing effects may be considered more valuable to the student than the somewhat undesirable side effect (Wagner, 1983). For example, a student receiving Benadryl for an itchy rash may experience drowsiness as a side effect. With this drowsiness, the student is less aware of the itching and does not scratch.

Persons giving medications to a student need to be aware of possible side effects of the medication, along with signs indicating that the student is receiving too much medication (i.e., signs indicating that the dose is toxic or harmful to the student). Information on possible side effects and signs indicating possible toxicity may be obtained from the student's parents or caregiver, the student's physician, or the health care worker in the school. Information on side effects is also available in reference books on medications, such as the *Physicians' Desk Reference* (PDR) (1989).

An allergy to a medication refers to hypersensitivity to a medication that does not normally cause a reaction (Thomas, 1985).   Signs of allergy to a medication are most often seen in the skin. Urticaria (hives) appears suddenly and may spread over the entire body. Itching occurs along with this rash. In addition to urticaria, other signs that may appear include: nausea, vomiting, diarrhea, irritability, and tired appearance (Whaley & Wong, 1987). If the student shows an allergic reaction to a medication, the medication should be discontinued.

Choking   The possibility of choking on a medication must be anticipated. The student with poor muscle control and/or coordination and the resistant student can be at great risk for choking. If the student begins to choke, medication administration must be stopped immediately. When the student begins to breathe normally and has completely recovered, medication administration can be resumed. If the student does not recover (i.e., continues choking, skin color turns blue), it is assumed that the student has an obstruction of the airway (see the next section, "Signs of an Emergency") (Whaley & Wong, 1987).

The health care worker in the school and the student's parents and/or caregiver must be notified of the occurrence of any of the above conditions: medication not received, wrong medication received, signs of side effects and/or toxicity, signs of allergy to medication, and choking on medication. The student's physician may also need to be contacted.

SIGNS OF AN EMERGENCY

Emergency situations generally arise when a student chokes on medication. If the student seems unable to recover from choking, the teacher should open the student's mouth and inspect to see if an object is plugging the airway. If the object is a tablet, capsule, or medication in food, and is visible, the fingers can be inserted in an attempt to remove the object. If the object is not visible, the Heimlich maneuver is used to force the medication out (see Chapter 8, Cardiopulmonary Resuscitation).

If the student is unable to recover from choking on medication that is liquid, the teacher must first open the mouth and look for and remove any object that is plugging the airway. If there is no visible object, the Heimlich maneuver is used to force out the material that is plugging the airway. A person trained in cardiopulmonary resuscitation should perform this maneuver (see Chapter 8, Cardiopulmonary Resuscitation, for more detailed information). The emergency procedure for the school must be followed, and the local emergency medical team must be notified immediately.

Additional emergency situations arise in connection with allergic reactions. School staff need to know if the child has had an allergic reaction to any medication in the past. Medications that have resulted in an allergic response should *never* be given to the student again. The student's medication log should indicate any allergies. When a student is started on a new medication, the school staff should refer to the report on allergies previously experienced. The new medication must be checked with the allergies listed to verify that the new medication has not resulted in an allergic reaction in the past. Verification that the new medication has not resulted in an allergic reaction in the past must be checked thoroughly. Since medications often have more than one name, the health care worker in the school can double check a new medication against a past allergy.

ADDITIONAL RESOURCES

School staff can find more information on administration of medication in the list of Literature Cited at the end of this chapter (King et al., 1983; Scipien, Barnard, Chard, Howe, & Phillips, 1986; Whaley & Wong, 1986; Wong & Whaley, 1987). Nurses in the school, the physician's office, public health department, or local hospital can provide assistance on methods of administration, side effects and toxic effects of medications, and setting up a medication log for the student. The occupational and physical therapist can provide guidance on proper positioning for medication administration and tips on oral-motor problems hindering medication administration. A pharmacist and the student's physician can provide information about the student's medication (i.e., side effects, toxic effects, interaction between medications).

LITERATURE CITED

Chard, M.A., & Scipien, G.M. (1986). Approaches to diagnostic and therapeutic procedures. In G.M. Scipien, M.U. Barnard, M.A. Chard, J. Howe, & P.J. Phillips (Eds.), *Comprehensive pediatric nursing* (pp. 217–235). New York: McGraw-Hill.

Dickey, S. (1987). *A guide to the nursing of children.* Baltimore: Williams & Wilkins.

Gadow, K.D. (1979). *Children on medication: A primer for school personnel.* Reston, VA.: Council for Exceptional Children.

Gadow, K.D., & Kane, K.M. (1983). Administration of medication by school personnel. *The Journal of School Health, 53*(3), 178–183.

King, E.M., Wieck, L., & Dyer, M. (1983). *Pediatric nursing procedures.* Philadelphia: J.B. Lippincott.

Mulligan-Ault, M., Guess, D., Struth, L., & Thompson, B. (1988) The implementation of health related procedures in classrooms for students with severe multiple impairments. *The Journal of The Association for Persons with Severe Handicaps, 13*(2), 100–109.

Physician's desk reference (43rd ed.). (1989). Oradell, N.J.: Medical Economics Co., Inc.

Scipien, G.M., Barnard, M.U., Chard, M.A., Howe, J., & Phillips, P.J. (Eds.). (1986). *Comprehensive pediatric nursing.* New York: McGraw-Hill.

Thomas, C.L. (Ed.). (1985). *Taber's cyclopedic medical dictionary.* Philadelphia: F.A. Davis.

Trahms, C., Affleck, J., Lowenbraum, S., & Scranton, T. (1977). The special educator's role on the health service team. *Exceptional Children, 43,* 344.

Wagner, M. (Ed.). (1983). *Nurse's reference library—drugs.* Springhouse, PA.: Intermed Communications, Inc.

Whaley, L.F., & Wong, D.L. (1987). *Nursing care of infants and children.* St. Louis: C.V. Mosby.

Wong, D.L., & Whaley, L.F. (1986). *Clinical handbook of pediatric nursing.* St. Louis: C.V. Mosby.

4

SKIN CARE

The most appropriate skin care treatment in the schools is that which is focused on preventing skin breakdown and preventing the development of pressure sores. Pressure sores heal slowly under the best of conditions. Once they have formed, all positioning strategies and programming for a student must be altered to accommodate their treatment. The purpose of skin care is, therefore, to ensure that the student either maintains or regains healthy skin.

OVERVIEW

To be able to understand the importance of and reasons for preventive skin care, it is helpful to first understand the structure and function of the skin, the body's largest organ. Second, it is necessary to be able to recognize healthy skin, unhealthy skin, and some of the causes for the breakdown of healthy tissue.

Structure and Function of Skin

The skin consists of three layers, the epidermis, the dermis, and sub-cutaneous tissue (Figure 4.1). The epidermis is the outer layer of skin and is considered to be a living, active structure. It is thought to be con-

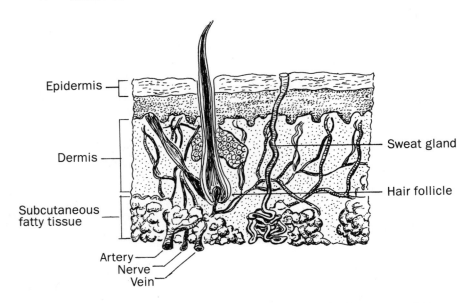

Figure 4.1.   The layers of skin: epidermis, dermis, and subcutaneous fatty tissue.

stantly involved in production of cells, movement of cells to the surface, and eventual maturing of cells. The outermost layer of the epidermis is composed of dead cells, which are continually being rubbed or washed away. This process of movement of cells from the innermost layer of the epidermis to the outermost layer takes approximately 28 days for every cell (Esterly, 1987).

The middle layer, the dermis, consists of connective tissue, blood vessels, nerves, hair follicles, sweat glands, and oil glands. The epidermis depends on the dermis for nutrients such as glucose, oxygen, amino acids, and vitamins (Humphrey, 1982). These nutrients help the epidermis carry out the work of replenishing itself as cells move from its innermost layer to its outermost layer. A hormone is thought to inhibit the production of the epidermis cells and the overall maturation rate of the epidermis. High levels of the hormone slow the maturation rate of the epidermis while low levels are associated with replenishment of the epidermis. The levels of this hormone are high during daytime activity and stress, and levels are lower during sleep or periods of rest. The healing of skin, or replenishment of epidermis cells, is thought to be promoted during rest and sleep when the levels of this hormone are low (Carpenito, 1983; Humphrey, 1982).

The subcutaneous tissue is the inner layer of skin. It is composed of loose connective tissue, blood vessels, and nerves. This layer loosely binds the dermis and epidermis to underlying structures of the body. It serves as a storage area for fat, insulation to conserve body heat, and a cushion to protect against trauma (Esterly, 1987; Innes, 1981).

Some functions of the skin include: 1) protecting inner tissues of the body from injury, drying, and invasion by bacteria or viruses; 2) assisting in regulation of body temperature; 3) assisting with excretion of substances from the body; and 4) assisting in production of vitamin D (Humphrey, 1982; Innes, 1981; Thomas, 1985).

The skin is the first line of defense for the body, protecting the body from the environment. The skin contains nerve receptors that provide the body with awareness of sensations of pressure, pain, and temperature. When the skin touches an object that is hot or sharp, nerve endings receive this message and, through complex neuromuscular activity, this message reaches the brain. The brain sends a message back to the area of the body experiencing the heat or sharpness resulting in the pulling away of the skin from the object. When nerves in the skin receive a message that there is pain, the brain receives this message and the student initiates activity to move away from or eliminate the pain.

The skin serves as a barrier to infection. Oils secreted by glands in the dermis help prevent the skin from drying and the resulting chapping and cracking of the skin. This chapping and cracking opens the skin, which usually serves as a barrier, to bacteria and viruses. Although bacteria can live on the surface of the skin, the relative dryness and acidity of the skin slows the growth of bacteria (Potter & Perry, 1985).

The skin also assists in regulation of body temperature, excretion, and reception of vitamin D. Blood vessels in the skin increase in size, allowing an increased flow of blood to the skin, and decreasing the temperature of the body. Sweat glands in the skin secrete increased amounts of moisture. This moisture, or perspiration, evaporates from the surface of the skin, cooling the skin. In order to increase the body temperature, blood vessels become smaller in size and perspiration decreases (Innes, 1981). The skin also has the ability to excrete substances from the body. During heavy perspiration, the skin excretes water and sodium chloride. As more water and sodium chloride are lost through the skin, an overall decreased amount of fluid in the body can result (Innes, 1981). Finally, the skin serves as a receptor for vitamin D from the sun (Carpenito, 1983) and assists in production of vitamin D for the body (Humphrey, 1982).

The Promotion of Healthy Skin

Skin reflecting a condition of health includes a color that is normal for the individual student, a smooth texture, no swelling, adequate turgor (elasticity), a temperature that is normal for the individual, and sensation present to the degree that is normal for the individual student. Healthy skin is characterized by having no bleeding or bruising; not being excessively oily or dry; having no breaks such as scratches or lacerations; and having no pressure sores, burns, or rashes.

Unhealthy skin may be skin that exhibits bleeding or bruising; is excessively oily or dry; has breaks such as scratches or lacerations; or has pressure sores, burns, or rashes. Characteristics of skin that may reflect an unhealthy condition include a color that is abnormal for the individual student, a rough texture, swelling, poor turgor (elasticity), a temperature that is abnormal for the individual student, and sensation that is absent or present to a degree that is abnormal for the individual student.

Factors to be considered when promoting healthy skin in the student with disabilities include the student's degree of bladder and bowel control, nutritional status, level of activity, ability to distinguish sensations, and ability to communicate to others the sensations experienced.

A student experiencing limited control over bladder and bowel functioning should be a candidate for an active skin care program. If the student wears clothing wet with urine or soiled with feces, the skin will not remain dry and clean. The constant presence of moisture can promote the growth of bacteria on the surface of the skin. Moisture, such as perspiration, urine, or feces, reduces the resistance of the skin and can make it more liable to breakdown (Horsley, 1981). This skin breakdown opens the body to possible infection.

Students with a questionable nutritional status are at risk for skin problems. If the student has poor general nutrition, there may be a reduction of subcutaneous tissue. This results in a reduction of the cushion effect provided by the subcutaneous tissue, which protects the body against trauma. The skin requires adequate nutrition and hydration to resist injury and disease (Potter & Perry, 1985).

The student's level of activity is another indicator of the need for a skin care program. In normally active persons, the skin and underlying tissue usually are not subjected to a high degree of pressure for long periods of time. Sustained pressure is avoided because of the discomfort (i.e., pain, tingling, or numbness) that is felt on the skin and subcutaneous tissue. As a result of discomfort, the person changes position, resulting in relief from pressure and discomfort.

Not all persons respond to sustained pressure on the skin. Some students do not interpret the pressure as painful because they may have decreased sensation in the skin and underlying tissues. In this case, nerve receptors in the skin do not receive messages that there is pressure on the skin and underlying tissues. Without the interpretation of pressure as painful, there is no reason to change position. Other students may perceive the discomfort, yet not be able to change position because of difficulty or inability to move certain parts of the body. In this case, the nerve receptors in the skin may receive the message that there is discomfort, yet the student may not be able to communicate this discomfort to others. The two major factors to be considered in the prevention of skin problems are the student's level of activity and ability to perceive sensations on the skin. The student having a decreased level of activity and decreased ability to perceive discomfort on the surface of the skin is at risk for developing skin problems. The most likely problem to develop is the pressure sore (also called decubitus ulcer or bedsore).

The Development of Pressure Sores

Normal cell activities, including activities of skin cells, depend on the reception of nutrients and the elimination of waste products. When pressure is applied to the surface of the skin, the ability of the blood to circulate to skin cells may be hindered. This reduces the ability of the cell to receive nutrients and eliminate waste. Pressure applied for as little as 1–2 hours to the skin and subcutaneous tissue over bony prominences can cause serious obstruction of blood flow. This can result in inability of the cell to function normally and result in death of the cell (Horsley, 1981). According to Rudd (1964), high pressures on the skin for a short time can be tolerated better than low pressures on the skin for long periods of time. It is believed that sustained pressure over an extended time causes more tissue damage since cells are without nutrients during that time (Innes, 1981).

Pressure sores develop in the following stages (Figure 4.2). Initially, pressure on the skin causes a reddening that disappears as the pressure is relieved. If pressure continues, the skin may have reddening that does not disappear when the pressure is relieved. The skin becomes hardened and warmer than surrounding skin. In the next stage,

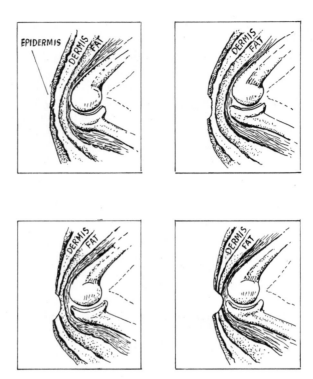

Figure 4.2.   Stages in the development of a pressure sore.

the skin continues to be reddened, hardened, and warmer than surrounding skin. The epidermis becomes broken and the dermis is exposed. During the third stage, an open sore develops as the dead tissue separates from the living tissue. The skin around the sore continues to be reddened and hardened and warmer than surrounding skin and there is drainage from the open sore. In the last stage, the open sore becomes deeper and has a foul smell. There may or may not be drainage present (Horsley, 1981).

PROCEDURES

Preparation for Skin Care

Preparation for skin care procedures first involves a determination of whether the teacher is dealing with healthy or unhealthy skin.

Healthy Skin   Preparation for the care of healthy skin requires that the teacher have knowledge of the condition of the student's skin through close observation of the skin during contact with the student in the classroom. This means specifically examining the student's skin, noting overall skin characteristics as well as examining portions of the body particularly susceptible to the development of pressure sores. A rating scale for determining the potential for pressure sore formation has been developed by Gosnell (1973). Figure 4.3 is an adaptation of the scale. A low score indicates great susceptibility to developing pressure sores and a high score indicates reduced risk for pressure sores. This scale should be completed annually as part of the overall assessment and program development process.

A general health plan should be developed for the student at risk for developing skin problems. The plan should include routine position changes, cleansing, maintenance of nutrition, and use of lotions or oils on the skin. The health care worker in the school should be consulted to develop a healthy skin care program. Methods of maintaining healthy skin may need to be clarified or endorsed by the health care worker in the school.

Unhealthy Skin   Preparation for care of unhealthy skin also includes having knowledge of the condition of the student's skin. For the student having unhealthy skin, school staff need to actually look at the skin and identify the extent of the problem. It is necessary to know what the skin disorder is, the natural course of the disorder and usual treatment. Any allergies the student has must be known to ensure that the student is not allergic to the prescribed treatment. A referral to a dermatologist (skin specialist) may be required for diagnosis and treatment.

The school staff involved in performing treatment for the skin problem must have a detailed treatment plan in writing. This includes information on the actual procedure along with the frequency and duration of treatment. The treatment plan must be discussed with the health care worker in the school and may require an order from the student's physician. Treatment should be kept as simple as possible (Esterly, 1987) but may involve changing dressings, the application of lotions, the use of heat lamps, and so forth. Any of these procedures may require specific techniques, the use of gloves or other special equipment, and attention to prevention of the spread of the condition to healthy skin.

Performing Skin Care

The type of skin care provided in the classroom will vary for procedures used to maintain healthy skin and those used to treat unhealthy skin.

RATING SCALE

Mental status	Continence	Mobility	Activity	Nutrition
5 Alert	4 Fully controlled	4 Full	4 Ambulatory	3 Good
4 Apathetic	3 Usually controlled	3 Slightly limited	3 Walks with assistance	2 Fair
3 Confused	2 Minimally controlled	2 Very limited	2 Remains in chair	1 Poor
2 Stuporous	1 Absence of control	1 Immobile	1 Remains in bed	
1 Unconscious				

Date	Mental Status Sub-score	Continence Sub-score	Mobility Sub-score	Activities Sub-score	Nutrition Sub-score	Total score

Figure 4.3.   Scale for identifying the potential for development of pressure sores. (Adapted from Gosnell, D. [1973]. An assessment tool to identify pressure sores. *Nursing Research, 22,* 55–59.)

Skin care procedures for healthy skin involve an overall program oriented toward assisting a student in remaining clean and healthy. Skin care procedures for unhealthy skin are specific treatments and responses to sores, rashes, bruises, and so forth on specific parts of the body.

Healthy Skin   The primary focus of care of healthy skin is prevention of the development of skin problems. Four areas must be considered when promoting healthy skin: 1) keeping the skin clean and dry, 2) maintaining proper nutrition, 3) maintaining adequate activity, and 4) reducing periods of continuous pressure on parts of the body across the day.

Keeping the skin clean and dry is necessary to keep skin healthy. This is important for skin all over the body, and particularly for skin that comes in contact with feces or urine. A primary skin care program should include efforts to reduce or eliminate incontinence, efforts to establish toilet training, catheterization, or frequent routines of checking and changing incontinent wear and cleansing the skin to reduce prolonged exposure of the skin to feces or urine. This exposure can result in softening of the skin or maceration. Softened skin is at an increased risk for development of sores. Moisture, from any source, accumulated in folds of the skin, around the genitals, thighs, or any place where the skin on parts of the body can rub together, will result in redness, irritation, and the eventual development of sores (Walker, 1971). Maceration of the skin by urine and feces adds the excoriating (skin cutting) effects of the decomposing substances in the urine and the infective organisms present in the feces to already damaged tissue, increasing the likelihood that sores will develop. For example, organisms producing ammonia from the urine will cause alkaline burns, especially if the skin is already weakened by moisture (Walker, 1971).

In addition to keeping the skin between the legs clean and dry, it is important to keep skin over the entire body clean. Maintaining proper hygiene can be effective in decreasing the bacterial population on the skin. If the student develops a break in the skin, bacteria tend to move to that area and grow (Horsley, 1981). Bathing the skin removes dirt and dead cells from the epidermis (Innes, 1981). Relief of prolonged pressure while ensuring that the skin is clean and free of excess moisture, and avoiding injury to the skin, are the essential methods of prevention of pressure sores (Walker, 1971).

Walker (1971) recommends the maintenance of adequate nutrition as an additional strategy in preventing development of pressure sores. The daily intake of appropriate nutrients is necessary to maintain healthy skin. If, for some reason, the intake of, or body's use of nutrients is decreased, then the student is more susceptible to development of sores. For example, if the student has a fever or other disease process taking place, body protein is being broken down to provide energy. The student may be unable to eat adequate amounts of food and necessary nutrients may not be available to replace those lost or those needed. Anemia, resulting from an inadequate amount of iron, reduces the body's resistance to infection and delays the repair of injured tissue. The tissue becomes weakened, vulnerable to mild pressure, and likely to develop sores (Horsley, 1981). Adequate intake of fluids is also important, especially in students who are dehydrated. Ensuring that the student has an adequate fluid intake can help prevent dry, cracked lips and skin. A diet from the basic four food groups and containing the proper number of calories is needed for normal day-to-day living. An illness or injury causes a decrease in one or more of the nutrients needed for healthy skin. Protein and vitamin C, important in preventing pressure sores (Innes, 1981), are utilized to fight infection or disease. (See Chapter 6, Nutrition Monitoring and Supplementation).

Optimal levels of activity must be encouraged as part of a proactive skin care program. Decreased activity can result in increased opportunities for the student to experience pressure on skin surfaces. The skin and subcutaneous tissue are squeezed between underlying bony prominences and a hard surface such as a bed or a chair. Certain parts of the body sustain more weight when a person is sitting and lying and are considered pressure areas. The most common pressure areas are identified in Figure 4.4. This pressure prevents circulation of blood from occurring normally so cells in the tissue are starved for nourishment. Normal cells can survive for a certain length of time, but if the pressure continues for a prolonged time, the cells will die, beginning skin breakdown and the development of pressure sores. Sustained pressure over a long period of time is thought to do more damage than great pressure for brief periods. In students whose general physical condition is poor, the length of time the skin cells can remain without adequate blood supply is less than the time acceptable for healthy skin. Students at risk for development of sores need to move, or be moved, frequently during the day. Figure 4.3 can be used to identify the student's risk level. A change in position should occur about every 20 minutes for students at high risk. The movement releases continuous pressure and also increases blood circulation (Walker, 1971).

The student, whether active or inactive, may also experience pressure from braces, shoes, or sitting in a wheelchair. The *same* concerns about pressure resulting from inactivity apply to pressure resulting from

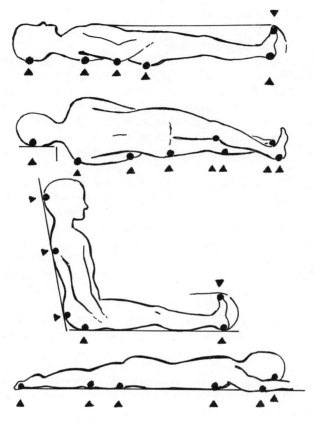

Figure 4.4.   Pressure areas most commonly susceptible to the development of pressure sores.

ill-fitting equipment. The skin underneath braces and splints or wheelchair seats should be checked *daily* to identify persistent red spots. If the spots do not fade within 20 minutes after the pressure is relieved, the health care worker should be notified of: 1) ill fitting equipment and 2) the potential for development of a pressure sore.

The final aspect of preventing development of skin problems for the student with disabilities is the need to identify methods the student uses to communicate the presence of discomfort. As discussed previously, uncomfortable pressure causes a student to move in order to relieve the discomfort. If the student cannot initiate movement to relieve the discomfort, methods need to be considered to assist the student in communicating with others. School staff need to be sensitive to changes in mood, movement, or posturing as indicators of pain.

Unhealthy Skin   When providing care to unhealthy skin, the focus is on treating the skin to promote a return to a healthy condition. Efforts should also be made to prevent development of further skin problems. The actual care of the unhealthy skin is prescribed by the student's physician or other health care professional, or endorsed by the health care worker in the school. Because of the great variation in skin disorders and resulting treatment plans, specific procedures are not described here; rather a general review of treatment of skin problems is covered.

Generally, treatment of skin disorders may involve application of a substance to the affected area, covering the area with a dressing, or leaving the area uncovered and open to the air. Treatments may include application of lotions, powders, creams, ointments, gels, aerosol sprays, or solutions (Esterly, 1987). Dressings may involve application of a substance to the area and then placement of a covering or dressing. This dressing may be dry, wet and allowed to dry while in place, or applied and maintained as a wet dressing.

Use of a wet dressing necessitates adding solution to the dressing to prevent drying out. Wet dressings are used with severe itching, burning, stinging sensations, or acutely inflamed moist or oozing dermititis. Lotions, creams, and ointments can be used for dry skin and as a method of carrying a medication to the surface of the skin. Powders are effective absorptive agents in areas of the skin where there is excessive moisture and are useful in reducing friction in those areas where skin surfaces touch and rub against each other. In some instances the student may need to be taken to surgery for removal of dead tissue from the sore and/or grafting of healthy skin to the area of the pressure sore.

If a pressure sore is being treated, the method of treatment should be written clearly and followed closely, and adequate supplies must be available at the school to perform the necessary treatment. Of utmost importance is the need to eliminate pressure from the sore to prevent further breakdown of the skin. A regular schedule for repositioning the student must be established using those positions that best allow the student to continue with other activities while avoiding pressure on the existing sore and sustained pressure on other areas at risk for development of sores.

Methods of skin care, described above under "Healthy Skin," should also be followed to prevent development of additional skin problems. Diligence in carrying out the established plan for skin care is crucial for the welfare of the student. It is thought that the specific methodology used for treatment is not as important as the regularity with which the skin treatment plan is carried out (Cameron, 1979).

Procedures Following Skin Care

Procedures for following up on skin care address two areas: 1) use of washing procedures before attending to another student and 2) adequately inspecting the student to note any changes, or lack of changes, in the condition of the skin.

School staff working with skin care for unhealthy skin must routinely, carefully, and thoroughly wash hands before and after treatment. Handwashing should be done at a sink that is not used for food preparation or toileting. Handwashing is recommended to prevent the carrying of bacteria and viruses to the student's skin and possibly infecting the student, and to prevent any bacteria or viruses on the student's skin from spreading to other students and school staff.

Changes in condition of the skin need to be identified and communicated to the student's parents and the health care worker in the school. In order to recognize changes, school staff need to know the condition of the skin initially. Changes include any deterioration in the status of a pressure sore, development of an open area on the skin, or a hard lump under the skin. Development of a lump may indicate damage to deep tissues, especially the fatty layer. If this condition is overlooked, the skin will break down with continued pressure. All students should be checked daily for changes in skin condition (Walker, 1971). Lack of improvement in the status of the student's skin needs to be noted and brought to the attention of the health care worker in the school and the student's parents and/or caregiver. The treatment plan may need to be altered to find the appropriate method of treatment. Any change in the student's general condition, such as anorexia, dehydration, general malaise, or onset of incontinence of urine or feces, places the student at risk for developing skin problems (Walker, 1971).

Warning Signs

The student may develop a skin disorder that is not responsive to treatment or may progress in severity and increase in size. Treatment may need to be changed. The student may be allergic to the substances being used for treatment. The student's physician needs to be contacted for recommendations.

In addition to an already existing problem, an alternate skin problem may develop. For example, an infection may develop in the irritated or open skin. If an infection is suspected, the health care worker in the school must be contacted to record the student's temperature and examine the skin for the presence of redness, swelling, heat, pain, disordered function (Thomas, 1985), and the presence of drainage. The student's physician may need to be contacted and antibiotics may need to be started. The student may need to be retained at home because of the potential for spreading infection to other students and school staff.

As noted before, a skin disorder may develop in the student who has had no previous problems. If there is suspicion that the student is developing a skin problem, the health care worker in the school and the parents and/or caregiver need to be notified, with efforts made to eliminate the conditions contributing to the problem.

SIGNS OF AN EMERGENCY

If the student has a sore that does not heal and that progresses in size, the potential exists for occurrence of septicemia or blood poisoning. This condition indicates that bacteria have entered the blood stream. If not treated with antibiotics, the infection can progress and cause an overwhelming infection and death. Infection can be avoided by keeping the student's skin in a healthy condition and maintaining the student's nutrition. Healing will not occur when a student lacks protein due to inadequate intake or unusual loss (Guyton, 1966). A student with an open, draining sore can lose protein with the drainage. If the fluid and nutrients lost through the drainage from the sore are not replaced, healing is further delayed.

The student may experience an allergic reaction to a substance applied to the skin. This may appear as reddening of the skin, a burning sensation, or severe itching. Referral needs to be made to the physician for prescription of treatments and medications to relieve these symptoms. Anaphylaxis is an extreme allergic reaction to a substance. This reaction can be life-threatening. Signs of anaphylaxis include: flushing of the skin followed by severe itching; swelling of the skin or mucous membranes; swelling of the upper airway, which can result in difficulty breathing or complete airway obstruction; decreased blood pressure; and increased heart rate (Graef & Cone, 1985). The student experiencing an anaphylactic reaction needs immediate medical attention. The emergency procedure in the school must be followed. This includes calling the local emergency medical services for immediate transport to the hospital.

ADDITIONAL RESOURCES

Parents are a valuable resource for school staff when there is a question about the condition of the student's skin. The student's physician or health care professional working with the physician can provide assistance and direction on prevention/treatment of skin problems. The enterostomal therapist from a local hospital can provide assistance in care of the student's skin and the physical therapist in the school system can help find positions that will be suitable for the student during certain activities, yet prevent prolonged pressure on a few skin areas.

LITERATURE CITED

Cameron, G. (1979). Pressure sores: What to do when prevention fails. *Nursing, 79*(9), 42–47.

Carpenito, L.J. (1983). *Nursing diagnosis: Application to clinical practice.* Philadelphia: J. B. Lippincott.

Esterly, N.B. (1987). The skin. In R.E. Behrman & V.C. Vaughan (Eds.), *Nelson textbook of pediatrics* (13th ed., pp. 1385–1446). Philadelphia: W.B. Saunders.

Gosnell, D. (1973). An assessment tool to identify pressure sores. *Nursing Research, 22,* 55–59.

Graef, J.W., & Cone, T.E. (1985). *Manual of pediatric therapeutics.* Boston: Little, Brown.

Guyton, A.C. (1966). *Textbook of medical physiology* (3rd ed.). Philadelphia: W.B. Saunders.

Horsley, J.A. (1981). *Preventing decubitus ulcers: CURN project.* New York: Grune & Stratton.

Humphrey, J.P. (1982). Skin. In D.C. Broadwell & B.S. Jackson (Eds.), *Principles of ostomy care* (pp. 74–78). St. Louis: C.V. Mosby.

Innes, B. (1981). Integumentary status. In P.H. Mitchell & A. Loustau (Eds.), *Concepts basic to nursing* (3rd ed., pp. 572–601). New York: McGraw-Hill.

Potter, P.A., & Perry, A.G. (1985). *Fundamentals of nursing: Concepts, process, & practice.* St. Louis: C.V. Mosby.

Rudd, T.N. (1964). *The nursing of the elderly sick* (4th ed). London: Faber.

Thomas, C.L. (Ed.) (1985). *Taber's cyclopedic medical dictionary.* Philadelphia: F.A. Davis.

Walker, K.A. (1971). *Pressure sores: Prevention and treatment.* London: Butterworth & Company, Ltd.

5

BOWEL CARE

The purpose of bowel care is to promote adequate and regular bowel functioning throughout the entire day. This includes the prevention of or management of diarrhea and constipation. Because of the daily ongoing nature of conditions or procedures related to healthy bowels, bowel care becomes a school issue. Bowel care not only addresses the issue of toilet training, a curricular area commonly addressed within the domain of self-care, it additionally addresses the areas of diet, exercise, medication, and skin care.

OVERVIEW

Preliminary to a discussion of bowel care is a presentation of the basic structure and function of the gastrointestinal tract. This provides a basic framework for understanding how different conditions may affect the function of the intestines. Second, a brief discussion of factors generally affecting the function of the intestines is presented. These factors have obvious implications for the problems students with disabilities may have in establishing a normal and healthy bowel routine.

Structure and Function of the Bowel

The bowel or intestine is part of the gastrointestinal tract (Figure 5.1), and consists of the small intestine and the large intestine. Although the emphasis of this chapter is the structure and function of the large intestine, functioning of the entire gastrointestinal tract is reviewed briefly.

Food is normally taken into the mouth, ground into small pieces, and swallowed. Saliva mixes with food to begin breaking it down, allowing for more effective use by the body. When food is swallowed, the opening between the vocal cords is closed, preventing food from going into the trachea. Food moves through the esophagus, into the stomach. Once in the stomach, it mixes with hydrochloric acid and several enzymes, which further aid in breaking it down.

This mixture leaves the stomach and moves into the small intestine. Muscles of the small intestine contract and relax allowing the partially digested food and digestive secretions to mix thoroughly. This activity also allows the mixture to come in contact with the intestinal wall so that absorption of nutrients can occur. Almost all digestion and absorption of food and water occur in the small intestine.

The material remaining then moves into the large intestine (Figure 5.2). The large intestine consists of the cecum, the ascending colon, the transverse colon, the descending colon, the rectum, and the anus. The major absorption process going on in the large intestine is the movement of water from the large intestine back into the blood stream. The primary function of the large intestine is to concentrate and store fecal material prior to defecation.

The muscle movement in the large intestine is generally slower than in the small intestine. Because of this slow movement, material entering the colon remains there for 18–24 hours. During sleep and most of the day there is little or no movement in the large intestine. Three to four times a day, generally after meals, a marked increase in movement occurs. This increased movement (gastrocolic reflex) may lead to mass movement, in which large sections of the colon contract and push this fecal material from one third to three fourths the length of the colon in a few seconds (Vander, Sherman, & Luciano, 1975).

The fecal material is moved into the rectum by this mass movement. Distention of the walls of the rectum by fecal material is a normal stimulus for defecation or the defecation reflex. The response to this stimulus consists of a contraction of the rectum, relaxation of the internal and external anal sphincters and increased wavelike movement in the colon (Figure 5.3). This movement is generally adequate to propel

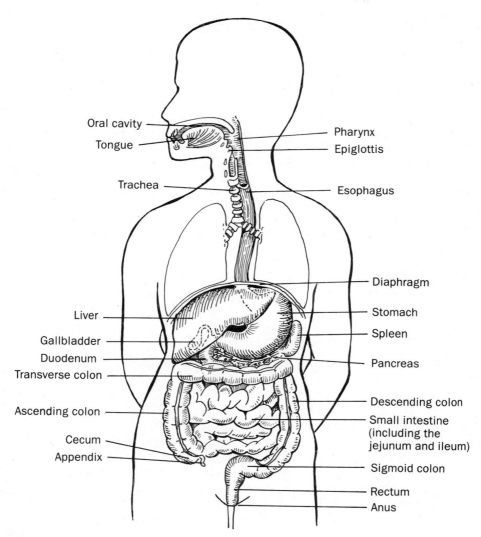

Figure 5.1.   The gastrointestinal tract.

feces through the anus (Vander et al., 1975). Defecation is normally assisted by deep breathing in of air followed by contraction of abdominal and chest muscles. This causes a marked increase in pressure inside the abdomen. This pressure is transmitted to the contents of the large intestine and assists in elimination of feces.

The conscious urge to defecate accompanies the initial distention of the rectum. If defecation does not occur, tension in the walls of the rectum decreases as the muscle relaxes. The urge to defecate subsides until the next mass movement pushes more feces into the rectum, increasing its volume and again initiating the defecation reflex.

Feces consist primarily of bacteria and food material that failed to be digested and absorbed while in the gastrointestinal tract. Feces are not waste products from inside the body. The lungs and kidneys eliminate wastes from processes going on inside the body. Feces are composed of material that has never been part of the body (Vander et al., 1975).

The following are expected characteristics of feces:

1. Amount is individual, depending on the intake of food and fluid.
2. Frequency of bowel movement is from 1 to 3 days.
3. Color is brownish.
4. Consistency is firm and formed.
5. Odor is individual depending on diet and intestinal flora.
6. Components are mucous threads—partially digested food (Brill & Kilts, 1980).

Factors Influencing Bowel Function

Each individual has unique patterns of bowel functioning, and the student with a disability brings additional complications to the issue of bowel control. The student may have oral-motor impairment resulting in inadequate intake of fiber and fluids; decreased levels of activity resulting in improper emptying of the intestines; delays in growth and development including an inability to walk and recognize the urge to defecate, or inadequate innervation of the rectal sphincters; or the student may receive medications that alter the consistency, color, and frequency of bowel movements. Factors generally influencing the pattern of bowel functioning and elimination include culture, early family life-style, diet, activity, growth and development, and anxiety and stress (Brill & Kilts, 1980).

Cultural and Family Influences   Persons in differing cultures place varying degrees of emphasis on the circumstances under which elimination occurs. The degree of privacy required, the frequency, the attitude toward odors and sounds of elimination, and methods used to promote elimination are a few factors that can be culturally determined. In the United States, high value is placed on complete privacy for elimination, along with separation of the sexes (Brill & Kilts, 1980).

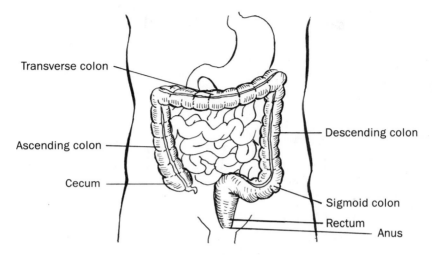

Figure 5.2.   The parts of the large intestine.

Early family life-styles also influence elimination patterns. For example, the availability of facilities, the number of people using a bathroom, and family habits contribute to a student's elimination pattern (Brill & Kilts, 1980).

Diet   A factor significantly affecting the pattern of bowel functioning is diet. The fiber content of the diet, the intake of fluids, and the intake of food affect the amount, frequency, color, consistency, and odor of feces. Foods with a high fiber content are those foods containing cellulose, such as fresh vegetables and fruits. These foods leave a residue in the colon. The amount of residue in the colon determines when the defecation reflex will occur. Diets high in fiber result in large amounts of residue remaining in the colon, with a resulting stimulation of the defecation reflex (Brill & Kilts, 1980).

If a student consistently has a low fiber diet, the time required to build up sufficient residue for initiating the defecation reflex is increased. Feces remain in the bowel for a longer period of time and water is removed from the feces. Feces are harder and drier and have difficulty moving along the intestines. This leads to constipation.

If, however, the movement of feces is speeded up by irritating foods, inflammation due to a virus or bacteria, drugs, or structural defects, then little water is reabsorbed by the bowel. Diarrhea results and the feces are watery and nonformed (Brill & Kilts, 1980). (Diarrhea and

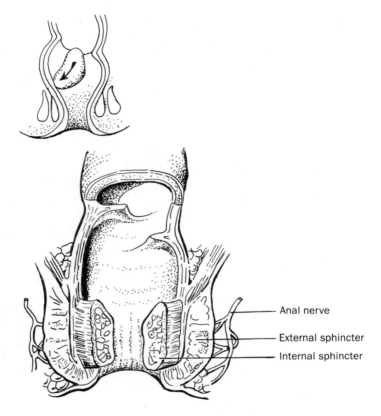

Anal nerve

External sphincter

Internal sphincter

Figure 5.3.   Response of the rectum to the presence of fecal material.

constipation are discussed further under the "Warning Signs" section of this chapter.)

Activity Levels   The student's level of activity is a significant factor in maintaining the muscle tone necessary for the processes of elimination. Inactivity due to weakness, paralysis, sedentary life-style, or medical conditions can result in weakening of all the muscles of the body. The weakened muscles specifically result in an improper emptying of the intestines (Brill & Kilts, 1980).

Growth and Development   The student's level of growth and development determines certain aspects of the elimination pattern. The infant (1–14 months) with normal development defecates 4–6 times a day and has pasty, loose, yellow feces if breast fed. The feces are firmer and darker yellow if the infant is fed a formula. Feces become more formed and fewer in number as the individual begins solid food. The toddler (15 months–3 years) begins to follow patterns of the adult in terms of the frequency and consistency of feces. Toilet training may begin during this time. The exact age when toilet training should begin depends on muscle tone and development of nerve tracts. The average preschooler (3–5 years) has almost complete voluntary control of elimination, but will have "accidents" when stressed or involved in activities. Schoolage children (6–12 years) have complete elimination control (Brill & Kilts, 1980).

Anxiety and Stress   Increased anxiety and stress can result in changed patterns of elimination. For example, changes in environmental routines, illness, and hospitalization are some stressors that can increase or decrease defecation (Brill & Kilts, 1980) and change the pattern of elimination.

PROCEDURES

Preparation for Bowel Care

Preparation for bowel care, including procedures involved in toilet training, consists of gathering information about the normal type and pattern of the student's elimination and factors that alter this pattern. This information will assist the teacher in developing strategies to assist the student in maintaining normal bowel functioning. Information on three aspects of bowel functioning are collected: 1) pattern of bowel functioning, 2) degree of bowel control, and 3) causes of abnormal bowel movements.

Information on the student's usual pattern of bowel functioning includes an identification of the usual times for defecation and the usual amount, color, and consistency of the feces. There must also be a determination of the position for the student that best facilitates defecation.

Information on the student's degree of bowel control includes the identification of any ongoing toilet training program and the steps of the toilet training program. This includes an awareness of the student's behaviors that may indicate that the student has an urge to defecate.

Causes of diarrhea or constipation, such as foods or medications, must also be identified. If diarrhea or constipation occur, it is important to know how these are managed. (Although this area of management is usually carried out in the student's home, school staff may need to be involved or find themselves involved in this aspect of bowel care.)

Performing Bowel Care

Bowel care includes promoting the student's usual pattern of bowel functioning. This may involve following the plan established by the student's parents and/or caregiver, physician, or other health care professional in the community. School staff may be involved in initiating a plan to promote adequate and regular bowel functioning. Factors that contribute to optimal functioning include: diet high in fiber, adequate fluid intake, schedule for elimination at regular times each day, continuation of established plan for toilet training (if applicable), environment conducive to elimination, proper positioning for elimination, and physical activity or exercise (Given & Simmons, 1979; Shaddix, 1986).

Fiber and Fluid Intake   When developing a program for the management of bowel functioning, fiber content in food and the regulation of fluids are the most important dietary considerations. Stool consistency can be regulated by diet (Coffman, 1986). Using diet, particularly fluid and fiber content, to maintain a firm stool increases the ability of the student and staff in managing the toileting process (Sullivan-Bolyai, 1986).

When the student has difficulty chewing and swallowing, an increase in fiber content may be difficult to achieve. Shaddix (1986) has recommended that the student progress from blended, pureed, or baby foods as rapidly as possible. Commercial baby foods contain very little fiber. To retain some of their fiber content, table foods can be placed in a baby food grinder or food processor to obtain the best texture for the student with oral-motor impairment. Shaddix (1986) also recommends serving bran cereal for breakfast or mixing unprocessed bran in food each day to supply additional fiber. Foods high in fiber are listed in the Appendix to this chapter.

Most children need between 1 and 2 quarts of fluid a day. Shaddix (1986) recommends limiting the amount of sweetened drinks such as carbonated beverages, tea, and fruit juices with added sugar and using unsweetened juice and water instead. Prune juice has a natural laxative effect and can be combined with another fruit juice to be more readily accepted by the student. Thickening liquids with items such as infant cereals, blended fruit, or unflavored gelatin, may change the consistency of the fluid to be more easily accepted by the student with oral-motor problems. The occupational therapist can be of assistance in finding appropriate methods to assist the child with oral-motor problems in taking fluids more easily.

Schedule of Elimination and Toilet Training   Normal bowel functioning implies that the student has a normal schedule of elimination. This developing or existing pattern may be incorporated into an ongoing, or new, toilet training program. Strategies for promoting the student's normal schedule of elimination include placement of the student on the toilet after meals and snacks to take advantage of the gastrocolic reflex that usually occurs after meals and careful communication with the student's parents and/or caregiver to identify the times during which defecation occurs. If toileting schedules are initially established at school, the schedule must be compatible with the student's life at home. Consistency between home and school is crucial.

Many toilet training programs are available. The function of this manual is not to summarize or present these alternatives (see Snell, 1987, or the list of Additional Readings at the end of this chapter for a summary), rather it is to suggest that an ongoing program, appropriate for the individual student, is important for the development of normal bowel functioning. Obviously, the method used for toilet training must be appropriate and individualized for the student, with the student's family and school staff working with the student.

When the student does not have control over elimination of feces, school staff need to check the student's underclothes or incontinent wear often. The frequency of checking will depend on the frequency of bowel movements and the condition of the student's skin. The student's skin is cleaned thoroughly after a bowel movement, with a soap that is mild and nonirritating. Ointments and creams are placed around the student's anal area only on the recommendation of the health care professional in the school or the student's physician.

Regression in the student's ability to control bowel functioning requires examination by all persons involved with the student's bowel training. Efforts are made to ensure that all persons are following the established plan and schedule. Other considerations should include: possibility of the student being ill, disruptions in the student's life at home or at school, or changes in the student's diet.

Facilitating Defecation   A student's defecation can be facilitated by environmental considerations, positioning of the student, and an increase in the student's overall muscle tone.

During toileting the environment should be as conducive as possible to defecation. Stimuli and/or activities that aid or detract in the process of defecation should be identified through discussion with the family and school personnel. For example, partitions may need to be set up in a bathroom, stalls may be used, bathroom facilities that are away from the classroom may be used, or students may use the bathroom individually in order to minimize distractions. Special techniques may be employed by individual students to facilitate defecation, such as leaning over in order to push down by blowing up a balloon, blowing bubbles, coughing, or pressing on the abdomen. Digital stimulation of the rectum may be needed to initiate defecation (Coffman, 1986). This procedure should be done only with the guidance of qualified health personnel.

Proper positioning on the toilet seat may facilitate defecation, and improper positioning can be a hindrance. A squatting position best facilitates defecation. When a student cannot sit up alone or assume a position similar to squatting, the student's head and trunk can be elevated with the hips flexed at 90° (Given & Simmons, 1979). An adapted toilet chair may be needed if the student has difficulty with balance or trunk control. Additionally, parents or the caregiver may have already discovered a useful device or method for positioning on the toilet. A special toilet chair can be constructed to sit over the toilet (Figure 5.4), or a stool for the student's feet may be used, with a support bar for the student to grasp (Figure 5.5).

Physical Activity and/or Exercise   An active approach to the implementation of a bowel care program includes physical activity and/or

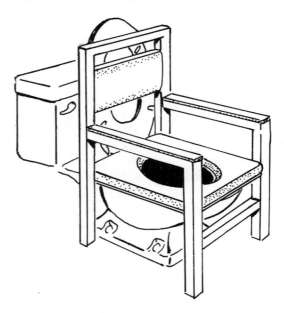

Figure 5.4.   One example of the many types of adaptations available to facilitate sitting on the toilet.

Figure 5.5.   One example of support for the feet and body, which can facilitate sitting on the toilet.

exercise. Physical activity can help the fecal material move through the
large intestine toward the rectum, facilitating normal bowel patterns.
Exercise as a component of bowel care should be conducted daily, in a
routine manner, and under the direction of a physician or physical
therapist.

Procedures Following Bowel Care

Procedures surrounding follow-up of bowel care involve what is done
immediately after any toileting activity, as well as correspondence with
school personnel and the family and/or caregiver to monitor bowel
patterns.

School staff assisting the student with toileting (getting to and from
the bathroom, changing incontinent wear, or cleaning after a bowel
movement) must carry out thorough handwashing afterward to prevent
bacteria from spreading to other students or school staff. Handwashing
after assisting with toileting must be carried out in a sink that is not used
for food preparation. This will require two sinks for use by staff working
with the students.

If the student deviates from the usual pattern of bowel functioning at school, parents and/or caregivers need to be notified using the established method of communication. If school staff and the health care worker in the school initiate a plan for bowel care, it will be necessary to communicate carefully with the student's parents and/or caregiver about what activities or methods promote or hinder bowel functioning. Parents and/or the caregiver may need to be taught to recognize what does and does not work for the student. School staff may also work with health care professionals in the community as the plan for bowel care is established and carried out. Communication with these persons verbally or in writing is necessary.

Warning Signs

Two of the most common bowel functioning problems that can develop are diarrhea and constipation.

Diarrhea   Diarrhea is defined as watery, copious bowel movements that are usually green in color and have a foul odor (Chow, Durand, Feldman, & Mills, 1984). Exactly which bowel movements can be considered diarrhea can be difficult to determine because of the great variations in bowel functioning in individuals. Characteristics of diarrhea include: 1) a noticeable or sudden increase in the number of stools, 2) change in consistency with an increase in water content, and 3) a tendency for stools to be greenish in color (Whaley & Wong, 1987). Food generally moves through the gastrointestinal tract, mouth to anus, in 2–3 days. Sometimes food and liquids, taken in by mouth, move through the body very quickly. Mouth to anus transit time for children 1–4 years of age is about 33 hours (Weaver & Steiner, 1984). When the student has diarrhea, this movement through the gastrointestinal tract is quicker than usual, resulting in a decrease in the amount of time for the intestinal tract to absorb water from the feces (Lifshitz, Ribeiro, & Silverberg, 1988).

During the first 3 years of life it is not unusual for a child to have one to three episodes of diarrhea, usually lasting no longer than 72 hours. The cause is usually viral (Feign & Stoller, 1987). Diarrhea may also be caused by diet, medications, milk allergy, food poisoning, parasitic infections, obstruction of the intestine by a large mass of hard stool, or other illnesses of which diarrhea is a symptom (Chow et al., 1984).

If a student is suspected of having diarrhea, the health care worker in the school should be contacted. When determining whether the student has diarrhea, consideration is given to the following: 1) the number and size of stools in a 24-hour period; 2) consistency and color of stools; and 3) the presence of other signs such as fever, irritability, cold, cough, lethargy, decreased appetite, vomiting, and abdominal pain. In addition to school staff communicating their concerns about the possibility of diarrhea to the health care worker, the student's parents and/or caregiver need to be notified. It is important to define characteristics of diarrhea stools for each student and determine if an appropriate treatment is being carried out at home (Chow et al., 1984).

Regardless of the cause, students with diarrhea, especially those students with problems swallowing foods and fluids, are at risk for developing dehydration. Signs of dehydration include crying without tears; dry skin; dry, cracked lips; concentrated urine; decrease in urination; weakness or sluggishness; and irritability (Blausey, Barton, & Dickie, 1984). If fluids cannot be replaced in adequate amounts, the student may need to be hospitalized for intravenous therapy. When providing fluids to the student with diarrhea, larger amounts of fluids should be given at less frequent intervals. Drinking and eating stimulate the gastrocolic reflex, and stool is likely to be passed (Murphy, 1984).

For the first 24 hours of diarrhea, clear liquids are usually given. Clear liquids such as flat, diluted ginger ale (or other caffeine-free soft drinks), apple juice, and flavored gelatin can be given (Chow et al., 1984; Questions and answers, 1986; Whaley & Wong, 1987). Murphy (1984) suggests flat 7-Up or ginger ale, Gatorade, popsicles, gelatin or gelatin water, or weak tea with sugar for the first 24 hours of diarrhea. After the first 24 hours, some foods may be introduced to the student. Foods such as rice, rice cereals, bananas, and potatoes are appropriate foods for refeeding (American Academy of Pediatrics, 1985).

The health care person in the school and the student's parents and/or caregiver must be notified if diarrhea does not improve after 24 hours; a fever develops; the student will not take fluids, cannot keep fluids down, or does not urinate; or the diarrhea stool contains blood (Murphy, 1984). Consideration should also be given to notifying the student's physician. Because of the possibility of diarrhea being caused by a virus, the student's parents may be asked to keep the student at home until the diarrhea ceases. The health care person in the school and the student's physician can assist in making this decision.

Constipation   Although constipation is a problem common in children, deviations from normal patterns of defecation, which might indicate constipation, are not clearly described. Constipation can be defined as the retention of feces in the intestinal tract or a delay in excretion of feces from the rectum. Constipation exists when the interval between bowel movements is greater than the time normal for the individual, when the volume is small and feces remain in the rectum, and when the consistency of feces is hard and dry (Given & Simmons, 1979).

Constipation is generally restricted to situations in which an individual has fewer than three bowel movements per week. When attempting to determine whether a student is constipated, remember that children who do not have a daily movement that is normal in size, shape, and consistency may be constipated. Less frequent movements are acceptable as long as stool is reasonably normal and easily passed. The size and consistency of stools must be considered. A change in the frequency of stools is more significant than the frequency itself (Johnson, Sessions, Snape, & Teichner, 1984).

In addition to the change in frequency, size, and consistency of stools, other signs of possible constipation include abdominal pain, enlargement of the abdomen, nausea, decreased appetite, no appetite, or painful defecation (Blausey, Barton, & Dicke, 1984; Dickey, 1987). An enlarged abdomen can also result from swallowing large amounts of air.

Constipation may be accompanied by liquid stools or what is thought to be diarrhea. A large mass of stool may be present in the rectum and/or colon. While semiliquid stools leak around the accumulated fecal mass, the student may have no awareness that there is stool in the rectum to be passed. However, the student may have an urge to defecate, yet ignore it and retain the stool in the rectum. The student ignoring the defecation reflex is described as having encopresis (Pettei & Davidson, 1988).

Constipation is not a disease, but it is a symptom associated with many conditions. The following conditions, among others, are associated with constipation: low fiber diet, inadequate fluid intake, dehydration, malnutrition, voluntary withholding of feces, defective innervation of muscles as in spina bifida and paraplegia, decreased muscle tone as in Down syndrome and cerebral palsy, and side effect of certain medications (Pettei & Davidson, 1988; Silverman & Roy, 1983). Medications such as antacids, anticonvulsants, antidepressants, decongestants, diuretics, iron preparations, or muscle paralyzers, may cause constipation in children (Pettei & Davidson, 1988).

Methods of treating constipation include: increasing fiber in the student's diet; increasing the student's intake of fluids; promoting a normal bowel pattern; minimizing the number of distractions while toileting; positioning properly on the toilet seat; following the established regime for the bowel program; ensuring that physical activity occurs as allowed; and using suppositories, laxatives, or enemas only if prescribed by a physician, nurse practitioner, or clinical nursing specialist. The first seven methods mentioned are described earlier in this chapter.

Laxatives are not recommended for use in children because of the potential for dependence and resultant abdominal cramps (Silverman & Roy, 1983). Chow et al. (1984) report, however, that laxatives should not be used with infants but are appropriate with schoolage children when constipation is a symptom of other conditions (i.e., encopresis and anal fissures). Stool softeners have been recommended and can be used over prolonged periods of time. Suppositories, stool softeners, or enemas have been used for children with neurologic disorders (Silverman & Roy, 1983). Mineral oil should never be given as a laxative because it decreases the absorption of fat soluble vitamins (Shaddix, 1986; Sondheimer, 1987). Mineral oil by mouth is also not recommended for children who are at risk for aspirating or choking because mineral oil aspirated into the lungs can cause pneumonia (Sondheimer, 1987).

A serious complication of prolonged constipation is urinary tract infection. Urinary tract infections are especially common in girls and may be present without any symptoms. Retention of a large mass of feces in the rectum and colon can block the flow of urine from the bladder. Urine remaining in the bladder allows the opportunity for bacteria to grow, resulting in a urinary tract infection (Sondheimer, 1987).

SIGNS OF AN EMERGENCY

Disturbances associated with severe diarrhea are dehydration and shock (Whaley & Wong, 1987). Diarrhea can continue until the amount of fluid lost results in moderate to severe dehydration. In moderate dehydration, the student's pulse increases, yet the blood pressure remains normal. When the student is in severe dehydration, the student's pulse becomes rapid and weak and the blood pressure decreases (Tucker & Sussman-Karten, 1987). If diarrhea continues and the circulation becomes disturbed, the student may develop shock. In addition to the rapid and weak pulse and decreased blood pressure, the student has sweaty skin that is ashen gray in color, decrease in urination, and changes in responsiveness. When shock is suspected, the health care worker in the school is notified, the student is placed flat on the floor (preferably with the head lower than the rest of the body), and the emergency procedure in the school is initiated. Emergency Medical System (EMS) needs to be summoned to transport the student to the hospital for immediate care (Chow et al., 1984).

Associated with severe diarrhea is a disturbance of sodium in the body. As water continues to be lost from the body, the concentration of sodium in the student's circulation becomes greater than usual. A student may develop seizures as a result of this excessive level of sodium in the body. Refer to Chapter 1, Seizure Monitoring, for more information on the student having a seizure.

Excessive use of enemas can deplete the student of fluids and result in an emergency situation (Potter & Perry, 1985). Emergency situations (i.e. dehydration, shock, and seizures) can occur as in the student having diarrhea. Administration of enemas to a student must be done only on the recommendation of the student's physician. It is generally recommended that no more than three enemas be given to clean the bowel at one time.

ADDITIONAL RESOURCES

The student's parents or caregivers are invaluable resources to school staff in promoting adequate and regular bowel functioning. They can provide information on the student's pattern of bowel functioning, diet, fluid intake, and level of activity as well as the cues given by the student indicating the need to defecate. These cues can be easily overlooked by others.

The student's physician can be helpful in solving problems with diarrhea, constipation, and skin irritation. Prescriptions may be needed to treat some of these problems. Changes in the fiber content of the student's diet are best made by a dietitian. The student's physician or other health care professional in the community may recommend a dietitian for this purpose. Shaddix (1986) provides helpful information on making changes in the student's fluid and fiber intake. For information about this publication, contact:

United Cerebral Palsy of Greater Birmingham, Inc.
2430 11th Avenue North
Birmingham, AL 35234
Telephone: (205) 251-0165

The physical therapist can provide much assistance in positioning the student during meals and elimination. The occupational therapist can provide assistance and information on feeding the student with oral-motor problems. Biofeedback therapy has been found to be helpful in managing bowel control in children with a physical disability such as spina bifida. The student must be able to understand and attend to what he or she is being asked to do (Richardson, Campbell, Brown, Masiulis, & Liptak, 1985). The student's pediatrician can recommend a pediatric gastroenterologist who can provide more information and assistance in this area.

LITERATURE CITED

American Academy of Pediatrics: Committee on Nutrition (AAP). (1985). Use of oral fluid therapy and posttreatment feeding following enteritis in children of a developed country. *Pediatrics, 75,* 358–360.

Behrman, R.E., & Vaughan, V.C. (Eds.). (1983). *Nelson textbook of pediatrics* (12th ed., pp. 610–612). Philadelphia: W.B. Saunders.

Blackwell, M.W. (1979). *Care of the mentally retarded.* Boston: Little, Brown.

Blausey, L.A., Barton, P.J., & Dicke, R.A. (1984). Development of nursing care guidelines: Putting the ONS outcome standards to work. *Oncology Nursing Forum, 11*(1), 54–58.

Brill, E.L., & Kilts, D.F. (1980). *Foundations for nursing.* New York: Appleton-Century-Crofts.

Chow, M.P., Durand, B.A., Feldman, M.N., & Mills, M.A. (1984). *Handbook of pediatric primary care.* New York: John Wiley & Sons.

Coffman, S. (1986). Description of a nursing diagnosis: Alteration in bowel elimination related to neurogenic bowel in children with myelomeningocele. *Issues in Comprehensive Pediatric Nursing, 9,* 179–191.

Dickey, S.B. (1987). *A guide to the nursing of children.* Baltimore: Williams & Wilkins.

Feigin, R.D., & Stoller, M.L. (1987). Diarrhea. In R.E. Behrman & V.C. Vaughan (Eds.). *Nelson textbook of pediatrics* (pp. 553–555). Philadelphia: W.B. Saunders.

Given, B.A., & Simmons, S.J. (1979). *Gastroenterology in clinical nursing.* St. Louis: C.V. Mosby.

Johnson, A.C., Sessions, J.T., Snape, W.J., & Teichner, V.J. (1984). Constipation: Is it functional, or...? *Patient Care, 18*(4), 128–130, 133, 137, 140–143.

Lifshitz, F., Ribeiro, H.C., & Silverberg, M. (1988). Childhood infectious diarrhea. In M. Silverberg & F. Daum (Eds.), *Textbook of pediatric gastroenterology* (2nd ed., pp. 284–329). Chicago: Year Book Medical Publishers, Inc.

Murphy, C. (1984). *Quick reference to pediatric nursing.* Philadelphia: J.B. Lippincott.

Pettei, M., & Davidson, M. (1988). Constipation. In M. Silverberg & M. Davidson, (Eds.), *Textbook of pediatric gastroenterology* (2nd ed., pp. 180–188). Chicago: Year Book Medical Publishers, Inc.

Potter, P.A., & Perry, A.G. (1985). *Fundamentals of nursing.* St. Louis: C.V. Mosby.

Richardson, K., Campbell, M.A., Brown, M.R., Masiulis, B., & Liptak, G.S.

(1985). Biofeedback therapy for managing bowel incontinence caused by meningomyelocele. *The American Journal of Maternal/Child Nursing, 10*(6), 388–392.

Shaddix, T. (1986). *Nutritional care for the child with developmental disabilities: Management of constipation.* Birmingham: United Cerebral Palsy of Greater Birmingham, Inc.

Silverman, A., & Roy, C.C. (1983). Constipation, fecal incontinence, and proctologic conditions. In A. Silverman & C.C. Roy (Eds.), *Pediatric clinical gastroenterology* (pp. 391–413). St. Louis: C.V. Mosby.

Snell, M. (1987). *Systematic instruction of persons with severe handicaps.* Columbus, OH: Charles E. Merrill.

Sondheimer, J.M. (1987). Resolving chronic constipation in children. *Patient Care, 21*(5), 108–118.

Sullivan-Bolyai, S. (1986). Practical aspects of toilet training the child with a physical disability. *Issues in Comprehensive Pediatric Nursing, 9,* 79–96.

Tucker, J.A., & Sussman-Karten, K. (1987). Treating acute diarrhea and dehydration with an oral rehydration solution. *Pediatric Nursing, 13*(3), 169–174.

Vander, A.J., Sherman, J.H., & Luciano, D.S. (1975). *Human physiology: The mechanism of body function* (2nd ed.). New York: McGraw–Hill.

Whaley, L.F., & Wong, D.L. (1987). *Nursing care of infants and children.* St Louis: C.V. Mosby.

ADDITIONAL READINGS

Barnard, K.E., & Erickson, M.L. (1976). *Teaching children with developmental problems.* St. Louis: C.V. Mosby.

Burkitt, D.P., Walker, A.R.P., & Painter, N.S. (1972, December 30). Effect of dietary fibre on stools and transit-times, and its role in the causation of disease. *The Lancet, 2*(7,792), 1408–1411.

Candy, C.E. (1987). Recent advances in the care of children with acute diarrhea: Giving responsibility to the nurse and parents. *Journal of Advanced Nursing, 12*(1), 95–99.

Dunlap, G., Koegel, R.L., & Koegel, L.K. (1984). Continuity of treatment: Toilet training in multiple community settings. *The Journal of The Association for Persons with Severe Handicaps, 9*(2), 134–141.

Foxx, R.M., & Azrin, N.H. (1973). *Toilet training the retarded.* Champaign, IL: Research Press.

Levitt, S. (1982). *Treatment of cerebral palsy and motor delay* (2nd ed.). Oxford: Blackwell Scientific Publications.

Mahoney, K., Van Wagenen, R.K., & Meyerson, L. (1971). Toilet training of normal and retarded children. *Journal of Applied Behavior Analysis, 4*(3), 173–181.

Mead, D. (1983). Chronic constipation and soiling. *Nursing Mirror, 157*(3), 23–24.

Powell, M.L. (1981). *Assessment and management of developmental changes and problems in children.* St. Louis: C.V. Mosby.

Questions and answers about diarrhea in children. (1986). *Patient Care, 20*(20), 171.

Raborn, J.D. (1978). Classroom appplication of the Foxx-Azrin toileting program. *Mental Retardation, 16*(2), 173–174.

Richmond, G. (1983). Shaping bladder and bowel continence in developmentally retarded preschool children. *Journal of Autism and Developmental Disorders, 13*(2), 197–204.

Smith, P.S., & Smith, L.J. (1987). *Continence and incontinence: Psychological approaches to development and treatment.* London: Croom Helm.

Sullivan-Bolyai, S., Swanson, M., & Shurtleff, D.B. (1984). Toilet training the child with neurogenic impairment of bowel and bladder function. *Issues in Comprehensive Pediatric Nursing, 7*(1), 33–43.

Weaver, L.T., & Steiner, H. (1984). The bowel habit of young children. *Archives of Disease in Childhood, 59,* 649–652.

Williams, F.E., & Sloop, E.W. (1978). Success with a shortened Foxx-Azrin toilet training program. *Education and Training of the Mentally Retarded, 13*(4), 399–402.

Appendix

HIGH FIBER FOODS

I.   BRAN

Raisin Bran, cornbread
All Bran
Fruit'n Fiber Cereal
Granola
Grape-Nuts
Most
Nutri-Grain
Oatmeal
Shredded Wheat

II.   RAW FRUITS

Prunes
Pears
Apples
Strawberries
Dried peaches
Raisins
Figs

III.   VEGETABLES

Spinach, lettuce
Cabbage
Turnip greens
Mustard greens
Corn

IV.   UNPROCESSED BRAN

Unprocessed bran may be purchased at most grocery stores, and mixed with foods. Begin by mixing 1–2 teaspoons daily, and slowly increase the amount to no more than 2 tablespoons daily. Bran may be easily mixed with such foods as cereals, mashed potatoes, and applesauce, or combined with hamburger or other ground meats (Shaddix, 1986).

6

NUTRITION MONITORING AND SUPPLEMENTATION

Sarah McCamman
Jane Rues

A growing number of children with special nutritional problems are entering schools, and at younger ages. Optimal nutrition for these students is essential for maximizing their mental and physical development and enhancing their ability to participate during the school day. A number of studies have documented that children with developmental disabilities do not receive adequate nutrition for growth and development. Half of the children with cerebral palsy studied by Peaks and Lamb (1951) lacked adequate protein, vitamin C, iron, and fiber. Palmer (1978) found that approximately 90% of the 500 children with developmental disabilities studied had nutritional disorders. In a recent survey of 2,457 special education students, 37% of the children needed special foods or diets and 32% required special feeding procedures, that is,

Sarah McCamman is Director of Training in Nutrition and Jane Rues is Interdisciplinary Training Coordinator at the Children's Rehabilitation Unit, University Affiliated Program, University of Kansas Medical Center, Kansas City, Kansas.

tube feeding, modified feeding equipment, or supervision at mealtime (Horsley, 1988).

Unfortunately, nutrition services have not been well integrated into the school system to help special educators deal with these challenging and complex problems. This is due in large part to a general lack of information regarding the role and function of a nutritionist which, when combined with our individual biases and familial and cultural folklore related to eating, contribute to the current underutilization of nutrition services. It is necessary, therefore, for the teacher to monitor the student's nutritional status and be aware of the nutritional resources available in the community.

OVERVIEW

The provision of adequate nutrients in appropriate amounts is essential for children to achieve their physical and developmental potential. The well-nourished child grows at an expected rate, has resistance to illness, and has the energy to take advantage of social and educational opportunities. To initiate appropriate intervention, the special educator must be aware of children at risk for nutrition problems and the simple screening methods used to identify these children.

The classroom is a unique environment for observing changes in eating patterns of children. The special education teacher, trained as an observer of behavior, can take on an important role in monitoring the child's feeding abilities, eating behaviors, food intake, and preferences. In addition, the teacher should be aware of factors typically affecting a student's nutritional needs and common nutritional problems associated with children having special health care needs.

Factors Affecting a Student's Nutritional Needs

A number of factors may affect a student's nutritional needs. These may include the actual characteristics of the student's disability or the treatment used to alleviate those characteristics.

The Specific Disabling Condition   Various medical conditions put children at high or established risk for having nutritional problems. For example, a child with Prader-Willi syndrome will have oral-motor difficulties in the first few months of life leading to failure to thrive. By

18–36 months the child will develop an almost insatiable appetite and become obese unless preventive treatment is implemented.

Students with oral-motor problems frequently have diets that are inadequate in calories or fluids, or that contain a limited variety of foods. For example, a student with cerebral palsy may exhibit increased tone around the mouth, lips, tongue, and jaw. This increased muscle tone will affect the fluidity of oral-motor movements, timing and rhythm of eating, ability to handle textures—all of which will limit the quantity eaten. Difficulty eating may also be associated with strong emotional reactions at mealtimes resulting in behavior problems that can also limit food intake. The dietary treatment for children with food allergies or inborn errors of metabolism can be so restrictive that it leads to specific nutrient deficiencies. Table 6.1 lists common medical conditions and their nutritional implications.

The Treatment   Medications can change the way foods are accepted or used by the body because a variety of different drug-nutrient interactions can occur. Side effects of drugs that can compromise a student's nutritional status include increased or decreased food intake; inhibition of nutrient synthesis; decreased absorption of nutrients; alteration in transport, utilization, or storage of metabolites; and increase excretion of nutrients.

The teacher, however, will be most concerned about the drugs that effect food intake. Some drugs change taste sensation; others can cause a dry mouth, nausea, or a stomach ache. These reactions may decrease the amount of food a student will eat. Common medications that cause alterations of food intake or that affect the way foods are used by the body include anticonvulsants (e.g., Dilantin, phenobarbital, Tegretol), which interfere with vitamin D metabolism and folate and calcium absorption; stimulants (e.g., Ritalin and Dexedrine), which can cause a decrease in food intake and subsequent slowing of growth; spasmolytics (e.g., theophylline), which can increase energy needs and result in weight loss if increased food intake does not occur; steroids (e.g., prednisone), which can result in increased appetite and weight gain or poor utilization of calcium resulting in osteoporosis; and diuretics, which can increase excretion of minerals from the kidneys. Table 6.2 lists the nutritional side effects of drugs commonly used for students receiving special education as well as some suggestions on counteracting the drug's effects.

Unless plans are developed that compensate for these factors that alter a student's nutritional status, malnutrition may result. Treatment

Table 6.1.   Medical conditions and related nutritional concerns

Medical condition	Nutritional concerns
Prader-Willi syndrome	Failure to thrive common in infancy due to low tone and poor suck Short stature Decreased energy needs for age Extreme hyperphagia, usually after 2 years of age (may eat trash, pet food, and so forth)
Short bowel syndrome (May be the result of midgut volvulus, congenital small bowel atresia, omphalocele, surgical resection, or necrotizing enterocolitis. The length of functional bowel, presence or absence of ileocecal valve, and whether the remaining bowel is primarily ileum or jejunun will affect nutrient needs.)	If the ileum is removed may see steatorrhea (foul smelling, foaming stools) due to malabsorption of fat If Ileocecal valve is missing, transit time is reduced and there is a greater chance for diarrhea and malabsorption (see Chapter 12, Colostomy or Ileostomy Care) At risk for anemia due to malabsorption and poor intake At risk for essential fatty acid and vitamin/mineral deficiencies (zinc, biotin, B vitamins)
Bronchopulmonary dysplasia (chronic lung disorder following ventilator therapy)	Increased calorie needs due to increased work of breathing Fluid restriction May have other medical problems (prematurity, intracranial bleeding, hydrocephalus, microcephaly) Increased risk for metabolic bone disease, especially children with low birth weight, immobility, chronic lasix, and low calcium intake Decreased ability to efficiently suck and swallow Increased risk for behavioral feeding problems: rumination, vomiting, impaired ability to tolerate spoon feedings, impaired ability to initiate self-feeding

(continued)

Table 6.1.   *(continued)*

Medical condition	Nutritional concerns
Cardiac disease	Growth delay common, most likely due to cardiac failure and malnutrition
	Poor voluntary intake
	Increased calorie needs due to increased cardio-respiratory work
	May tire during feedings
	Weak suck
	Restricted fluid intake to avoid congestive heart failure
	Prolonged hospitalization
	Chronic illness
	May have other medical problems (prematurity, cleft lip/palate, esophageal atresia, Down syndrome, intrauterine growth retardation)
	Increased risk for behavioral feeding problems
Cerebral palsy	Possible increase in calorie needs; at increased risk for protein-calorie malnutrition, secondary to low intake and increased needs
	Constipation possible due to decreased mobility and/or dehydration
	Possible vitamin and mineral deficiencies due to low intake and limited variety of foods
	At risk for oral-motor feeding problems
	May tire with feedings
	At risk for behavioral feeding problems
Cleft lip/cleft palate	Difficulty sucking, swallowing, breathing; if palate area is decreased more difficult to create negative pressure between the tongue and roof of mouth

(continued)

Table 6.1. *(continued)*

Medical condition	Nutrition concerns
Cleft lip/cleft palate *(continued)*	At risk for poor growth
	Swallowing of excessive air
	Hypersensitive mouth
	At risk for behavioral feeding problems
	The greater the extent of the cleft, the more feeding problems
Down syndrome	May have weak suck during infancy
	At risk for oral-motor feeding problems
	Constipation
	May have other medical conditions (cardiac defects)
	At risk for behavioral feeding problems
	Abnormal growth pattern, short stature and tendency toward obesity
Fetal alcohol syndrome	Intrauterine growth retardation (birth weight, length and head circumference below 3rd percentile)
	Short stature
	Small head circumference
	Poor growth
	At risk for failure to thrive
	Increased incidence of oral malformations (cleft lip, cleft palate)
	Developmental delay
	Poor suck, uncoordinated swallow
Myelomeningocele (spina bifida)	May have poor suck during infancy from complications of hydrocephaly
	During infancy may have many soft stools; not to be mistaken for malabsorption
	Difficulty measuring length due to orthopaedic complications
	At risk for behavioral feeding problems

Adapted from Ohio Neonatal Nutritionists. (1985). *Nutrition care for high risk newborns.* Philadelphia: George F. Stickley.

Table 6.2. The nutritional and physical side effects of drugs commonly used for students receiving special education, and the nutritional prevention of the effect

Major drugs	Possible nutritional effect	Prevention of nutritional effect	Possible physical effect
Analgesics			
Aspirin	Depresses serum vitamin C and folic acid. Increases urinary loss of vitamin C, potassium, and amino acids.	Add 50–100 mg/day vitamin C as in broccoli, citrus juice, strawberries. Increase fresh greens and raw fruits.	GI irritations, nausea, upset stomache, heartburn, prolonged bleeding time
Antacids			
Maalox	Decreases iron absorption; depresses serum phosphate.	Increase intake of liver, molasses, wheat germ, whole grains, peanuts, green vegetables.	Decreased stomach acidity, edema from high sodium content, constipation, passage of fat in feces
Antibiotics			
Neomycin	Decreases lactase activity.	Decrease milk intake or give Lact-Aid.	Decreased appetite and taste acuity, diarrhea, nausea
Chloramphenicol	Hinders all intestinal absorption.	Give a well-balanced vitamin and mineral supplement and high calorie fruit juice.	Vomiting, general malabsorption of nutrients
Tetracycline	(Dairy products inhibit absorption.)	Avoid dairy products and iron supplements for 2 hours.	Diarrhea, nausea, vomiting
Anticonvulsants			
Phenobarbital Dilantin	Disturbs vitamin D metabolism resulting in poor calcium utilization, producing osteoporosis and rickets.	Give appropriate daily vitamin as prescribed by an M.D.	Swelling of gums, G.I. distress, constipation, anorexia, osteomalacia

(continued)

Table 6.2.   *(continued)*

Major drugs	Possible nutritional effect	Prevention of nutritional effect	Possible physical effect
	Increases need for folic acid to prevent megaloblastic anemia. May lower blood level of vitamins K, B_6, and B_{12}.	Give appropriate daily multivitamin, with folic acid, as prescribed by an M.D.	Contributes to megaloblastic anemia
Cathartics (laxatives)			
Mineral oil	Vitamins A, D, E, K absorbed in oil and excreted	Give supplement of fat-soluble vitamins 12 hours after each dose of oil.	Abdominal cramp, steatorrhea, GI distress
Exlax	Decreases absorption of vitamin D. Depletes potassium. Causes poor nutrient absorption due to increased transit time.	Give multivitamin supplement if used regularly. Give liberal fruits and vegetables.	Abdominal cramps due to hyperperistalis
Corticosteroids			
Prednisone	Increases need for protein and vitamin B_6, C, D, and folic acid. Increases retention of sodium. Increases loss of potassium, calcium, and zinc.	Give diet liberal in dairy products and meat. Restrict intake of salt (sodium). Give multiple vitamin-mineral supplement.	Edema and increased weight, weakness, dizziness, growth suppression in children, impaired wound healing, osteoporosis, GI distress, insulin-resistance, glucose intolerance

(continued)

Table 6.2.   *(continued)*

Major drugs	Possible nutritional effect	Prevention of nutritional effect	Possible physical effect
Diuretics			
Thiazides: (Diamox Re-serpine)	Increases loss of potassium	Feed foods high in potassium such as po-tatoes, ba-nanas, carrots, celery, broc-coli, and citrus fruits.	Thirst, anorexia, increased urine output, sugar/ blood in urine, drowsiness, GI distress
Stimulants			
Methyl-phenidate (Ritalin) Dextroam-phetamine (Dexedrine)	Suppresses ap-petite and therefore growth.	Give drug *with* rather than *be-fore* meals. Re-duce dosage to minimum re-quired.	Decreased ap-petite, growth rate, and weight in chil-dren; nausea; dizziness; drowsiness
Tranquilizers			
Mellaril	Increases ap-petite to pro-duce weight gain.	Monitor calories.	Increased weight, increased ap-petite, edema, dry mouth, drowsiness, constipation, GI distress, blurred vision

Adapted from Crump, M. (1987). *Nutrition and feeding of the handicapped child.* Boston: College-Hill.

may address the need for vitamin and mineral supplement. This should be considered if the diet is restrictive due to inborn errors of metabolism or food allergies, if a prescribed drug alters nutrient utilization, or if the diet is low in calories.

Common Nutritional Problems

Common nutritional problems result in disorders in growth and weight gain. Often these may be caused by poor eating skills or eating habits, or other unrelated factors.

Disorders in Growth and Weight Gain   Slower than expected linear growth might indicate that a child is malnourished, has a chronic disease (e. g., kidney or heart disease), an endocrine problem, or a genetic or chromosomal abnormality (e.g., Down syndrome).

Lack of appropriate weight gain is one of the more common problems found in children with special health care needs. Slower than desired weight gain usually results from inadequate intake of calories. This may be due to poor appetite as a side effect of medication, feeding problems, or chronic illness. Inadequate intake of calories can cause a student to be irritable and withdrawn. It can delay linear growth, motor abilities, and learning capacity.

Children who gain weight too fast are more likely to be overweight as adults. This can lead to a number of health problems, including high blood pressure, diabetes, cancer, and heart disease. In addition, very young children who are obese can show delayed gross motor development due to the extra fat their muscles must support. A number of children in special education have a tendency to be overweight, including those students with Down syndrome, Prader-Willi syndrome, or spina bifida.

Poor Eating Skills or Eating Habits   Some students may refuse to eat foods from certain food groups. Other students, because of delayed oral-motor skills or dietary restrictions, are frequently limited in the variety of foods eaten. The reduced range of foods eaten can result in a limited nutrient intake. For example, a child who does not consume milk might have a deficiency in protein, calcium, and riboflavin. If breads and cereals are not eaten, a deficiency in thiamin, niacin, and fiber might result.

Many students will not progress in their eating skills or will have disturbances in their feeding skills, which may lead to a less than optimal volume, texture, or variety of foods eaten. This narrowed food choice may limit nutrient or calorie intake, resulting in slow growth, inadequate weight for height, or a nutrient deficiency. Infants and children are particularly vulnerable to dehydration and resulting electrolyte imbalances because of difficulty in swallowing or reduced opportunities to drink. These conditions can contribute to irritability due to thirst or constipation, and if left unidentified, can be life threatening.

Some of these students may require assistance in meeting their nutritional needs via a nasogastric or gastrostomy tube (see Chapter 13, Nasogastric Tube Feeding or Chapter 14, Gastrostomy Tube Feeding). Tube feedings do not necessarily preclude oral feeding, but consultation with the physician and/or a feeding team will assist the educational staff in determining the quantity, type, and timing of oral feedings. In general, oral feedings should precede tube feeding to capitalize on the student's hunger as a motivator. When liquid formula for tube feedings contains all the requisite nutrients and calories, the teacher can use preferred foods to increase anticipation, compliance, and pleasure during oral feedings. Periodic measurement of the amount and type of food consumed orally, as well as through the tube, will assist the nutritionist in adjusting the ratio of amount of food taken orally to food presented through the tube for continued optimal nutrition.

Constipation   Constipation, a very common problem, can occur due to a number of factors including: 1) the child's neuromuscular problem, 2) inadequate fluid or fiber intake, 3) lack of exercise, and/or 4) drugs that decrease intestinal motility. Constipation can cause a child to be uncomfortable and may decrease appetite as well as develop into a serious chronic condition (see Chapter 5, Bowel Care).

Gagging, Vomiting, and Rumination   Gagging, vomiting, or rumination often result from overfeeding, food intolerances, improper feeding techniques, or gastrointestinal abnormalities. Occasionally a child will gag or vomit to control his or her environment. Gagging, vomiting, or rumination can alter the acid-base balance of the body, cause irritation to the throat and mouth, and destroy the enamel on the teeth.

Summary   Students who are well-nourished feel better. A child who is losing weight or not gaining weight at the expected rate can be irritable, have a short attention span, and thus have poor interactions with his or her environment. These children do not have the energy to take advantage of the educational opportunities offered. The well-nourished child, in addition to learning more easily, also resists infections better and has fewer illnesses. Given the variety of nutrition disorders experienced by special education students and the impact of nutrition on their health outcomes, the special educator must take an active role in identifying nutrition problems and seeking assistance from appropriate disciplines.

PROCEDURES

Monitoring Growth

Feeding skill development and use of special feeding equipment have traditionally been the focal points of nutrition concerns for special educators. Monitoring the nutritional status of a student, as reflected by his or her growth, is also important. Growth is a sensitive measure of health and development. Trends revealed through repeated height and weight measurements can be used to detect growth abnormalities, monitor nutritional status, or evaluate the effects of nutritional or medical interventions.

Measuring Weight   Growth measurements must be made accurately and recorded correctly at least three times a year. A beam scale with nondetachable weights is recommended for measuring weight accurately. This type of scale is commonly found in a physician's offices and in the school health office. The major error made by practitioners in monitoring weight occurs when the scale is not "zeroed" before use. Many apparent fluctuations in weight are due to measurement error rather than actual weight loss or gain. The importance of obtaining accurate measurements by using standardized equipment cannot be over-emphasized. In order for the accuracy of the scales to be maintained, they should be checked three times per year by an inspector of weights with a set of standard weights to ensure accuracy of the scale.

The student is weighed in light clothing with shoes removed, wearing as little clothing as possible with consideration given to privacy needs. If possible, the student should stand quietly in the middle of the platform with arms at the side. The weight measurement should be repeated and compared so that the weight measurements are within ¼ pound of each other in order to exclude any obviously erroneous measurements. If the child is unable to bear weight in standing, an adult may hold the student and obtain a combined weight. The adult then subtracts his or her weight obtained on the same scale at that time from the combined weight. Larger or older students, for whom this method is not appropriate, may have weights obtained by using a sling scale or chair scales. These scales are often available in hospitals or medical centers.

Measuring Height   A measure of weight does not provide maximum information without corresponding measures of height. Both are needed for an accurate analysis of growth. In measuring height, a metallic tape or yardstick attached to a flat wall should be used. Measuring rods attached to a platform scales and plastic or cloth tapes are considered inaccurate and should not be used. Ideally the student should be able to cooperate and stand upright. Otherwise, measures of length may be taken with the student lying down. (See the following section, "Measuring Length.") The measurement of height is taken without shoes, making sure that clothing and hairstyle do not interfere with obtaining an accurate height. The student should stand tall and straight, with eyes straight ahead and with shoulder blades, buttocks, and heels touching the vertical surface. Both feet should be flat on the floor, heels slightly apart, knees together, legs and back straight, hands hanging naturally at the sides. The headboard used for measuring is lowered until it touches the crown or top of the head and makes a right angle with the measuring tape and the wall. The measurement is then read at the same level as the headboard so that error due to the angle of observation is avoided. Repeat measurements should read within ¼ inch.

Measuring Length   If a student is less than 2 years of age, or is unable to stand unassisted and straight, then he or she may be measured lying down on a measuring board. One person (possibly a parent) holds the student's head so the eyes are looking vertically upward with the crown of the head firmly against the fixed headboard. A second person holds the student's feet; knees and hips are extended and toes pointed directly upward (Figure 6.1). A movable footboard is brought firmly against the heels. Individualized methods of assessing length are necessary when a student is unable to lie with shoulder, hips, and heels aligned. Students with this degree of disability should be referred to a dietitian for assessment. Length measurements of students unable to lie with shoulders, hips, and heels aligned may be obtained by using a soft tape measure. As above, repeat measurements should be within ¼ inch.

Recording and Plotting Height and Weight   Recording and plotting a child's height and weight at the beginning, middle, and end of the school year will help monitor the student's growth. The health care worker in the school can assist in obtaining and assessing these data. A variety of growth charts are available for assessing the growth of children. The growth charts adapted from the National Center for Health

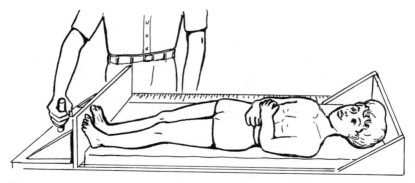

Figure 6.1.   Measuring length while the student is lying down.

Statistics (NCHS) (Hamill, Wright, Johnson, Reed, Roche, & Moore, 1979) can be used to assess the growth of most children and should be a permanent part of a child's record. A sample growth chart for boys and girls is presented in Appendix A.

Recognizing that children with disabilities may have different growth expectations than children who do not have disabilities has prompted the recent development of separate growth charts for children with Down syndrome, Prader-Willi syndrome, Turner syndrome and achondroplasia (dwarfism). The Additional Resources section of Appendix B identifies the sources of specialized growth charts.

When accurate measurements are taken and then plotted on appropriate growth charts, a visual representation of growth status emerges. In order to accurately plot the growth data, first obtain the correct growth chart for the student's age and sex. Use the chart for birth to 36 months as long as length is measured while lying down and use the charts for ages 2–18 years when the student is measured while standing. Record the date, height, and weight on the chart. Plot weight for age by first locating the student's age on the horizontal axis at the bottom or top of the chart. Appendix A includes procedures for calculating age. Draw a straight line on the vertical line extending up from the designated age in years and months. Locate the student's weight at the side of the chart. Draw a straight line on the horizontal line from the weight across the chart until it intersects with the vertical line from the age. Mark the spot where these two lines intersect, making sure to use the column with the corresponding units of measurement (metric or U.S.). Repeat any measurements immediately that show a sharp increase or decrease in percentile.

In order to plot a height-for-age, use the same chart and again locate the child's age at the bottom of the chart. Draw a line on this vertical line. Identify the child's height at the left side in the column marked in inches or centimeters and draw a horizontal line. Mark the intersection of these two lines.

In addition to weight-for-age and height-for-age, weight-for-height provides information about a student's nutritional status. The weight-for-height measurement compares a student only to others of the same height, not age. It is of particular importance in monitoring many students with health care needs because these students frequently do not grow at the same rate as other individuals of the same age. A graph for weight-to-height is found on the lower back of the growth charts in Appendix A. Locate the child's current height at the bottom, the weight at the side, and plot where these two lines intersect.

A series of plots, rather than a single set of measurements, will reveal more information about a child. This involves continuous measures on a monthly or bimonthly basis. If a growth curve is flattening out and the student's percentile score is decreasing over time (e.g., 25%–5%), further evaluation by a dietitian is warranted. Appendix A also includes sample age, weight, and height information for practice.

For determining whether a child is underweight, overweight, or has short stature, the data gathered for a particular student is compared to standard data. If the length-for-age data or weight-for-age-data fall below the 5th percentile, a referral for a nutritional assessment is necessary. The acceptable ranges for age, height, and weight are indicated by the lighter areas on the chart. If the weight-for-length is at or below the 5th percentile or at or over the 95th percentile, it shows significant underweight or overweight respectively. A referral for a nutritional assessment is warranted. Possible reasons for an underweight condition include improper nutrition due to poor caloric intake, chronic disease, dehydration, iron deficiency, infectious disease, or measurement error. Possible reasons for an overweight condition include higher calorie intake than the child's energy expenditure (common in Prader-Willi syndrome and Down syndrome), edema, and measurement error.

A referral to a nutritionist should be made when weight-for-age is at or below the 5th percentile or at or above the 95th percentile, length for age is at or below the 5th percentile, weight for length is at or below the 5th percentile or at or above the 95th percentile. In students over 1 year of age, if weight has not increased during a 3-month period or height has not increased in any 6-month period, a referral is needed. For more complete information on the accurate assessment of growth see Appendix B.

Monitoring Feeding Behavior

In addition to height and weight measures, feeding behavior is a very important component affecting overall nutritional status and should be monitored. Many children with special health care needs have disturbances in their feeding skills. This may be due to chronic health problems, early negative oral experiences (e.g., tube feedings, intubation, suctioning), neurological problems, or fatigue during meals due to poor nutrition. School personnel should note any changes in feeding behavior or changes in volume of foods consumed. Information about these aspects of feeding should be passed from school to home. Due to the complexity of factors causing these types of problems, an interdisciplinary team approach is suggested if significant problems occur.

Many hospitals affiliated with a university have a Feeding Team.

This team generally includes a dietitian, nurse, occupational therapist, speech pathologist, and behavioral psychologist. For a school age child, the special educator should also be a team member. Issues addressed by a Feeding Team include nutritional adequacy of current diet (via a 3-day food record); physical growth including weight, length, weight-for-length, and body composition; postural and oral-motor reflexes; quantity, type, and timing of oral feedings; special health care needs of the student; and affective responses of student during feeding. Such a comprehensive and functional approach to feeding assessment will identify the strengths and positive behaviors the student brings to the feeding situation, as well as deficit areas. Involvement of the teacher and parents with the Feeding Team is essential to develop a feeding program that can be implemented across educational and home environments. Similarly, prioritization of recommendations by the team is critical in the formulation of short- and long-term goals for the feeding program. Priority is obviously given to ensuring adequate nutrition and growth and then to the development of correct and independent feeding skills. It is important to note that occasionally recommendations related to increasing food texture or oral-motor responses may have to be deferred until the student is adequately nourished. These are complex issues that are best resolved by an interdisciplinary Feeding Team.

Increasing Caloric Intake   Strategies to assist in weight gain do not always involve getting the student to eat more. Often the extensive amount of time spent at mealtime or the functioning level of the student negates a simple solution of taking more bites. School food service personnel are responsible for making modifications in foods, that is, changing food texture, or providing specific foods to help increase the calories offered.

There are several techniques to increase the number of calories a student consumes when not enough food is consumed to maintain an appropriate rate of growth. Figure 6.2 presents a list of foods that may be added to the student's meal that increase the caloric and nutrient intake without requiring the student to eat more food. The addition of fats, which are a particularly concentrated source of calories; evaporated milk; wheat germ; or eggs into the preparation of foods or added at the table will promote growth. A regular meal pattern with two or three snacks per day is also recommended to promote weight gain. The inclusion of these additives must be done with cooperation of a dietitian/physician who is aware of food allergies and the student's health issues. Additional suggestions are found in a series of pamphlets by Shaddix (1986).

Food Additive	Rationale
Undiluted evaporated milk	This supplies approximately 25 calories per tablespoon. It may be used in place of whole milk in creamed soups, cooked or cold cereals, puddings, cocoa, or milkshakes.
Powdered non-fat dry milk	This supplies approximately 25 calories per tablespoon. Super milk can be made by adding 1/4 cup powdered milk to 1 cup fluid milk. Be sure to refrigerate this before drinking. You can also add 1/4 cup powdered milk to cereal such as oatmeal or cream of wheat, 2 tablespoons powdered milk to 1/2 cup mashed potatoes, or 1/4 cup powdered milk to a container of yogurt. *In children under 2 years of age, it is not recommended to use either the undiluted evaporated milk or the powdered non-fat milk because the high protein content places a burden on their developing kidneys.*
Vegetable oils, margarine, or mayonnaise	These supply approximately 35–40 calories per teaspoon. They may be added to sandwiches, puddings, soups, potatoes, rice, hot cereal, casseroles, or vegetables to significantly increase the calorie intake without altering the volume, taste, or texture of food to which they are added. Mayonnaise may be used as dressing on vegetables or salads including gelatin salads. The kitchen at the school may be asked to send a stick of margarine or a few ounces of salad oil to be added to underweight students' meals.
Dry infant cereal	This supplies approximately 9 calories per tablespoon. It may be added to yogurt, potatoes, and beverages.
Cheese	This supplies approximately 100 calories per ounce. It may be served grated over eggs, pasta, rice, soups, and cooked cereals.

(continued)

Figure 6.2.   Food additives that increase caloric value. (Adapted from Shaddix, T. [1986]. Meal planning for the childhood years. Nutritional care for the child with developmental disabilities. Birmingham, AL: United Cerebral Palsy of Greater Birmingham, Inc.)

Figure 6.2.   *(continued)*

Food Additive	Rationale
Table or whipped cream	This supplies approximately 50 calories per tablespoon. It may be used unsweetened in soups, fruits, pancakes, puddings, or folded into potatoes or vegetable purees. It can be substituted for milk in recipes, poured on chicken or fish while baking, or mixed with pork or rice.
Peanut butter	This supplies approximately 100 calories per tablespoon. It can be used with all grains, spread on fruits, blended in milkshakes, yogurt, puddings, or ice cream.

Food Preparation

The calorie and nutrient intake of food can be increased by such procedures as using less water than recommended when reconstituting frozen juices, using whole milk instead of water in soups or cooked cereals, and by using instant breakfast powder in milk or yogurt.

It might be difficult to maintain or increase a student's rate of weight gain because of impaired oral function or because of excessive energy requirements due to high levels of movement, heavy braces, or other orthotic devices. Frequent illness or infections may decrease a child's appetite, as do certain medications. Commonly used foods, such as those shown in Figure 6.2, may help facilitate weight gain and are safe and inexpensive. It is a myth that the failure to thrive or an underweight condition in many children with disabilities is a necessary part of having a disability. The reason for a child's weight or height being less than the 5th percentile is frequently that the child does not get enough calories.

Increasing Fluid Intake   Adequate fluid intake is essential for maintaining health. Children with oral-motor problems often have difficulty consuming sufficient liquids. This may be caused by an inability to communicate thirst, problems with hand-to-mouth coordination, problems with sucking or swallowing, or heavy drooling. Fruits and vegetables are excellent sources of water. Canned fruit, watermelon, cucumbers, greens, and squash are examples of foods high in water content. Many students with oral-motor difficulties are able to consume thickened liquids more successfully than thin liquids. A recipe such as: mix 1 cup whole milk, 1½ cups baby rice cereal (dry), 1½ cups fruit (any type), 2 teaspooons corn oil, and 6 ounces of milk in a blender thickens milk and provides 260 calories. Other products commonly used to thicken thin liquids in order to facilitate swallowing include pureed fruit, baby cereal, yogurt, dehydrated fruits and vegetables, mashed potato flakes, gelatin (added to warm liquids), or commercially available products designed specifically for thickening foods.

Utilizing Snacks and Meals   In addition to using food fortifiers, providing high calorie fluids and using extra fat in the foods, the teacher must ensure that students are fed on a frequent and regular basis. High calorie snacks play an important role in contributing to a student's overall nutritional status. Snacks should be served from the Basic Four Food Groups and served no less than 2 hours before a main meal, otherwise the student's appetite for the main meal may be decreased. Some suggestions for high calorie snacks include milkshakes or eggnogs, Instant Breakfast, sliced cheese and crackers, dried fruit, cookies. Additionally, yogurt can be mixed with instant breakfast powder, wheat germ, or dry powdered milk for extra calories.

Minimizing Side Effects of Medications   Drug therapy is very common in children with developmental disabilities. Some medications cause undesirable side effects in addition to the desired changes. For example, methylphenidate (Ritalin) and dextroamphetamine (Dexedrine) can cause nausea and therefore suppress the appetite. Giving these medications during the meal, rather than before, might help eliminate some of the problem. Consideration should also be given to providing the student with several minimeals throughout the day instead of three larger meals. Refer to Table 6.2 for examples of common drugs and their possible side effects; also consult the health care worker at school for other methods of minimizing side effects of medications.

Being Aware of Food Allergies   Food is often blamed for many undesirable behaviors in students, such as hyperactivity, irritability, or poor attention span. Food is also blamed for many gastrointestinal, respiratory, neurological, and skin conditions. The diagnosis of food allergy, however, must be made by a physician, and verification of food allergy is by agreement of diagnostic tests and clinical impression. The special educator has the opportunity to observe symptoms of food allergy in a setting other than the home. The additional help of a dietitian is important to avoid an unnecessarily limited diet, which can result in malnutrition. Under no circumstance should a student be maintained on a restricted diet without convincing, objective documentation that a food allergy exists.

Mealtime Goals and Guidelines   Students who enjoy mealtime are more likely to have a good appetite. The following is a list of suggestions for making mealtime as pleasant an experience as possible:

1. Ensure that the student with motor difficulties is positioned correctly so that eating, rather than maintaining body position, is the focus of the mealtime.
2. Provide the student with a variety of foods and textures from all the basic food groups.
3. Recognize that all children refuse foods.
4. Introduce new foods gradually and when a student is most hungry in order to create optimum conditions for acceptance.
5. When rejected, offer the food again at frequent, regular intervals.
6. Serve portions that are appropriate for the child's needs.
7. Provide appropriate serving sizes (see Table 6.3 for suggestions).
8. Allow 10–20 minutes of rest before a meal if a child has been playing vigorously, in order to help improve appetite.
9. Encourage independent feeding whenever possible.

Procedures Following Mealtime

Accurate record-keeping will assist school personnel in assessing various nutrition and/or oral-motor interventions. The amount of food or drink offered is frequently much less than that ingested, particularly when a child has oral-motor difficulties. Thus, it is not only important to measure the volume of food served, but also that lost from spillage. This can be done by weighing the luncheon plate and bib before and after the meal and subtracting to find the amount spilled or not eaten. These data are essential in the attempt to identify the reasons for a student's weight gain or loss.

Warning Signs

Many of the warning signs for dehydration, that is, thirst; loss of appetite; drowsiness; flushed skin; and an increase in body temperature, pulse rate, and breathing rate are also symptoms of a number of other illnesses. In order to factor out the cause and treatment, consultation with a school nurse and/or referral to a health care provider is indicated. It is important that school personnel be sensitive to each child's health

Table 6.3. Basic food guide

To ensure that the child receives adequate amounts of nutrients to promote growth and weight gain, the Basic Food Guide has been established to serve as a simple food selection guide. Follow the chart below and include in the daily diet the recommended number of servings from each of the four groups. If the child is smaller than normal for chronological age, the nutrient requirements should be based on height rather than age.

Food group	Serving size for age/height			
	1–2 years 29"–34" in height	2–3 years 34"–37" in height	3–6 years 37"–45" in height	6–12 years 45"–57" in height
Milk group				
Include three to four servings daily of the following foods:				
Milk	1/2 cup	1/2–3/4 cup	3/4 cup	3/4–1 cup
Cottage cheese	1/4–1/2 cup	1/2 cup	1 cup	1 cup
Cheddar or American cheese	1 oz.	1 oz.	1 oz.	1 1/2 oz.
Yogurt	1/4 cup	1/4 cup	1/4 cup	3/4 cup
Ice cream	1/2 cup	3/4 cup	1 cup	1–1/4 cup
Pudding	1/2 cup	3/4 cup	3/4 cup	1 cup
Meat group				
Include two or more servings daily of the following foods:				
Meat, fish, poultry	1 oz.	1–2 oz.	1 1/2–2 oz.	2 oz.
Eggs (limit to three per week)	1	1	1	1
Peanut butter	1 tbsp.	1–2 tbsp.	3 tbsp.	4 tbsp.
Cheese	1 oz.	1 oz.	1 oz.	2 oz.
Legumes	1/4 cup	1/4 cup	1/2 cup	1 cup
Bread and cereal group				
Include four or more servings daily of the following foods:				
Enriched white or wheat bread or rolls	1/2	1/2	1	1–2
Ready-to-eat cereals	1/4 cup	1/3 cup	1/2 cup	1 cup
Cooked cereals	2 tbsp.	2 tbsp.	1/4 cup	3/4 cup
Pasta, rice	2 tbsp.	2 tbsp.	1/4 cup	1/2 cup
Crackers	3	3	5	5
Fruit and vegetable group				
Include four or more servings daily of the following foods:				
Unsweetened juice	1/4–1/2 cup	1/2 cup	1/2 cup	1/2 cup
Citrus fruit, berries, tomato, cabbage	1/4 cup	1/4 cup	1/2 cup	1/2 cup
Other fruits (fresh or canned)	2 tbsp.	2 tbsp.	2–4 tbsp.	1/2 cup
Green vegetables	2 tbsp.	2 tbsp.	2–4 tbsp.	1/2 cup
Other vegetables (e.g., potatoes, squash, carrot)	2 tbsp.	2 tbsp.	2–4 tbsp.	1/2 cup

Reprinted with permission from Shaddix, T. (1986). *Meal planning for the childhood years. Nutrition care for the child with developmental disabilities.* Birmingham: United Cerebral Palsy of Greater Alabama.

and behavioral state, as many students are unable to communicate verbally their physical status. The symptoms listed above may be early indicators for a prompt referral.

ADDITIONAL RESOURCES

A registered dietitian can be contacted through a local hospital, a hospital clinic, county or state extension service, or state or local chapter of the Dietetic Association. The request should be for dietitians who work with children who have special health care needs. In addition, the state's Services for Children with Special Health Care Needs and University-Affiliated Programs can offer consultation and technical assistance for the development of nutrition services in schools.

LITERATURE CITED

Crump, M. (1987). *Nutrition and feeding of the handicapped child.* Boston: College-Hill.

Hamill, P.V.V., Wright, T.A., Johnson, C.L., Reed, R.B., Roche, A.F., & Moore, W.M. (1979). Physical growth: National Center for Health Statistics percentiles. *American Journal of Clinical Nutrition 32,* 607–629.

Horsley, J.W. (July 1988). Nutrition services for children with special health care needs within the public school system. *Topics in Clinical Nutrition, 3*(3), 55–60.

Palmer, S. (1978). Nutrition and developmental disorders: An overview. In S. Palmer & S. Ekvall (Eds.), *Pediatric nutrition in developmental disorders* (pp. 21–24). Springfield, IL: Charles C Thomas.

Peaks, S., & Lamb, M.W. (1951). Comments on the dietary practice of cerebral palsied children. *Journal of the American Dietetic Association, 27,* 870–876.

Shaddix, T. (1986). *Meal planning for the childhood years. Nutritional care for the child with developmental disabilities.* Birmingham: United Cerebral Palsy of Greater Birmingham, Inc.

Appendix A

PROCEDURE FOR CALCULATING AGE

When plotting measurements on the birth to 36 months chart, age must be determined to nearest month. When plotting on 2–18 year charts, round to the nearest ¼ year. Calculate first days, then months, then years.

Example:	Year	Month	Day
Date of measurement	88	9	29
Birthdate	− 86	− 11	− 27
	1	10	2

As this example shows, it is sometimes necessary to borrow days from the month column or months from the year column to complete the subtraction.

Example of Plotting on Growth Chart:

Name: Meg
Date of Birth: May 26, 1980
Date of Measurement: January 20, 1989
Weight: 20 kg
Height: 125 cm

Following are blank growth charts. Calculate that this youngster is 8 years 8 months old. After plotting her you can see that she falls below the 5th percentile for weight and just below the 25th percentile for height. She is in less than the 5th percentile weight for height.

**BOYS: PREPUBESCENT
PHYSICAL GROWTH
NCHS PERCENTILES***

NAME_____   RECORD #_____

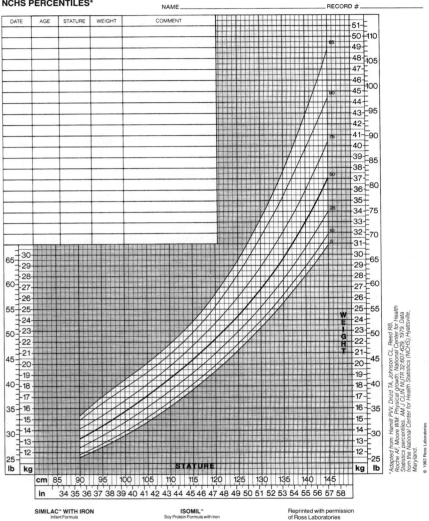

STATURE

*Adapted from: Hamill PVV, Drizd TA, Johnson CL, Reed RB, Roche AF, Moore WM. Physical growth: National Center for Health Statistics percentiles. AM J CLIN NUTR 32:607-629, 1979. Data from the National Center for Health Statistics (NCHS) Hyattsville, Maryland.

© 1982 Ross Laboratories

SIMILAC® WITH IRON
Infant Formula

ISOMIL®
Soy Protein Formula with Iron

Reprinted with permission
of Ross Laboratories

Used with permission of Ross Laboratories, Columbus, OH 43216.

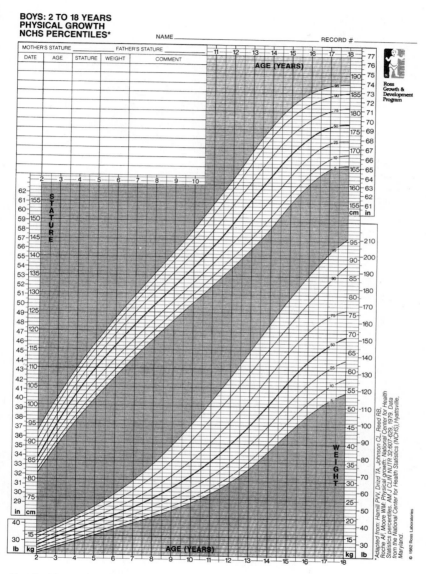

BOYS: 2 TO 18 YEARS
PHYSICAL GROWTH
NCHS PERCENTILES*

Used with permission of Ross Laboratories, Columbus, OH 43216.

GIRLS: PREPUBESCENT
PHYSICAL GROWTH
NCHS PERCENTILES*

NAME _____ RECORD # _____

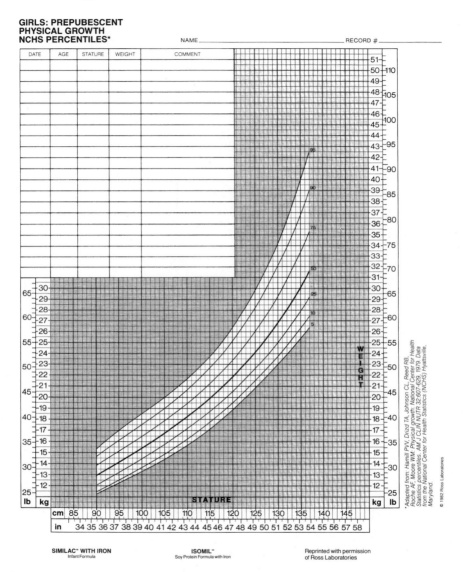

SIMILAC™ WITH IRON
Infant Formula

ISOMIL™
Soy Protein Formula with Iron

Reprinted with permission
of Ross Laboratories

*Adapted from: Hamill PVV, Drizd TA, Johnson CL, Reed RB, Roche AF, Moore WM: Physical growth: National Center for Health Statistics percentiles. AM J CLIN NUTR 32:607-629, 1979. Data from the National Center for Health Statistics (NCHS) Hyattsville, Maryland.

© 1982 Ross Laboratories

Used with permission of Ross Laboratories, Columbus, OH 43216.

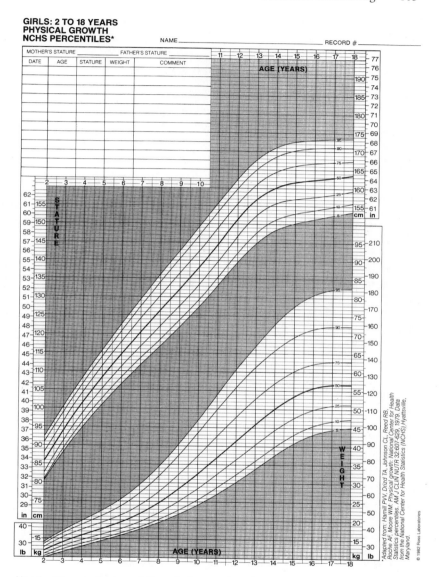

**GIRLS: 2 TO 18 YEARS
PHYSICAL GROWTH
NCHS PERCENTILES***

Used with permission of Ross Laboratories, Columbus, OH 43216.

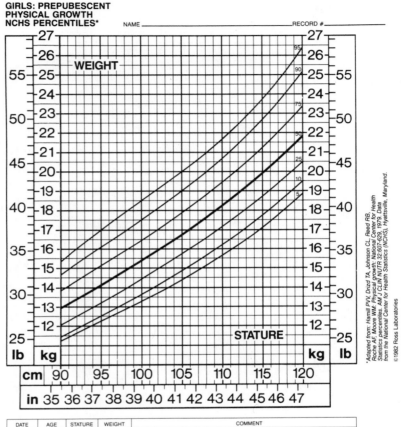

GIRLS: PREPUBESCENT PHYSICAL GROWTH NCHS PERCENTILES*

Used with permission of Ross Laboratories, Columbus, OH 43216.

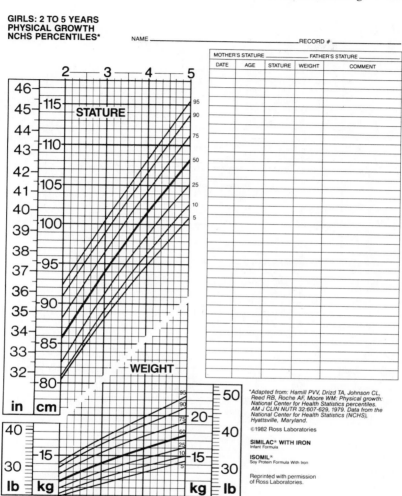

GIRLS: 2 TO 5 YEARS
PHYSICAL GROWTH
NCHS PERCENTILES*

Used with permission of Ross Laboratories, Columbus, OH 43216.

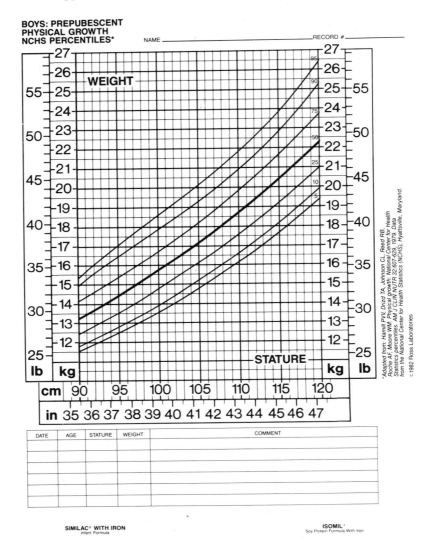

BOYS: PREPUBESCENT PHYSICAL GROWTH NCHS PERCENTILES*

Used with permission of Ross Laboratories, Columbus, OH 43216.

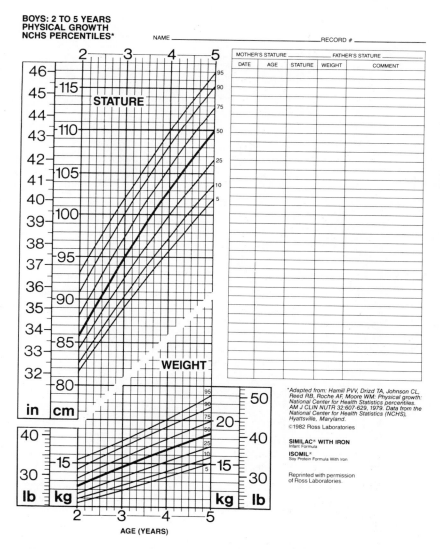

BOYS: 2 TO 5 YEARS PHYSICAL GROWTH NCHS PERCENTILES*

STATURE

WEIGHT

AGE (YEARS)

*Adapted from: Hamill PVV, Drizd TA, Johnson CL, Reed RB, Roche AF, Moore WM: Physical growth: National Center for Health Statistics percentiles. AM J CLIN NUTR 32:607-629, 1979. Data from the National Center for Health Statistics (NCHS), Hyattsville, Maryland.

©1982 Ross Laboratories

SIMILAC® WITH IRON
Infant Formula

ISOMIL®
Soy Protein Formula With Iron

Reprinted with permission of Ross Laboratories.

Used with permission of Ross Laboratories, Columbus, OH 43216.

BOYS: BIRTH TO 36 MONTHS
PHYSICAL GROWTH
NCHS PERCENTILES*

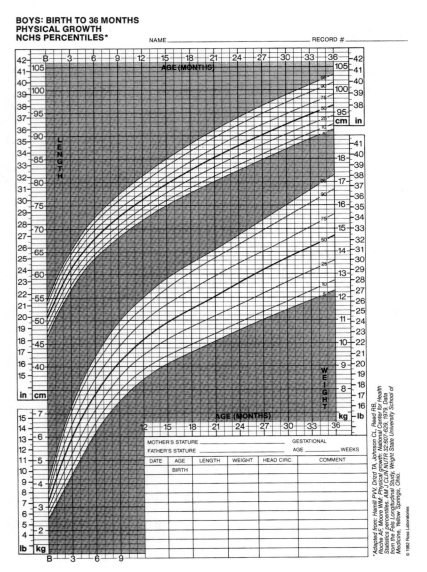

Used with permission of Ross Laboratories, Columbus, OH 43216.

**BOYS: BIRTH TO 36 MONTHS
PHYSICAL GROWTH
NCHS PERCENTILES***

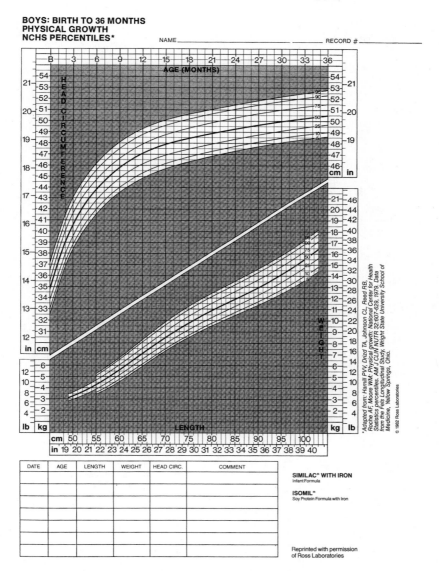

NAME _____   RECORD # _____

*Adapted from: Hamill PVV, Drizd TA, Johnson CL, Reed RB,
Roche AF, Moore WM: Physical growth: National Center for Health
Statistics percentiles. AM J CLIN NUTR 32:607-629, 1979. Data
from the Fels Longitudinal Study, Wright State University School of
Medicine, Yellow Springs, Ohio.

© 1982 Ross Laboratories

DATE	AGE	LENGTH	WEIGHT	HEAD CIRC.	COMMENT

SIMILAC® WITH IRON
Infant Formula

ISOMIL®
Soy Protein Formula with Iron

Reprinted with permission
of Ross Laboratories

Used with permission of Ross Laboratories, Columbus, OH 43216.

**GIRLS: BIRTH TO 36 MONTHS
PHYSICAL GROWTH
NCHS PERCENTILES***

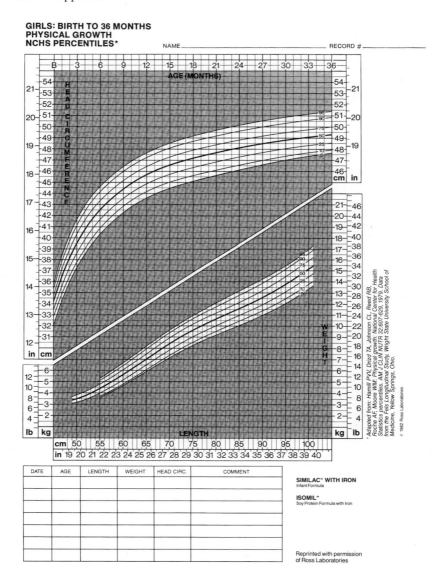

Used with permission of Ross Laboratories, Columbus, OH 43216.

**GIRLS: BIRTH TO 36 MONTHS
PHYSICAL GROWTH
NCHS PERCENTILES***

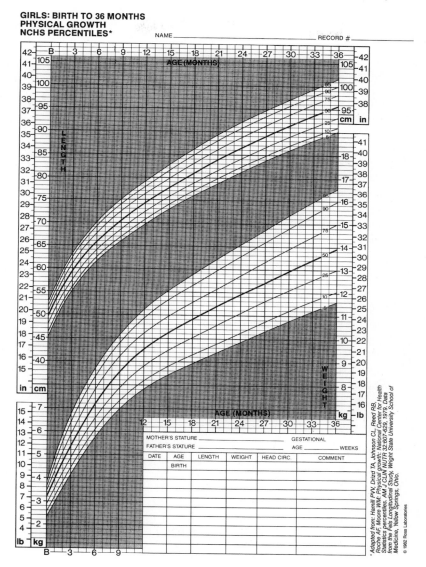

Used with permission of Ross Laboratories, Columbus, OH 43216.

Appendix B

GENERAL RESOURCES

Identified by the CHEWS Nutrition Project, Nutrition Bureau, Public Health Division, Santa Fe, New Mexico 87503

General materials
Title: *Child of Mine: Feeding with Love and Good Sense*
Author: Ellyn Satter, R.D., M.S.S.W., M.S.
Form: Book
Length: 200 pages
Date published: 1986
Available from: Bull Publishing Company
P.O. Box 208
Palo Alto, CA 94302
(415) 322-2855

Title: *Feed Me, I'm Yours*
Author: Vicky Lansky
Form: Book
Length: 152 pages
Date published: 1974
Available from: Simon & Schuster, Inc.
Simon & Schuster Building
1230 Avenue of the Americas, Department MBA,
New York, NY 10020

Title: *How to Get Your Kid to Eat . . . But Not Too Much*
Author: Ellyn Satter, R.D., M.S.S.W., M.S.
Form: Book
Length: 396 pages
Date published: 1987
Available from: Bull Publishing Company
P.O. Box 208
Palo Alto, CA 94302
(415) 322-2855

Title: *Nutrition in Infancy and Childhood, 3rd Edition*
Author: Peggy Pipes, R.D., M.P.H.
Form: Book

Length: 303 pages
Date published: 1985
Available from: The C.V. Mosby Company
                  St. Louis, MO

Materials related to food and food preparation

Title: *Non-Chew Cookbook*
Author: Randy J. Wilson
Form: Book
Length: 195 pages
Date published: 1985
Available from: Wilson Publishing Inc.
                  P.O. Box 2190
                  Glenwood Springs, CO 81601-2190

Title: *Blender-Full, High Protein, High-Calorie Recipes*
Author: Dietetic Internship Program
          Memorial Hospital of Glendale
          Glendale, CA
Form: Booklet
Length: 24 pages
Date published: 1985
Available from: Los Angeles District
                  California Dietetic Association
                  P.O. Box 3506
                  Santa Monica, CA 90403

Title: *The Joy of Snacks*
Author: Nancy Cooper, R.D.
Form: Book
Length: 269 pages
Date published: 1987
Available from: Diabetes Center
                  P.O. Box 739
                  Wayzata, MN 55391

Materials related to developmental disabilities

Title: *Nutritional Care for the Child with Developmental Disabilities*
Author: Tina Shaddix, R.D.
Form: Brochure(s), series
        "Promoting Weight Gain"

"Weight Control for the Overweight Child"
"Oral-Motor Development and Feeding Techniques"
"Management of Constipation"
"Meal Planning for the Childhood Years"
Length: 11–27 pages
Date published: 1986
Available from: United Cerebral Palsy
2430 11th Avenue North
Birmingham, AL 35234
Attn: Tina Shaddix, R.D.

Title: *Medical Aspects of Developmental Disabilities in Children Birth to Three: A Resource for Special-Service Providers in the Educational Setting*
Author: James A. Blackman, M.D.
Form: Book
Length: 231 pages
Date published: 1984
Available from: Division of Developmental Disabilities, Department of Pediatrics
University Hospital School
The University of IA
Iowa City, IA 52242

Title: *Nutrition and Feeding of the Handicapped Child*
Author: Iris Crump, R.D., M.S.
Form: Book
Length: 178 pages
Date published: 1987
Available from: College-Hill Press/Little, Brown and Company
Order Department
200 West Street
Waltham, MA 02254-9931

Title: *Nutrition Education for Retarded Children—A Program for Teachers*
Author: Virginia Stewart Johnson, M.S., R.D., Mary Ann Harvey-Smith, Ph.D., R.D., Joyce B. Bittle, Ph.D., R.D., Lee Jane Nuckolls, M.S., R.D.
Length: 183 pages
Date published: 1980
Available from: Publications Department
Boling Center for Developmental Disabilities
711 Jefferson Avenue
Memphis, TN 38105

ADDITIONAL RESOURCES INCLUDE

Material for measuring growth

Title: *A Guide to Pediatric Weighing and Measuring*
Author: Centers for Disease Control and Health Services Administration
Form: Booklet
Length: 28 pages
Date published: Unknown
Available from: U.S. Department of Health and Human Services

Title: *Growth References from Conception to Adulthood*
Author: Proceedings of Greenwood Genetic Center
Form: Spiral bound
Length: 220 pages
Date published: 1988
Available from: Greenwood Genetic Center
                  1 Gregor Mendel Circle
                  Greenwood, SC 29646

Growth charts for specific disabilities

Cronk, C., Crocker, A., Pueschel, S., Shea, A., Zackai, E., Pickens, G., & Reed, R. (1988). Growth charts for children with Down syndrome: One month to eighteen years of age. *Pediatrics, 81*(1), 102–110.

Holm, V.A. (1988). Appendix A: Growth Charts for Prader-Willi Syndrome. In Greenswag, L.R. & Alexander, R.C. (Eds.), *Management of Prader-Willi Syndrome* (pp. 237–240). New York: Springer-Verlag.

7

THERAPEUTIC MANAGEMENT

The ability to move about freely provides one way in which persons define and express themselves, as well as being a measure of health and physical fitness. Gestures and mannerisms are forms of communication that depend on movement. Motor activity is a primary means of discharging emotion, particularly for children (Mitchell, 1981). The purposes of therapeutic management are to improve the general health of the student, promote functioning of the body within the limits of the student's condition, maintain or improve joint mobility, and prevent deformity or the development of further deformity.

OVERVIEW

Movement depends on proper functioning of the central nervous system, the muscles, and the bones. Change or injury to any of these three parts of the body may cause a loss or a change in the ability to move. This lack of movement may result in additional systems of the body being affected. Systems at risk include the respiratory, urinary, and gastrointestinal systems, as well as the overall health of the skin.

The Effect of Restriction of
Movement on the Muscles, Joints, and Bone

The functioning and movement of the muscles may be affected for a variety of reasons. A student may experience damage to a portion of the brain, resulting in an interruption of the transmission of impulses to muscles and impairment of the overall ability of muscles to function. Muscles may also lose the ability to contract because of a disease, such as muscular dystrophy, or the muscle may deteriorate through lack of use or through loss of innervation, which is a decrease in the number of nerves acting upon a muscle.

When joints are not used, movement is decreased or lost. This loss is due to a process that usually contributes to the strength and flexibility of joints and the related muscles. A network of fibers is continually being "laid down," that is, deposited or formed, in the muscles and joints. Normal daily activity maintains the range of motion of joints and the related muscles, keeping the fibrous network of muscles and joints loose, pliable, and capable of moving with ease. The fibrous network stretches to accommodate the maximum movement of the joint. When movement is less frequent and limited, however, the fibrous network becomes less pliable and shortens to the length to which muscle is stretched. In less than a week of immobilization, fibrous tissue can be "laid down," causing restricted movement in a joint (Kottke, 1966). This is referred to as fibrosis.

Fibrosis within a muscle leads to shortening of the muscle. These shortened muscles pull the joint to which they are attached into an abnormal position, creating a contracture (Mitchell, 1981). A contracture is the permanent shortening of a muscle, with resulting shortening of surrounding tendons and ligaments. Joints that are most likely to develop contractures are those to which large muscles are attached, such as the hip and knee joints. If a student develops contractures of the hips or knees, greater effort of the muscle is required for standing and walking. There is also increased wear on the surfaces of the joints (Kottke, 1966).

Normal muscle movements also provide desired stresses to bone, making bone dense and hard. When normal muscle movements are absent, bone tends to become less dense, more porous, and softer. Therefore, joint movement must be maintained to contribute to healthy bones. Joint movements alone, however, do not ensure strong bones. Joint movements can ensure continued ability to move and *may* contribute to (or encourage) increased density of bones. It is thought that normal activities such as walking, running, and standing provide stresses on bones resulting in more calcium being deposited in the bones and stronger, more dense bones forming. If bone becomes too porous through disuse, a pathologic fracture may occur. This occurs when a force that would not have fractured a healthy bone results in a fracture of the weakened, porous bone (Mitchell, 1981).

The Effect of Lack of Movement on Other Systems of the Body

Lack of movement also affects other bodily functions and systems. These may include the respiratory, urinary, and gastrointestinal systems as well as the health of the skin.

The Respiratory System   The immobile student can develop problems with the lungs because more effort is required to expand the lungs and exchange air when a person is immobile than is required of an active person. Muscles used in breathing may be decreased in strength due to immobility, resulting in a decrease in the expansion of the chest. In addition to muscle weakness, the pressure of a bed or chair against the chest can also lead to decreased chest expansion and shallow breathing. As a result of limited chest expansion, the normal secretions produced in the lungs collect, rather than leaving the lungs. Secretions collected in the lungs provide an excellent environment for growth of bacteria, often resulting in pneumonia. Coughing, deep breathing, and changing positions can aid in moving the secretions from the lungs and preventing pneumonia (Mitchell, 1981).

The Urinary Tract   Retention of urine in the bladder may occur as a result of the student's decreased activity. The upright position (sitting or standing) promotes emptying of the bladder. If a student remains immobile and cannot initiate urination, urine may be retained in the bladder and the bladder will distend (i.e., become enlarged). Occasionally, just enough urine will dribble out of the bladder to relieve pressure and the urge to urinate. This, however, does not allow for complete emptying of the bladder. The stagnant urine remaining in the bladder provides an environment for growth of bacteria. Placing the student in an upright position may promote emptying of the bladder (Mitchell, 1981). Changing the student's position can prevent urinary tract infections by preventing the urine from remaining stagnant (Potter & Perry, 1985).

The Gastrointestinal System   The effect of lack of movement upon normal bowel functioning is addressed in Chapter 5, Bowel Care. In summary, lack of movement weakens muscle tone. This results in a reduced ability of the bowels to empty completely, increasing the risk of constipation or the development of an impaction.

The Condition of the Skin   Lack of movement can affect the health of the skin by causing pressure on the skin and underlying tissues. Continued pressure can cause an area to be deprived of normal blood supply and necessary nutrients for the cells in the skin and underlying tissue. If an area continues to be deprived of nutrients, cells in that area die. If enough cells die, the skin and tissue inevitably break down and an ulcer or pressure sore develops. Changing the student's position can help prevent skin problems by periodic relief of pressure and distribution of pressure over as wide an area as possible (Mitchell, 1981). (See Chapter 4, Skin Care.)

The Use of Therapeutic Management

Therapeutic management techniques focusing on improving health and maintaining movement capacity include postural drainage, joint range of motion, positioning, therapeutic handling, and relaxation (Fraser, Hensinger, & Phelps, 1987). Postural drainage, joint range of motion, positioning, and therapeutic handling are presented in the following discussion.

Postural Drainage   The ability of the student with multiple disabilities to expand the lungs may be decreased because of generalized muscle weakness and/or weakening of the muscles associated with coughing. Alternately, a student may lack the muscle control or coordination necessary to cough effectively and clear fluid from the lungs. The resulting decrease in lung expansion or inability to cough leads to an increased pooling or accumulation of secretions in the lungs. To avoid development of pneumonia or other infections, postural drainage or chest physiotherapy is administered. This is considered the best method to prevent pooling of secretions in the lungs.

Postural drainage is performed to promote the drainage and coughing up of secretions from the lungs. The student is placed in various positions to allow gravity to be used as an aid to promote drainage of secretions from the lungs, bronchi, and trachea (Figure 7.1). Postural drainage may be performed to treat lung conditions such as bronchitis, cystic fibrosis, pneumonia, and asthma (Wong & Whaley, 1986).

Joint Range of Motion   Joint range of motion refers to exercises in which parts of the body are moved in specific directions. The range of motion of joints is maintained in active persons by the movements and exercises that occur daily with walking, running, working, and playing. Many students with multiple disabilities have restricted movement.

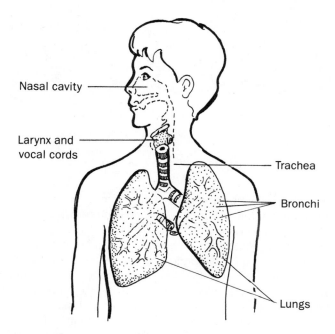

Figure 7.1.   Portions of the respiratory system.

These students may be able to move some or all joints through complete range of motion, but the joints that the student is unable to move must be moved by another person. This movement is referred to as passive range of motion exercise. Common range of motion exercises are presented in the Appendix to this chapter.

Positioning   For the student with multiple disabilities, positioning becomes the basis, *not the goal,* of an effective physical management or educational program. Positioning includes efforts to maintain the body in the most symmetrical alignment possible. Positions that the student may assume or in which the student may be placed include the supine (Figure 7.2), prone (Figure 7.3), and sidelying positions (Figure 7.4). In the supine position, the student is lying on the back. In the prone position, the student is lying on the abdomen (stomach). Recumbent or lying down positions, although difficult to adapt to functional educational programming, are helpful for the student with multiple disabilities because they are conducive to relaxation, requiring minimal muscle control of the posture (Fraser et al., 1987). The student should most often be placed in, or assisted to, positions in which the trunk and head are supported upright (i.e., sitting, kneeling, and standing). These

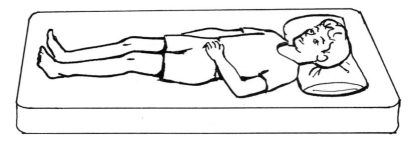

Figure 7.2.   One example of a student positioned in supine (i.e., on the back).

are, overall, healthier positions in that they increase circulation and levels of awareness, while producing some weight bearing and contributing to lung expansion.

Therapeutic Handling   Therapeutic handling is described by Fraser et al. (1987) as a dynamic process in which the therapist responds to the student's every shift in posture and mobility. Therapeutic handling may be very involved when assisting students with multiple disabilities because of the extensive deformities often present and rigid postures. For these students, therapeutic handling includes proper lifting methods and body mechanics (Fraser & Hensinger, 1983). Emphasis should be placed on handling techniques that prevent injury to the student and to the persons providing care for the student (Fraser et al., 1987).

PROCEDURES

Preparation for Therapeutic Management

When preparing to perform postural drainage, joint range of motion, positioning, or therapeutic handling, school staff must know the proper

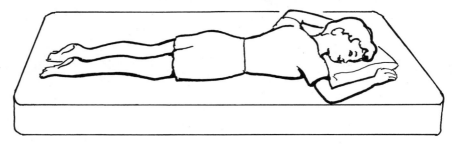

Figure 7.3.   A student positioned in prone (i.e., on the stomach).

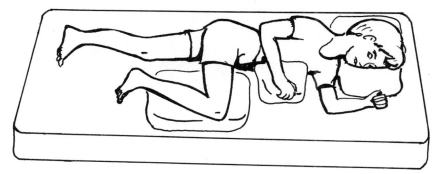

Figure 7.4.   A student in side-lying.

methods and techniques used to complete the procedure, the desirable position of the student, the frequency with which the procedure is performed, and the student's ability to tolerate the procedure.

Postural Drainage   When performing postural drainage, school staff must be trained in performing the cupping, vibration, and other steps of the procedure. Postural drainage must be prescribed by the student's physician with evidence of this prescription documented in the student's school records. The teacher should receive training both in implementing the procedures and managing the situation in case of an emergency. In most instances, postural drainage is performed twice a day (early in the morning and just before bedtime) (Scipien, Barnard, Chard, Howe, & Phillips, 1986). For some students, postural drainage may be performed three to four times a day (Wong & Whaley, 1986).

Joint Range of Motion   When joint range of motion is performed, school staff must know how to position the student, which joints are to be moved, how the joint is to be moved, the extent of pressure to apply against resistance, and the number of times each joint is to be moved. School staff must also identify functional movements to use to facilitate range of motion, either actively or passively. In active range the student performs the action, in passive range the motion is performed by the teacher or therapist. Before initiating joint range of motion, the student is most likely placed on a mat on the floor with the staff person at the side of the student. Ensuring that the student is comfortable and relaxed is helpful to both the student and staff person. Careful observation of the student's facial responses or overall body movements can provide information about the student's level of comfort. Informing the student before movement occurs can help promote relaxation as well as encourage active participation.

Joint range of motion generally is performed a minimum of two times daily, with the frequency prescribed by the student's physician and reflected in the school records. As much as possible, the process of ranging joints should be included in the performance of functional activities as well as conducted during specified times. For example, the range of motion of the elbow can be conducted during all attempts at reaching during the school day.

Positioning   When positioning the student, school staff need to know how to properly place and align the student and the special equipment necessary to ensure that the student is properly positioned. The physical therapist provides input on positioning based upon the level and type of the student's activities and the need for rest. Activities that necessarily occur throughout the day, such as feeding and toileting, also determine the student's position. Brill and Kilts (1980) recommend that the student's position be changed a minimum of every 2 hours. More position change may be necessary depending on the student's risk level for developing pressure sores (see Chapter 4, Skin Care).

Therapeutic Handling   Therapeutic handling includes lifting methods and body mechanics (Fraser & Hensinger, 1983). School staff need to be able to demonstrate the methods recommended for lifting and moving the student that will prevent injury to the student and the staff, as well as facilitate participation in the movement by the student. Staff must know what constitutes and how to implement good body mechanics when lifting and moving the student.

When implementing any therapeutic management procedure the ability of the student to tolerate a procedure needs to be assessed. It is important to know the student's responses to the procedure, especially how the student with limited verbal communication reveals discomfort and pain (e.g., facial expressions, withdrawal, a crying sound), when a rest period may be needed, and what positions are most and least tolerated by the student.

Performing Therapeutic Management

Postural Drainage   The student is placed in the desired predetermined position (Figure 7.5). Small students can be placed on the lap of a staff person. Older and larger students can be placed on a padded slant board or padded wedge board. A bed or couch can be used with pillows to position the larger student comfortably.

After the student is placed in position, deep breathing is encouraged. The student can be encouraged to blow up a balloon or blow bubbles to facilitate deep breathing. The shaded areas shown in Figure 7.5

on the chest and back are then cupped. Cupping is accomplished by rapidly striking the student's chest with a cupped hand (Figure 7.6) for 1 minute. The opposite side of the chest is cupped in the same area for 1 full minute. After cupping is completed in one position, the student is encouraged to breathe deeply and is vibrated. Vibration can be created by placing one hand on top of the other on the student's chest wall and rapidly tightening and loosening muscles of the lower arm. A gentle, firm pressure on the student's chest occurs as the staff person's lower arm muscles are tightened and loosened. The student is then encouraged to cough.

These steps are performed for each of the positions in Figure 7.5, on the right and left side of the chest. The entire procedure generally requires 20–30 minutes (Wong & Whaley, 1986). Postural drainage should be performed 1–1½ hours before meals to decrease the chance of vomiting and so the student has time to rest and develop an appetite (Wong & Whaley, 1986). This procedure should not be performed after meals.

Joint Range of Motion   When moving the student's limbs and joints through range of motion, the movements are carried out smoothly, slowly, and should not push excessively against resistance of the joint causing pain. The body part is held with a secure yet gentle grasp (Killingsworth, 1976). If a body part is to be lifted or moved, the staff person places one hand under the joint for support (Figure 7.7a), or supports the joint by holding the body part on either side of the joint (Figure 7.7b), or supports the joint with one hand while another part of the extremity is cradled with the other arm (Figure 7.7c) (Potter & Perry, 1985). While moving the joint, the staff person observes for signs of discomfort and pain as well as the amount and ease of joint movement. The types of movements that are performed on the student's joints are recommended by the student's physician and the physical therapist. Types of movements for joint range of motion are described in the Appendix to this chapter.

Positioning   Efforts are made to maintain the student in a position as near normal as possible for comfort, to prevent deformity (Mitchell, 1981), for general health, and to encourage interaction with the environment. Staff should give consideration to positioning of the student for all activities including those performed during grooming, feeding, dressing, toileting, and work. Feeding, dressing, and toileting are presented as examples. As described previously, the student may be placed in a supine (Figure 7.2), prone (Figure 7.3), sidelying (Figure 7.4), sitting (Figure 7.8), kneeling (Figure 7.9), standing position (Fig-

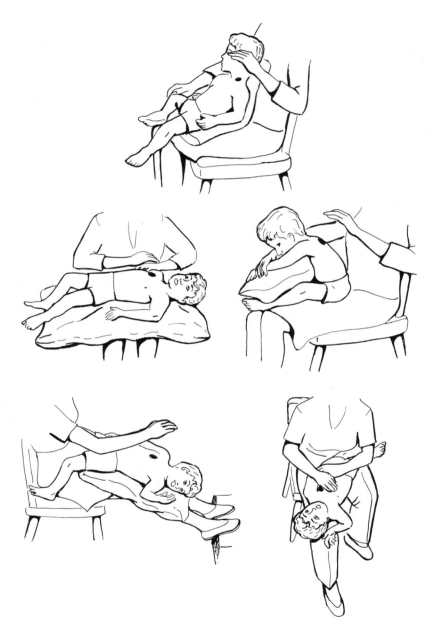

Figure 7.5. Strategies for performing postural drainage, including the position of the student and areas of the student's body that receive percussion.

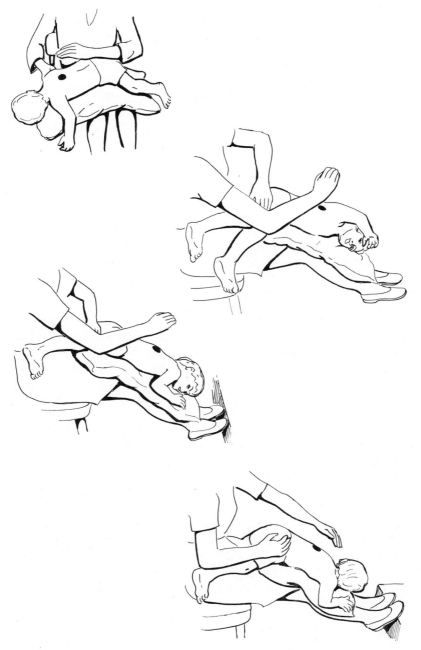

Figure 7.5.   *(continued)*

Figure 7.6.   The structure of the teacher's hand during percussion.

ure 7.10), or modifications of these. It is important to note that the position should not be considered the goal of any activity. Rather, positioning should be considered the basis for assisting the student in performing any activity as close to optimally as possible.

During feeding, the student may sit in a wheelchair or feeding seat (Figure 7.11) with support to either side of the head. Positioning during mealtime should provide the student with support of the trunk, head, legs, and arms and allow the student to focus attention and energy on oral-motor skills. The staff person sits in front of the student to allow eye-to-eye contact to take place. The jaw may need to be controlled during feeding. The jaw may be controlled manually from the front (Figure 7.12a) or from the side (Figure 7.12b). Control from the side provides the staff person the opportunity to cradle and stabilize the student's head during feeding (Fraser et al., 1987). Manual control of the jaw facilitates oral control, minimizes loss of food, and hopefully aids in ensuring an adequate nutritional intake.

If the student is capable of participating in the dressing process, the greatest level of independence is encouraged. Efforts are made to support the trunk of the body while the student reaches to place the arm into the sleeve of a coat (Fraser et al., 1987). This can occur in sidelying, sitting, or standing positions.

If the student is unable to dress independently, school staff will be involved with dressing. The student with cerebral palsy may stiffen up and become more difficult to handle when lying on the back. The student may tend to push the head and shoulders back, and straighten and stiffen the hips and legs. Placing the older student's head and shoulders on a hard pillow, flexing the neck, allows the arms to move forward and the hips and legs to bend more easily. Dressing the student may then be easier (Finnie, 1975).

Finnie (1975) suggests placing the student with cerebral palsy in sidelying for dressing. This allows the student to be rolled from side to

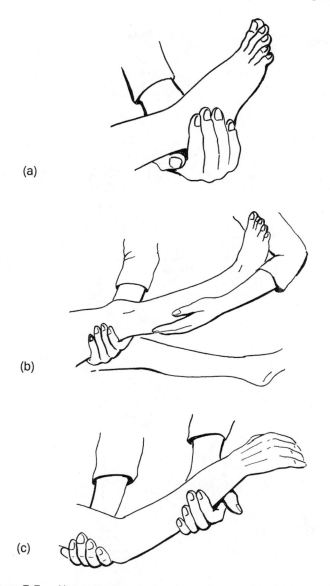

(a)

(b)

(c)

Figure 7.7.   Alternate ways to provide support to a joint while performing range of motion.

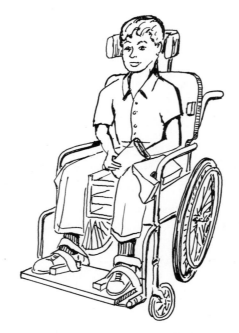

Figure 7.8.   One way to position a student in sitting.

Figure 7.9.   One way to position a student in kneeling.

Figure 7.10.   One way to position a student in standing.

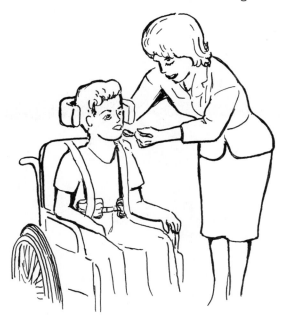

Figure 7.11.   One example of the many different types of support possible during mealtime.

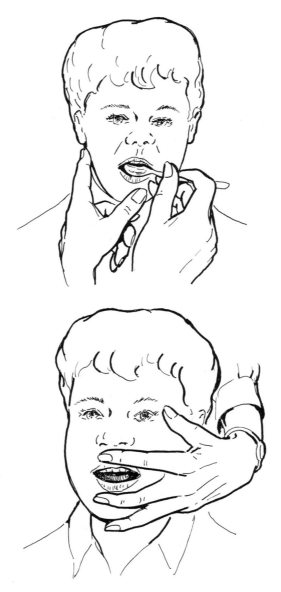

Figure 7.12.   Jaw control methods used to facilitate normal chewing during mealtime.

side, keeping the head bent forward and the knees and hips flexed. The student thus has less of a tendency to push the head back, and the shoulders and head are more easily brought forward. Stiffness of the body is also decreased.

Finnie (1975) has other suggestions for positioning during dressing. Clothes are placed on the more involved arm or leg first, and removed from the least involved arm or leg first. Bending the student's leg makes putting on socks and shoes easier. When the leg is straight, the ankle and foot are stiffer and the toes are more likely to turn under. When putting on a diaper, the hips and knees are more easily bent and the knees spread if a pillow is placed under the student's head or hips.

Since many students with multiple disabilities do not have control of the bladder and bowels and do not acquire control, school staff will be assisting with positioning the student for toileting. The student who cannot tolerate a sitting position usually uses incontinent wear. Toilet chairs may be used for the student who sits or can be assisted to sitting. A toilet chair that provides support for the back and along the sides has been recommended for the student with more severe disabilities (Figure 7.13). The triangle chair or corner chair can be used as a toilet chair for the younger student (Figure 7.14). Positioning the student in an upright position can help prevent constipation by making defecation easier. The upright position can also allow the bladder to empty more completely (see Chapter 5, Bowel Care).

Additional equipment used in positioning the student includes a wheelchair (Figure 7.15), wedge (Figure 7.16), and prone board or prone-stander (Figure 7.17).

The student may require a device for supporting a joint or certain other part of the body. An orthosis is an appliance that is used to correct, prevent, support, or align deformities or improve the function of movable body parts. The student with multiple disabilities may require a spinal orthosis (Figure 7.18), and less often needs an orthosis for the legs and feet (Figure 7.19), or the arms and hands (Fraser et al., 1987). Staff persons working with the student need to know how to remove and replace the orthosis.

Therapeutic Handling   School staff working with the student requiring positioning must understand the importance of lifting and moving the student in a way that protects the student and the staff person while encouraging student participation. School staff should use good body mechanics when bending to pick up or lift a student, work with a student on the mat, or assist a student up from the floor. General rules for maintaining good body mechanics include: flexing the knees and

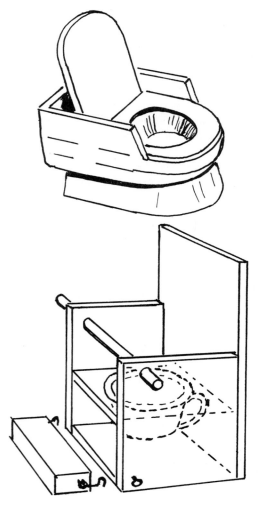

Figure 7.13.   Two of the many types of adaptations possible to facilitate a student sitting on the toilet.

hips, keeping the back straight, keeping shoulders in line with the pelvis, keeping the feet apart, placing one foot slightly in front of the other, avoiding twisting movements of the spine when lifting, and never carrying an impossible load (Killingsworth, 1976).

When lifting and carrying a student, school staff must lift by using the strong thigh muscles rather than the back muscles. Squat, then stand to lift, lift and carry heavy objects close to the body, and carry

Figure 7.14.   A triangle chair used to provide support to a student during toileting.

objects using muscles that pull shoulder blades together to lessen fatigue and avoid back strain (Killingsworth, 1976). It is important to work with the force of gravity by pushing, pulling, and lowering, rather than against the force of gravity by lifting (Brill & Kilts, 1980).

Procedures Following Therapeutic Management

After performing postural drainage, joint range of motion, positioning, and therapeutic handling, the student's responses to and ability to toler-

Figure 7.15.   An example of a wheelchair adapted to support a student while sitting.

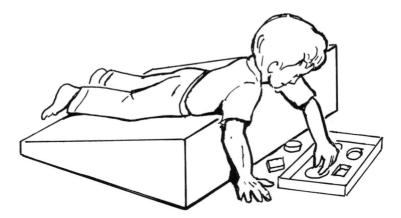

Figure 7.16.   A wedge—a piece of equipment used to support a student while in prone.

Figure 7.17.   A prone-stander—a piece of equipment used to support a student while standing.

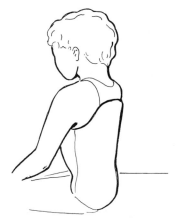

Figure 7.18.   A spinal orthosis used to help provide support to a student's trunk.

ate the procedure are considered. If the student experiences difficulty with a procedure, staff need to consider the problem and its differences or similarities to past responses. School staff persons may need to consult with therapists and/or the health care worker in the school to evaluate the problem. The problem may be caused by changes in the student or improperly managed procedures. Changes may need to be made in the procedure to accommodate the student. Parents and/or caregivers, may also need to be notified of the student's behaviors related to the procedures, and parents can provide school staff with insight into the student's responses to the procedure and suggestions for changes.

After completing postural drainage, the student may be placed into a comfortable position, allowed to rest, or participate in a relaxing activity. Any mucus coughed up by the student is disposed of in a lined wastebasket. Thorough handwashing must be carried out after disposal of the mucus. Hands are washed at a sink that is not used for food preparation. Any joint swelling or discomfort should be noted and reported to the school health care worker and parents.

School staff should also consider their own responses and ability to tolerate therapeutic handling of the student. Staff need to *take care of themselves* and be aware of discomforts (e.g., back pain). The staff may try alternate methods of moving the student, and should recognize when additional assistance may be needed. If a staff person is experiencing difficulty in moving or applying any procedure, the steps used in moving the student need to be evaluated and may need to be changed.

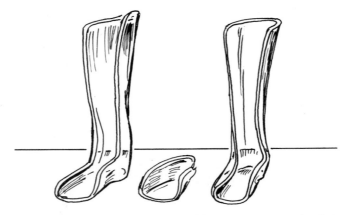

Figure 7.19.   A leg orthosis used to provide support to a student's knees or ankles.

More assistance or a different method of moving the student may be needed.

Parents need to be notified when a particular procedure was not performed. For example, if the class spends an afternoon out of the classroom and the student remains positioned in the wheelchair until returning to school several hours later, joint range of motion may have been omitted because of the change in class schedule. Informing the parents of this may allow them to work the joint range of motion into the child's schedule for the remainder of the day.

Warning Signs

Postural Drainage   Vomiting can occur during or after postural drainage. Efforts must be made immediately to remove vomitus from the student's mouth and prevent choking and aspiration (pulling of secretions into the trachea and lungs). Secretions can be removed from the mouth by wiping out the mouth with a clean tissue or cloth, or by suctioning the mouth using a bulb syringe, a portable suction machine, or a DeLee suction trap (see Chapter 16, Tracheostomy Care). The health care worker in the school and the student's parents and/or caregiver need to be notified of an episode of vomiting.

Vigorous coughing and the downward position of the student during postural drainage could result in increased intracranial pressure (pressure inside the skull). If vigorous coughing develops, the student should be allowed to sit up until coughing subsides. The sitting position is less frightening to the student and allows the student to produce a deeper cough. (See Chapter 9, Monitoring a Shunt, for indicators of increased intracranial pressure.)

Inability of the student to relax can hinder efforts made in postural drainage, or joint range of motion and positioning. Techniques that promote relaxation include: supportive, comfortable, and restful atmosphere; a confident and reassuring therapist; the use of pillows to support body parts; massage; and heat (Killingsworth, 1976). The physical therapist can provide recommendations of techniques that promote relaxation of the student.

As previously described, the student may develop pneumonia when percussion and postural drainage is utilized. Signs indicating pneumonia vary depending on the age of the student, the organism causing pneumonia (bacterial, viral), the presence of other health problems, and the amount of the lung surface affected (Whaley & Wong, 1987). General symptoms include chills, fever, pain in the chest, and cough (Thomas, 1985). The student may also cough up yellow, green, or blood tinged mucus that has an odor. If pneumonia is suspected, the health care worker in the school and the student's parents and/or caregiver must be notified. The student will need the attention of a physician and appropriate medications.

Therapeutic Positioning and Joint Range of Motion   Pain, swelling, or warmth of a joint may indicate inflammation in the joint. An inflamed joint may need to rest while other joints continue to be moved. If one or all of these symptoms occur, the health care worker in the school, the physical therapist, and parents and/or caregiver must be notified. The student's physician may also need to be notified of these signs.

A contracture may develop in a joint evidenced by limitation of movement in the joint. The joint feels stiff or tight or there is resistance to movement by the staff person. Joint range of motion and proper positioning can maintain the movement in a body part. It may be that the development of contractures cannot be prevented, but the student can be assisted to have as much movement in the joint as possible.

If the student develops redness that does not disappear after a position change, there may be excessive pressure on the skin resulting in the beginning stages of a pressure sore. Normal tissues have been shown to begin to degenerate in 2 hours of unrelieved pressure (Krusen, Kottke, & Ellwood, 1971). The presence of redness or signs of pressure sores (see Chapter 4, Skin Care) is a concern. The health care worker in the school, the physical therapist, and the student's parents and/or caregiver need to be notified. Efforts must be made to relieve pressure on the student's skin while positioning the student in the most normal and natural positions as possible, with changes in positioning at least every 2 hours.

Equipment used in positioning the student will become too small as the student grows. School staff and therapists should routinely check the fit of the equipment to the student. Equipment may need to be adapted for the student or new equipment purchased.

SIGNS OF AN EMERGENCY

Postural Drainage

The student may experience a blockage of the airway by secretions that are being loosened during postural drainage. The student becomes unable to move air into the lungs. Management of this problem is described in Chapter 8, Cardiopulmonary Resuscitation. The staff person must call for assistance from other staff in the classroom and follow the established plan for an emergency in the school.

Aspiration can be a concern with the student receiving postural drainage or with the student being fed. Vomiting during or after postural drainage provides an opportunity for vomitus to be pulled into the trachea or lungs. Because the student may assume a position in which the neck and head are extended during feeding, swallowing is difficult. Extension of the head increases the possibility of aspiration of food and fluids into the lungs (Howison, 1983). If attempts to suction the aspirated material from the airway are unsuccessful, the staff person calls for assistance from other staff in the classroom. The procedure described in Chapter 8, Cardiopulmonary Resuscitation, is followed. The established plan for an emergency in the school must be followed.

Range of Motion and Therapeutic Positioning

The occurrence of a fracture or dislocated bone is considered an emergency in that the student needs immediate attention to place the broken or dislocated bone(s) back into a proper position. The bone(s) needs to be stabilized with a cast, splint, or device surgically placed to allow for healing in the most normal position.

A fracture or dislocation could occur during joint range of motion, positioning, or therapeutic handling. If a fracture or dislocation is suspected by school staff, the health care worker in the school should be contacted to evaluate the student. Indicators of a fracture may be a change in joint range of motion (limited or excess movement), swelling around area of fracture, pain or tenderness, and bruising. There may be a grating sensation at the point of fracture, as broken bone ends move over each other. A student may have no difficulty with moving the fractured area (Whaley & Wong, 1987). After evaluation by the health care worker, the student may be referred to a physician. The student should be transported to the physician's office or hospital by persons who can provide proper support to the body part that is thought to be injured. The student may need to be transported by the local emergency medical services. The health care worker in the school and the student's physician can assist in determining the best method of transportation. The student's parents and/or caregiver must also be notified.

ADDITIONAL RESOURCES

Parents can be an invaluable resource to school staff working with the student. Parents provide much information about the student's abilities, techniques that do and do not work, and information about the student's daily activities.

Physical therapists in the school can provide assistance and information about joint range of motion, positioning, and therapeutic handling. Physical therapists working with children in hospital settings may be a resource to the school physical therapist and school staff in the classroom.

Manufacturers and distributors of equipment can provide information about the use of equipment and new or different equipment that can be more effective for the student. The physical therapist and occupational therapist will most likely have names and addresses of manufacturers and distributors.

Respiratory therapists and nurses can instruct school staff in techniques of postural drainage. Respiratory therapists can be contacted at a local hospital. The nurses working in the physician's office, a public health nurse, or clinical nursing specialist working with children can teach postural drainage techniques to school staff.

The orthopedic surgeon who has performed surgery on a student can provide specific information about proper positioning of the student after surgery, and positioning to prevent development or further development of deformity.

The orthotist, the person who made an orthotic device for the student, may need to be contacted for information about the use of the device. When the device does not fit properly, the orthotist should be contacted.

LITERATURE CITED

Brill, E.L., & Kilts, D.F. (1980). *Foundations for nursing.* New York: Appleton-Century-Crofts.

Finnie, N.R. (1975). *Handling the young cerebral palsied child at home* (2nd ed.). New York: E.P. Dutton.

Fraser, B.A., & Hensinger, R.N. (1983). *Managing physical handicaps: A practical guide for parents, care providers, and educators.* Baltimore: Paul H. Brookes Publishing Company.

Fraser, B.A., Hensinger, R.N., & Phelps, J.A. (1987). *Physical Management of multiple handicaps.* Baltimore: Paul H. Brookes Publishing Co.

Howison, M.V. (1988). Cerebral palsy. In H.L. Hopkins & H.D. Smith (Eds.), *Willard & Spackman's occupational therapy* (7th ed., pp. 675–706). Philadelphia: J.B. Lippincott.

Killingsworth, A. (1976). *Basic physical disability procedures.* Oakland, CA: Amy Killingsworth and CAL-SYL Press.

Kottke, F.J. (1966). The effects of limitation of activity upon the human body. *Journal of the American Medical Association. 196*(10), 117–122.

Krusen, F.H., Kottke, F.J., & Ellwood, P.M. (1971). *Handbook of physical medicine and rehabilitation* (2nd ed.). Philadelphia: W.B. Saunders.

Mitchell, P.H. (1981). Motor status. In P.H. Mitchell & A. Loustau (Eds.), *Concepts basic to nursing* (3rd ed., pp. 343–390). New York: McGraw-Hill.

Potter, P.A., & Perry, A.G. (1985). *Fundamentals of nursing.* St. Louis: C.V. Mosby.

Scipien, G.M., Barnard, M., Chard, M.A., Howe, J., & Phillips, P.J. (1986). *Comprehensive pediatric nursing.* (1986). New York: McGraw-Hill.

Thomas, C.L. (Ed.). (1985). *Taber's cyclopedic medical dictionary* (15 ed.). Philadelphia: F.A. Davis.

Whaley, L.F., & Wong, D.L. (1987). *Nursing care of infants and children* (3rd ed.). St. Louis: C.V. Mosby.

Wong, D.L., & Whaley, L.F. (1986). *Clinical handbook of pediatric nursing.* St. Louis: C.V. Mosby.

Woods, G.E. (1983). *Handicapped children in the community.* Bristol: John Wright & Sons Ltd.

Appendix

RANGE OF JOINT MOTION EXERCISES

TYPE OF MOVEMENT

BODY PART

Neck **Flexion:** Chin is brought to rest on chest.
    Extension: Head is returned to erect position.
    Hyperextension: Head is bent back as far as possible.
    Lateral flexion: Head is tilted as far as possible toward each shoulder.
    Rotation: Head is turned as far as possible to the right and to the left.

Shoulder **Flexion:** Arm is raised from side position forward to a position above head.
    Extension: Arm is returned to position at side of body.
    Hyperextension: Arm is moved behind the body, keeping elbow straight.
    Abduction: Arm is raised to side to a position above head with palm way from the head.
    Adduction: Arm is lowered sideways and across the body as far as possible.
    Internal rotation: With elbow flexed, shoulder is rotated by moving the arm until thumb is turned inward and toward the back.
    External rotation: With elbow flexed, the arm is moved until thumb is upward and lateral to the head.
    Circumduction: Arm is moved in a full circle.

Elbow **Flexion:** Elbow is bent so that the lower arm moves toward its shoulder joint and the hand is level with the shoulder.
    Extension: Elbow is straightened by lowering the hand.
    Hyperextension: Lower arm is bent back as far as possible.

Adapted from Potter, P.A., and Perry, A.G. (1985). *Fundamentals of nursing.* St. Louis: C.V. Mosby.

Forearm	**Supination:**	Lower arm and hand are turned so that palm is up.
	Pronation:	Lower arm is turned so palm is down.
Wrist	**Flexion:**	Palm is moved toward inner aspect of forearm.
	Extension:	Fingers are moved so that fingers, hands, and forearm are level.
	Hyperextension:	The back of the hand is brought back as far as possible.
	Abduction:	Wrist is bent toward the thumb.
	Adduction:	Wrist is bent toward the fifth finger.
Finger	**Extension:**	Fingers are straightened.
	Hyperextension:	Fingers are bent back as far as possible.
	Abduction:	Fingers are spread apart.
	Adduction:	Fingers are brought together.
Thumb	**Flexion:**	Thumb is moved across palm of hand.
	Extension:	Thumb is moved straight away from hand.
	Opposition:	Thumb is touched to each finger of the same hand.
Hip	**Flexion:**	Leg is moved forward and up.
	Extension:	Leg is moved back beside other leg.
	Hyperextension:	Leg is moved behind body.
	Abduction:	Leg is moved laterally away from body.
	Adduction:	Leg is moved back toward center of body and beyond if possible.
	Internal rotation:	Foot and leg are turned toward other leg.
	External rotation:	Foot and leg are turned away from other leg.
	Circumduction:	Leg is moved in a circle.
Knee	**Flexion:**	Heel is brought toward back of thigh.
	Extension:	Leg is returned to floor.
Ankle	**Dorsal flexion:**	Foot is moved so that toes are pointed upward.
	Plantar flexion:	Foot is moved so that toes are pointed downward.

Foot	**Inversion:**	Sole of foot is turned in toward middle of the body.
	Eversion:	Sole of foot is turned out away from middle of the body.

Toes	**Flexion:**	Toes are curled downward.
	Extension:	Toes are straightened.
	Abduction:	Toes are spread apart.
	Adduction:	Toes are brought together.

8

CARDIOPULMONARY RESUSCITATION

Cardiopulmonary resuscitation (CPR) is an emergency procedure used in life-threatening situations when breathing, or breathing and the heart, have stopped. CPR is not considered a procedure that is routinely implemented in the classroom. It is a response to an emergency situation. Teachers and other professionals who interact on a consistent basis with children who have disabilities should, however, be routinely certified in administering CPR in order to be prepared to give emergency care when the need arises. Although any individual may, at some time, need CPR, students with heart defects, seizure disorders, cerebral palsy, medically fragile conditions, and so forth, may be at additional risk since many of these students experience conditions such as prolonged seizures, aspiration of fluids or objects, and anaphylactic shock.

The administration of CPR is intended to: 1) restore breathing and blood circulation, 2) provide oxygen to the brain and other vital organs until breathing or circulation is restored, or 3) provide oxygen to the brain and other vital organs until appropriate medical treatment can restore the normal action of the heart (*Heartsaver manual,* 1987).

OVERVIEW

In the adult population sudden death from heart attack is "the most prominent medical emergency" or situation requiring lifesaving measures (Standards for CPR and ECC, 1986, p. 2908). The rescue efforts, CPR, are made to cause blood to continue to move through the heart to the brain and lungs and to move air into the lungs to provide enough oxygen to the heart, brain, and lungs.

For children, unlike adults, heart attack is not the most prominent medical emergency. Difficulty with breathing is the most frequent medical emergency for children ("Standards and guidelines," 1986). Children may also require CPR for injuries; suffocation caused by toys, foods, or plastic covers; smoke inhalation; sudden infant death syndrome; and infections, especially of the respiratory tract (Statistical Resources Branch, Division of Vital Statistics, 1981). The majority of emergency situations requiring CPR for children are preventable. Special attention must be paid to providing environments that are safe and protective ("Standards and guidelines," 1986) while fostering independence.

This caution is particularly applicable for students with disabilities who are at greater risk for requiring CPR than other children. Characteristics of some conditions, for example, tracheostomies, excess fluids, pica, and so forth, make students with disabilities more susceptible to accidental deaths than the general population (Batshaw & Perret, 1981). For example, immature chewing and swallowing abilities and abnormalities of the structure and sensation of the mouth and throat result in a student being at a higher risk for choking on certain foods. Children are additionally at a higher risk for choking, when compared with an adult, because the child's airway is smaller and the cough is weaker (Harris, Baker, Smith, & Harris, 1984).

The student experiencing difficulty moving oxygen into the lungs may have a decrease in the supply of oxygen to the brain, heart, and other vital organs. It is this lack of oxygen, due to breathing difficulty, that is usually the cause of cessation of the pulse, that is, cardiac arrest (*Heartsaver manual*, 1987). The heart can continue to pump blood for several minutes after breathing has ceased and the oxygen stored in the lungs and blood will continue to circulate to the brain and other vital organs (Safar, 1986). By starting CPR quickly after the student has stopped breathing or the airway has been blocked, cessation of the pulse, that is, cardiac arrest, can be prevented (Standards for CPR and ECC, 1986).

CPR begun within 4 minutes (or less) after the pulse and breathing have stopped can be lifesaving for the student. When CPR is begun within 4 minutes, the student's chance of leaving the hospital alive are four times greater than for the student who does not receive CPR until after 4 minutes. After 4 minutes and without CPR, brain damage begins. After 10 minutes have passed without CPR, brain death is certain due to lack of oxygen (*Heartsaver manual*, 1987).

PROCEDURES

The procedures described here are intended to provide the teacher, or other related service personnel, with an understanding of what is involved in implementing CPR. This includes why the procedure is done and what is included in using CPR on a child who has stopped breathing and whose heart has stopped. A review of the procedures described is not sufficient training for an individual to be able to perform CPR on an adult or child in distress. Professionals should be trained by qualified personnel and should maintain an active certification.

How to Perform CPR

CPR includes three basic rescue skills referred to as the ABC's of CPR. These include opening the **A**irway, restoring **B**reathing, and restoring **C**irculation. These skills can be performed by persons properly trained in CPR until more advanced life support can be made available. The advanced life support is conducted by the Emergency Medical Services (EMS) or local rescue unit. Advanced life support includes special techniques, special equipment, and the use of drugs and fluids. If there is no EMS available in the community, the student should be taken immediately to the nearest hospital emergency room (*Heartsaver manual*, 1987). Procedures need to be identified for each classroom specifying who is trained, the location of the emergency equipment, and a designation of whom to call in the event of an emergency.

The CPR procedure described below is for the student from 1 to 8 years of age. The procedure for children over 8 years old is the same procedure for adult CPR and is not described here.

Opening the Airway   When it is suspected that the student's breathing or pulse has stopped, the rescuer makes an attempt to arouse the student by, for example, gently shaking the student's shoulder and shouting, "Are you okay?" The rescuer then calls out for help. The rescuer then positions the student on his or her back, with care being given to support the head and neck in case of injury. The rescuer then opens the airway by tilting the head and lifting the chin (Figure 8.1).

Restoring Breathing   The rescuer determines whether or not the student is breathing by looking, listening, and feeling for a breath while holding the airway open (tilting the head and lifting the chin). If it is determined that there is no breath, the rescuer gives the student two breaths.

Restoring Circulation   The rescuer determines whether or not a pulse is present by feeling for the carotid pulse (Figure 8.2) while tilting the head to open the airway with the other hand. If another person has come to assist, that person should first contact the EMS system. If the pulse is absent, the rescuer begins repeated compressions of the chest. Five compressions are given, then one breath, repeating five compres-

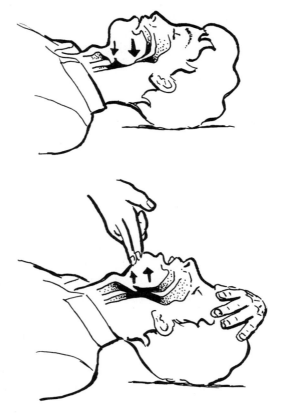

Figure 8.1.   Opening the airway by tilting the head and lifting the chin.

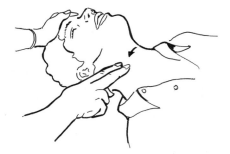

Figure 8.2.   Feeling the neck for the carotid pulse.

sions with one breath. The rescuer feels for the pulse at specific intervals. If no pulse is felt, the cycle of five chest compressions and one breath is continued. If the pulse returns, the rescuer checks for spontaneous breathing. If there is no breathing, the rescuer gives one breath every 4 seconds. If the student begins breathing spontaneously, the rescuer remains beside the student, monitoring the breathing and pulse carefully (*Heartsaver manual,* 1987).

Managing an Obstructed Airway

The procedure for managing an obstructed airway in a child is similar to management of an adult with an obstructed airway. The procedures described below are appropriate for a child from 1 to 8 years of age. The procedure for the child over 8 years of age is the same as for adults (*Heartsaver manual,* 1987).

Managing an Obstructed Airway in the Conscious Student
When the student is choking, the rescuer identifies if there is complete airway obstruction by determining if the student can speak or cough. If the student can speak or cough effectively, the rescuer does not interfere with the student's own attempts to force out the object or material blocking the airway. If the student is unable to speak or cough, the rescuer performs the Heimlich maneuver until the object or material is forced out. The Heimlich maneuver can be conducted with the student in either the standing or prone position. Figure 8.3 shows the procedure being applied to a child standing (Figure 8.3a), a child lying down (Figure 8.3b), to an adult standing (Figure 8.3c), and an adult lying down (Figure 8.3d). Depending on the weight of the student or the student's ability to maintain his or her own weight, the rescuer may wish to position the student on the floor or use the approach shown in Figure 8.3a in

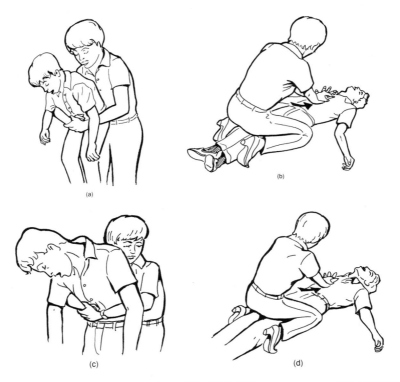

Figure 8.3.   Different examples of the Heimlich maneuver, performed on a choking child while standing (a) and lying down (b) and a choking adult while standing (c) and lying down (d).

a modified sitting position. This manuever is continued until the object or material is forced out of the student's airway or until the student becomes unconscious.

Managing an Obstructed Airway in the Student Who Becomes Unconscious   The rescuer places the unconscious student on his or her back, giving support to the head and neck (Figure 8.1). The rescuer calls out for help and initiates procedures to restore breathing. The rescuer looks down into the mouth and airway for an object or material blocking the student's airway. If the object or material is seen, the rescuer uses his or her fingers to remove it. If thé rescuer is unable to see and remove the object or material, the airway is opened and an attempt is made to breathe into the student. The rescuer then gives six to ten upward thrusts over the abdomen (the Heimlich maneuver for unconscious student lying on the floor as in Figure 8.3b, or 8.3d). The rescuer looks for the object or material blocking the airway. If the object or material is not seen or is not removable, the rescuer gives the student a breath, then six to ten upward thrusts over the abdomen. The cycle of looking for the object or material blocking the airway, opening the airway and breathing, and performing abdominal thrusts, is continued.

Managing an Obstructed Airway in the Unconscious Student
The rescuer finds an unconscious child and begins to follow the procedure for CPR. When attempting to give the student a breath, the rescuer notices that the student's chest does not rise. The rescuer repositions the student's head and again attempts to give a breath. When this is unsuccessful a second time, the rescuer gives six to ten upward abdominal thrusts. The rescuer looks for an object or material blocking the airway. If the object or material is seen, the rescuer uses his or her fingers to remove it. If the object is seen and removed and the student begins spontaneous breathing, the rescuer remains close by to monitor. If the object has been removed and the student does not begin spontaneous breathing, the rescuer applies CPR as described under "Restoring Breathing." If the rescuer is unable to see the object or material in the aairway, the cycle of looking for an object or material blocking the airway, attempting to breath into the student, and performing abdominal thrusts is repeated (*Heartsaver manual,* 1987).

Warning Signs

When CPR is improperly performed, compressions on the chest and breathing by the rescuer may not be effective in supporting life. Incorrect placement of the hands during chest compressions can cause fractures of ribs; bruising or bleeding of the liver, lung, and spleen. Chest compressions that are performed too deeply can cause bruises of the heart (*Heartsaver manual,* 1987).

Rescue breathing can cause distention or enlargement of stomach as air moves into the stomach, and vomiting can result. This abdominal distention occurs especially in children when: 1) the volume of air breathed into the child by the rescuer is too great, 2) the airway is not opened completely, and/or 3) the rescue breathing is too rapid. If the student vomits, the rescuer turns the student's head and body to the side to prevent choking. The vomitus is cleaned out of the mouth with a cloth (e.g., clothing or handkerchief). After the mouth and airway have been cleared, the rescuer immediately continues CPR (*Heartsaver manual,* 1987).

Transmission of disease when performing CPR may be a concern to the rescuer. The greatest concern over spread of disease from mouth-to-mouth rescue breathing should be for those persons who perform CPR frequently. These persons include health care workers, public safety personnel, and emergency health care providers. Generally the layperson most likely will perform CPR in a familiar setting, be familiar with the recipient, and have knowledge of the recipient's health. Transmission of the hepatitis B virus during the CPR procedure has not been documented. If a student is considered at risk for the AIDS virus, disposable airway equipment or resuscitation bags (Figure 8.4) should be used. This is recommended because of the theoretical risk of transmission of the AIDS virus via saliva during mouth-to-mouth resuscitation (*Recommendations for preventing*, 1985).

SIGNS OF AN EMERGENCY

CPR is performed as a means of saving a life. The use of CPR indicates that an emergency situation exists.

If a rescuer is alone and finds a student who is not breathing or has no pulse or both, the rescuer begins CPR. If the student's pulse or

Figure 8.4.   An example of a resuscitation bag used instead of mouth-to-mouth resuscitation.

breathing has not been restored after 1 minute, the rescuer takes the least amount of time to go telephone for help. The rescuer returns to the student as quickly as possible (*Heartsaver manual,* 1987). CPR is not to be interrupted for more than 5 seconds for any reason except for calling the Emergency Medical System or transporting the student to a hospital for continued care (Montgomery & Herrin, 1981).

CPR must be attempted by a person who is adequately trained. If a person who is trained in CPR does somehow injure the victim, that person is protected in a number of states by Good Samaritan laws. These laws prevent a recipient (or the recipient's family) from suing someone who attempted to perform lifesaving techniques (Batshaw & Perret, 1981). According to the 1985 National Conference on Cardiopulmonary Resuscitation and Emergency Cardiac Care, there is no known instance in which a layperson who has performed CPR has been successfully sued (*Heartsaver manual,* 1987). Laypersons are protected under most Good Samaritan laws if they perform CPR and if they have had no formal training (Standards for CPR and ECC, 1986).

Once CPR has been initiated by the rescuer, it should be stopped only when: 1) the student recovers or pulse and breathing are restored, 2) another trained individual takes over, or 3) the rescuer is too exhausted to continue (*Heartsaver manual,* 1987).

ADDITIONAL RESOURCES

CPR and management of airway obstruction classes are conducted by the American Heart Association, local hospitals, and other local agencies. Standards and guidelines were updated at the 1985 National Conference on Cardiopulmonary Resuscitation and Emergency Cardiac Care. These standards and guidelines are used as reference for proper training in CPR. A recommendation from this conference includes the need to train families, neighbors, and coworkers of high-risk persons. In addition, facilities such as schools should have the capability to give basic life support immediately and advanced life support should be available immediately or within 6–10 minutes ("Standards and guidelines," 1986).

LITERATURE CITED

Batshaw, M.L., & Perret, Y.M. (1981). *Children with handicaps: A medical primer.* Baltimore: Paul H. Brookes Publishing Company.

Harris, C.S., Baker, S.P., Smith, G.A., & Harris, R.M. (1984). Childhood asphyxiation by food. *Journal of the American Medical Association, 251*(17), 2231–2235.

Heartsaver manual: A student handbook for cardiopulmonary resuscitation and first aid for choking. (1987). Dallas: American Heart Association.

Montgomery, W.H., & Herrin, T.J. (1981). *Student manual for basic life support: Cardiopulmonary resuscitation.* Dallas: American Heart Association, Office of Communications.

National Conference on Cardiopulmonary Resuscitation and Emergency Cardiac Care. (1985). Dallas.

Recommendations for preventing transmission of infection with human T-lymphotropic virus type III/lymphadenopathy-associated virus in the workplace. (1985). *Morbidity and Mortality Weekly Report, 34,* 681–696.

Safar, P. (1986). The pathology of dying and reanimation. In G. Schwartz, P. Safar, & J. Stone, (Eds.), *Principles and practice of emergency medicine* (2nd ed., pp. 2–41). Philadelphia: W.B. Saunders.

Standards and Guidelines for Cardiopulmonary (CPR) and Emergency Cardiac Care (ECC), (1986). *The Journal of the American Medical Association, 255*(21), 2905–2989.

Statistical Resources Branch, Division of Vital Statistics. (1981). *Final mortality statistics.* Hyattsville, MD: Author.

9

MONITORING
A SHUNT

Students who have a shunt in place require routine monitoring in order to ensure the proper functioning of the shunt. The student with hydrocephalus is at risk for fluid collecting in the ventricles of the brain should the shunt malfunction. This fluid buildup will result in an increase of intracranial pressure and possible brain damage. Shunt monitoring involves attending to behaviors that may indicate the shunt is not functioning, in order to avoid complications related to the shunt.

OVERVIEW

The buildup of fluid in the brain is called hydrocephalus. A shunt is a method of treatment of hydrocephalus to drain this excess fluid. Hydrocephalus occurs in approximately 3–4 out of every 1000 births, including cases recognized during the first 3 months of life. Hydrocephalus is present before or at the time of birth more often than it is acquired after birth (Milhorat, 1978).

The fluid present in the brain is called cerebrospinal fluid. It is a clear, colorless, odorless fluid that is continuously formed primarily in the ventricles of the brain (Conway, 1978; Milhorat, 1978). The ventricles are cavities in the interior portion of the brain. There are two lateral ventricles, a third ventricle, and a fourth ventricle (Figure 9.1a).

Causes of Hydrocephalus

Hydrocephalus is considered to be a disorder caused by the imbalance in the formation and absorption of cerebrospinal fluid (Milhorat, 1978). This imbalance results in the accumulation of cerebrospinal fluid in the brain (Figure 9.1b). Cerebrospinal fluid is continuously formed in children at the rate of approximately 1 pint per 24 hours (Cutler, Page, Galicich, & Watters, 1968). The total volume of cerebrospinal fluid in the newborn is almost 2 ounces, and increases to 5 ounces in the adult (Menkes, 1985). The volume of cerebrospinal fluid is renewed every 8 hours. In children with hydrocephalus, the rate of cerebrospinal fluid formation is normal or only slightly reduced (Lorento, Page, & Watters, 1970).

Cerebrospinal fluid normally continuously flows from the ventricle where it is produced, to the dural sinuses where it is absorbed by the body (Milhorat, 1978). This movement of cerebrospinal fluid is diagrammed in Figure 9.2. The normal flow of cerebrospinal fluid, however, may be blocked or obstructed. The fluid may not flow out of the ventricles, or the fluid may flow out of the ventricles but be obstructed after leaving the fourth ventricle. There may be a number of reasons for the obstruction, including lesions that are present at birth or acquired after birth, or deformities present at birth. These cause a narrowing or blocking of the passageways that connect the ventricles or that lead from the fourth ventricle into the space surrounding the brain and the spinal cord (Menkes, 1985).

For other students with hydrocephalus, the cerebrospinal fluid may appropriately leave the ventricles but may not be absorbed properly by the membrane that encloses the brain and spinal cord. This can be caused by bleeding in the space between the membrane and the brain, damage to the membrane from infection (meningitis), or damage to the membrane from a malignant tumor or cyst (Menkes, 1985). Hydrocephalus can also result from the overproduction of cerebrospinal fluid. This overproduction has been reported when a tumor exists in the area of the ventricles responsible for production of cerebrospinal fluid (Milhorat, 1978).

If hydrocephalus is not treated in the child under 2 years of age, the head becomes enlarged. This is possible because, prior to 2 years of age, the bones of the child's skull are not united. When fluid begins to

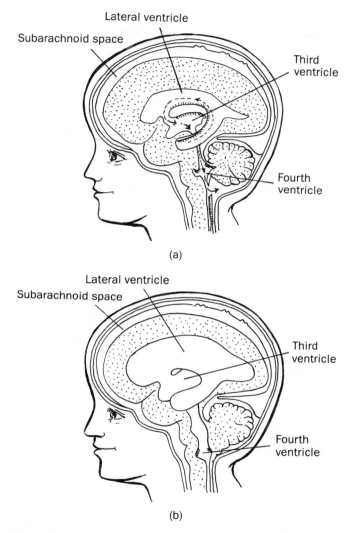

Figure 9.1.   A comparison of the ventricles of the brain when normal size (a) and when enlarged due to the accumulation of cerebrospinal fluid (b).

build up in the child's ventricles, there is increased pressure in the ventricles, and the child's head increases in size as the bones are forced apart. The enlarged head is usually the first sign of hydrocephalus in the child under 2 years of age. The forehead is unusually large, the soft spot

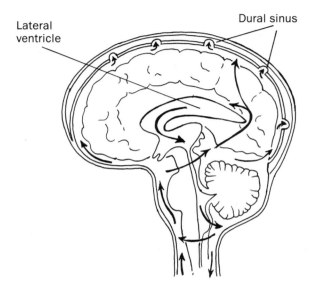

Lateral
ventricle

Dural sinus

Figure 9.2.   The movement of cerebrospinal fluid during absorption and
flow down the spinal column.

is tense or bulging, the veins on the scalp are enlarged, the eyes have a
downward gaze or "sunset gaze" with the white of the eyes being more
visible. The child may be irritable or lethargic (sluggish), and experience vomiting, increased muscle tone, or seizures (Grant, 1984;
Menkes, 1985).

If hydrocephalus develops in the child who is 2–10 years old,
change in head size is not the first sign. The signs of hydrocephalus in
the child over 2 years of age include: lethargy, nausea, vomiting, headache, decreased level of activity, seizures, and nystagmus (constant, involuntary, cyclical movement of the eyeball) (Grant, 1984).

For the children developing hydrocephalus after infancy, the symptoms are identical to those of increased intracranial pressure (Menkes,
1985). Increased intracranial pressure means that there is increased
pressure inside the skull. This will be discussed further in this chapter
under "Warning Signs."

Diagnosis and Treatment

Diagnosis of hydrocephalus is made by measuring the circumference of
the head over a period of time. The increase in head circumference

varies from a rapid increase over a few days to a slow increase over months. The measurements are plotted on a chart. Other methods for diagnosis are computerized axial tomography (CAT scan) and ultrasonography, the use of ultrasound (Menkes, 1985).

Treatment of the child with hydrocephalus includes surgical correction of the cause of the obstruction, decreasing the production of cerebrospinal fluid with drugs or surgery, or placing a tube into the ventricle to remove the excess cerebrospinal fluid (Menkes, 1985). The focus of discussion in this chapter is on the last method of treatment.

A shunt is a plastic tube that is placed into the child's ventricle to allow the flow of cerebrospinal fluid to be directed to another part of the body. The shunt consists of a ventricular catheter, a valve, and a distal catheter (Figure 9.3). Most shunts have a valve that allows fluid to move in one direction only and prevents the back-flow of fluid (Madsen, 1986). The distal catheter is placed into the area of the body that will receive the excess cerebrospinal fluid. This area will be either the per-

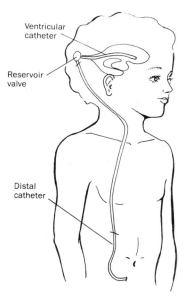

Figure 9.3.   The major parts of a shunt: the ventricular catheter leading into the ventricle of the brain accumulating the cerebrospinal fluid; the reservoir valve, which allows the fluid to flow only away from the ventricles; and the distal catheter, which is placed in the cavity of the body, where the excess fluid will be received.

itoneal cavity or the right atrium of the heart. The peritoneal cavity is the cavity that holds the abdominal organs. When a shunt is placed into the peritoneal cavity, it is called a ventriculoperitoneal shunt. The right atrium of the heart is the right upper chamber of the heart. When the shunt is placed into the right atrium, it is called a ventriculoatrial shunt.

A shunt is placed using the following steps: 1) an incision is made, 2) a small burr hole is drilled over the lateral ventricle on the right side of the head, 3) a catheter with multiple perforations is passed through the burr hole into the right ventricle, 4) the valve or pump is attached to this catheter. If the shunt is a ventriculoperitoneal shunt, the distal catheter is placed into the peritoneum and loosely sutured in place. Extra tubing is left in the peritoneal cavity to allow the shunt to uncoil as the child grows (Milhorat, 1978). If the shunt is a ventriculoatrial shunt, the distal catheter is placed into the right atrium and secured in place. As the child grows, the shunt is revised. Therefore ventriculoatrial shunts require more frequent revisions than ventriculoperitoneal shunts. Ventriculoperitoneal shunts are used more often than ventriculoatrial shunts (Madsen, 1986). These two options are illustrated in Figure 9.4.

Although some children with shunts become shunt-independent (do not require the presence of a shunt to control hydrocephalus), most persons with hydrocephalus continue to require the shunt to control the hydrocephalus (Holtzer & DeLange, 1973). There are generally no restrictions on the student's activities with the exception of exclusion from contact sports where there is a high incidence of head injury (Jackson, 1980). Care should be taken to prevent head injuries for the student having hydrocephalus and a seizure disorder; for example, carpet in classrooms could protect the student with hydrocephalus who falls during a seizure.

PROCEDURES

Since there is no actual contact with the components of a shunt, either the valve or the tubing, shunt monitoring involves identifying for each student behaviors that would indicate an increase in intracranial pressure, and establishing a routine procedure for documenting the student's condition.

Preparation for Monitoring a Student with a Shunt

Preparation for monitoring a shunt involves identifying the behaviors that are normal for the student and the behaviors that indicate that there

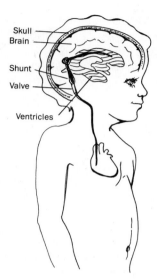

Skull
Brain
Shunt
Valve
Ventricles

Figure 9.4a.   The placement of a ventriculoatrial shunt from the ventricles of the brain to the right upper chamber of the heart, which is the right atrium of the heart.

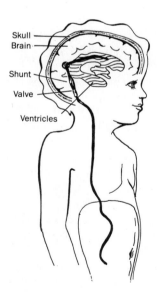

Skull
Brain
Shunt
Valve
Ventricles

Figure 9.4b.   The placement of a ventriculoperitoneal shunt from the ventricles of the brain to the abdomen or peritoneal cavity.

may be a malfunction with the shunt. Obstruction and malfunction of the shunt are the most frequent complications. Infections following the placement of the shunt is also a complication (Madsen, 1986). Symptoms of these complications are discussed in this chapter under "Warning Signs." School staff must be prepared to identify the early signs of complications in order to prevent brain damage.

Monitoring a Student with a Shunt

Care of the student having a ventriculoperitoneal or ventriculoatrial shunt includes making careful observations and reporting signs of complications to the student's parents and/or the physician. Weekly observations of the student should be made in the following areas: 1) behavior, 2) level of activity, and 3) response to and awareness of the environment.

Using knowledge of the student's usual behavior, school staff can learn to discriminate between usual behavior and unusual behavior. Signs indicating the possibility of complications are watched for and reported to the health care worker in the school and the parents and/or caregiver. School staff who are uncertain about their observations can consult with the health care worker in the school for assistance.

Warning Signs

The presence of a ventriculoperitoneal shunt or a ventriculoatrial shunt can result in complications including obstruction or malfunction of the shunt and infection (Menkes, 1985; Milhorat, 1978).

When a shunt becomes obstructed, or malfunctions, the cerebrospinal fluid begins to build up in the ventricles. A shunt malfunction may include a disconnection in the tube, leakage, a kink in the tubing, or problems with the pumping chamber (valve). This buildup of fluid results in increased pressure in the ventricles, or increased intracranial pressure. The following may be indicators that the student is experiencing increased intracranial pressure: headache, nausea, vomiting, double vision, blurred vision, irritability, restlessness, personality change, lethargy, drowsiness, inability to follow simple commands, decreased orientation to time and place, and seizures. In the student whose soft spot can still be felt, the soft spot becomes full (Bell & McCormick, 1978; Hausman, 1981; Madsen, 1986).

If the obstruction is not relieved and the pressure continues to increase inside the brain, the student's pupils (dark area in the center of the eye) may become smaller and react very slowly to light. If the pressure continues to build, the student's pupils may enlarge and become fixed when exposed to light. The pulse may decrease, breathing may become irregular, and eventually death may occur (Hausman, 1981).

When there is evidence of increased intracranial pressure, school staff should notify the health care worker in the school and the student's parents. Discussions with the health care worker and parents may help determine whether the health care professional must be notified. Pumping the valve of the shunt may be recommended by the health care professional to reduce intracranial pressure. The risks involved with the process of pumping the shunt are great. If too much cerebrospinal fluid is removed, there is a resulting decrease in the amount of pressure in the brain. The ventricles may collapse inward, resulting in additional brain damage. Only a person who has been specifically instructed in the procedures should attempt to pump the shunt.

The student having seizures must be monitored by school staff and treated according to the protocol established for the student by the health care professional. Care of the student experiencing seizures has been described in Chapter 1, Seizure Monitoring.

For the student who is unable to communicate the presence of a headache, double vision, or blurred vision, or is unable to follow simple commands, the school staff must rely on their own observations. By closely communicating with the student's parents and others working with the student, school staff can learn what behaviors are usual for the student and what behaviors indicate the presence of increased intracranial pressure.

Infection related to a shunt occurs most often within the first 2–4 months after placement of the shunt or surgical revision of the shunt (George, Leibrock & Epstein, 1979; Madsen, 1986; Schoenbaum, Gradner, & Shillito, 1975). The presence of a foreign body, the shunt, extending from the ventricles of the brain to the heart or the peritoneal cavity, makes the potential for serious infections more likely (Madsen, 1986).

Indicators of the presence of a shunt infection are often subtle and include: nausea, vomiting, headache, lethargy, feeding problems, and fever. If the student develops any of these signs, the health care worker in the school must be notified. A shunt infection requires administration of antibiotics. The shunt may eventually need to be replaced if the infection is not successfully treated (Jackson, 1980; Milhorat, 1978).

SIGNS OF AN EMERGENCY

The student may experience a sudden obstruction of the flow of cerebrospinal fluid with resulting increase in ventricle size within hours. If the student is over 2 years old, the bones in the skull are fused and the skull is unable to expand as the intracranial pressure increases. Nausea, vomiting, and severe headache are most commonly seen first. If the pressure is not relieved, the student can worsen progressively and death may occur (Milhorat, 1978).

Attention must be given to the student having a shunt when he or she experiences nausea, vomiting, and headache, or other evidence that there is increase in intracranial pressure. The health care worker in the school and the student's parents must be notified of the student's condition. If the student's condition worsens, the health care professional must be notified immediately. The student may need to be transported by the emergency medical team for immediate removal of excess cerebrospinal fluid.

ADDITIONAL RESOURCES

The student's health care professional can provide specific information for school staff working with the student having a shunt. The health care professional and the student's parents can inform the school staff of the student's usual behaviors and behaviors that will indicate development of complications.

The list of Literature Cited at the end of this chapter can also provide useful information for persons working with a student having hydrocephalus and a shunt.

LITERATURE CITED

Bell, W.E., & McCormick, W.F. (1978). *Increased intracranial pressure in children: Diagnosis and treatment* (2nd ed.). Philadelphia: W.B. Saunders.

Conway, B.L. (1978). *Carini and Owens neurological and neurosurgical nursing.* St. Louis: C.V. Mosby.

Cutler, R.W.P., Page, L., Galicich, J., & Watters, G.V. (1968). Formation and absorption of cerebral spinal fluid in man. *Brain, 91,* 707–720.

George, R., Leibrock, L., & Epstein, M. (1979). Long-term analysis of CSF shunt infections: A 25-year experience. *Journal of Neurosurgery, 31,* 804–811.

Grant L. (1984). Hydrocephalus: An overview and update. *Journal of Neurosurgical Nursing, 16*(6), 313–318.

Hausman, K.A. (1981). Nursing care of the patient with hydrocephalus. *Journal of Neurosurgical Nursing, 13*(6), 326–332.

Holtzer, G.J., & DeLange, S.A. (1973). Shunt—Independent arrest of hydrocephalus. *Journal of Neurosurgery, 39,* 698–701.

Jackson, P.L. (1980). Ventriculo-peritoneal shunts. *American Journal of Nursing,* *80*(6), 1104–1109.

Lorento, A.V., Page, L., & Watters, G.V. (1970). Relationship between fluid formation, absorption, and pressure in human hydrocephalus. *Brain, 93,* 679–692.

Madsen, M.A. (1986). Emergency department management of ventriculo-peritoneal cerebrospinal fluid shunts. *Annals of Emergency Medicine, 15*(11), 1330–1343.

Menkes, J.H. (1985). *Textbook of child neurology* (3rd ed.). Philadelphia: Lea & Febiger.

Milhorat, T.H. (1978). *Pediatric neurosurgery.* Philadelphia: F.A. Davis.

Schoenbaum, S.C., Gradner, P., & Shillito, J. (1975). Infections of cerebrospinal fluid shunts: Epidemiology, clinical manifestations and therapy. *Journal of Infectious Disease, 131,* 543–552.

10

CAST CARE

$\mathbf{O}$ccasionally students will require a cast as a result of a fracture or during recovery from a surgical procedure. Cast care is an ongoing process designed to protect the cast from damage. The cast itself must be monitored so that it continues to support and protect, and does not further injure the affected part of the body. Because a cast is susceptible to dampness, soil, or breakage throughout the day, the teacher, and other personnel, must be aware of procedures to maintain its correct positioning and composition.

OVERVIEW

Types and Structure of Casts

Almost any part or parts of the body can be supported in a cast. Types of casts include the short arm cast, the long arm cast, the short leg cast, and the long leg cast (Figure 10.1), the body cast, and the hip spica cast (Figure 10.2). Hip spica casts can be single spica (a), one and one half spica (b), or double spica casts (c). Spica refers to the way the pieces of cloth are laid or woven onto the body. The strips of plaster of Paris are layed in a slightly overlapping pattern and resemble a stylized ear of wheat.

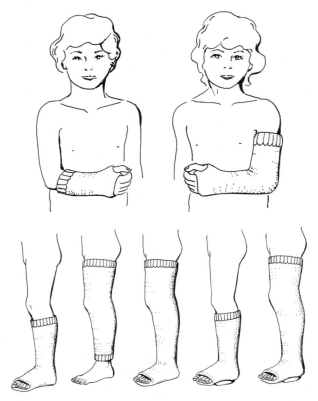

Figure 10.1.   Examples of short and long arm casts and short and long leg casts.

A plaster of Paris cast is usually composed of the following layers of materials: stockinette, cotton padding, and rolls of gauze soaked with plaster of Paris. Stockinette, a cotton woven material that is open at both ends, is placed over the body part to be casted. Cotton padding is then applied to protect the bony prominences beneath the cast. Plaster of Paris is then applied and makes up the hard outer surface of the cast.

The edges of a plaster of Paris cast are covered with a stocking or cotton-like material extending from inside the cast, or with adhesive tape (Figure 10.3). If the tape becomes loose, it should be replaced. The edges of the cast must be covered to prevent injury to the student or damage to the cast. The covering prevents: 1) rough edges from irritating the student's skin, 2) the student from pulling the padding out of the

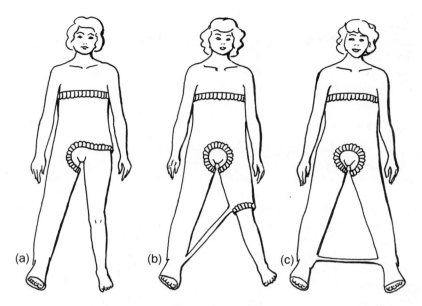

Figure 10.2.   An example of a single spica cast (a), a one and one-half spica cast (b), and a double spica cast (c).

cast, and 3) the plaster of Paris from crumbling and falling beneath the student's cast and irritating the skin (Hilt & Schmitt, 1975).

Although most casts for children are made of plaster of Paris, casts can also be made of fiberglass saturated with polyurethane resin. Fiberglass casts are most commonly used for arm or short leg casts (Iversen & Clawson, 1987). Plaster of Paris casts are less expensive than

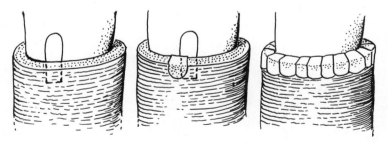

Figure 10.3.   An example of covering the raw edges of a plaster of Paris cast with tape extending from the inside of the cast and overlapping the edge.

those made of fiberglass, and fiberglass casts are lighter and less bulky than those made of plaster of Paris, allowing for a greater range of activity. Fiberglass casts, unlike plaster of Paris casts, can tolerate being wet. Differences in care for the two kinds of casts depend only slightly on the composition of the cast and the body part casted.

Purpose of Cast

Casts provide both support and protection to injured parts of the body. These generally include preventing movement of broken bones or dislocated bones that have been placed into proper position, and supporting injured ligaments and joints to decrease pain and promote healing. Casts also allow for movement, such as walking, to occur as early as possible after an injury. Casts can be used to prevent or reduce the severity of deformities that result from conditions such as scoliosis (curvature of the spine to the side of the body) and to correct deformities such as clubfoot (deformity of the foot) (Iversen & Clawsen, 1987) or congenital dislocation of the hip. Short leg casts may be applied to correct the abnormal position of the foot (Figure 10.4). A hip spica cast may be applied after the hip is placed in proper position (Figure 10.5). The need for a cast is determined by the student's physician, who applies the cast or directs the application of the cast by a technician.

Children usually experience a fractured bone as a result of household or automobile accidents, sports injuries, or child abuse. Some children experience fractures even though there does not seem to be suffi-

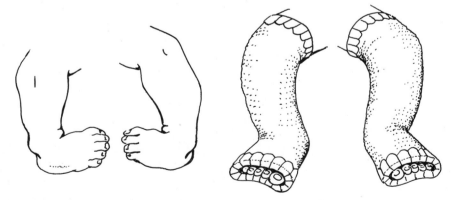

Figure 10.4.   An example of a short leg cast applied to correct the position of the foot.

Figure 10.5.   An example of a hip spica cast applied to hold the hips in a correct position.

cient force to break the bone. This is referred to as a pathological fracture and may occur as the child is being lifted to a sitting position. Nonambulatory children have frail bones and frequently experience these fractures (Batshaw & Perret, 1986) (see Chapter 7, Therapeutic Management).

The time required for healing of a fracture in a child is usually shorter than the time required in an adult. Healing time for a fractured femur (large bone in the thigh) is about 4 weeks during early childhood (1–6 years), 6 weeks during later childhood (6–11 or 12 years), and 8–10 weeks during adolescence (Whaley & Wong, 1987). The healing of bones for students with disabilities generally takes 8–12 weeks (Batshaw & Perret, 1986). For these students, casts may remain in place longer.

Students with cerebral palsy can experience dislocation of the hip as muscles tighten and pull the hip out of proper position. Partial or complete surgical resection of muscles, nerves, and tendons may be carried out to correct this problem (Turek, 1984). After surgical correction, a spica cast may be applied to maintain the desired position. Students with cerebral palsy may also develop contractures (a fixed position of a joint). Surgical resection of muscles and tendons may be carried out to allow for improved movement of the joint (Turek, 1984). Afterwards, a cast is applied to support the joint, tendons, and muscles during healing.

Since the cast provides support and maintains the position of a specific body part, damage to a cast can result in a change in the support given to the body part. Preserving a cast is important because application of a cast is time-consuming and expensive, and a damaged cast can alter the desired position of the body part resulting in pain and injury. While the cast is in place on the student's body, the student's skin and circulation to the area beneath the cast must remain healthy. Care must be taken to ensure that there is no pressure to cut off circulation to the casted area and that the casted area remains healthy.

PROCEDURES

Preparation for Cast Care

The school staff need to know the purpose of the cast, whether the cast is new or has been in place for a period of time, the type of cast material used, the activities that are appropriate for the student, and the activities from which the student is restricted.

Four major requirements are included in cast care: 1) protecting and cleaning the cast, 2) assisting the student with a cast in toileting activities, 3) checking the condition of the skin around and underneath the cast, and 4) checking for the continued correct positioning of the cast. The first three procedures require additional materials.

Cleaning the cast requires a mild abrasive cleanser and water. The cast is kept clean using plastic wrap on those areas susceptible to soiling. A flashlight is needed for determining whether the area underneath the cast is free of foreign objects. For those students in a hip cast, a bed pan and urinal (for males) are required instead of the usual toileting facilities. Alcohol is used on the skin surrounding the edges of the cast to reduce the liklihood of the skin being injured.

Performing Cast Care

The purpose of cast care is to preserve the cast while allowing the student to participate in as many activities as possible. Daily cast care involves care of the new cast, preventing cast soiling, bathing the student with a cast, managing the activity of the student with a cast to prevent any harm or injury to the student as a result of wearing the cast, and monitoring the fit of the cast.

The New Cast   The new cast must be protected to preserve the life of the cast itself. If the plaster cast is less than 72 hours old, it should be handled carefully because indentations are created more easily during this period. Indentations made in a new cast can create unnecessary pressure on areas beneath the cast. Additional indentations may also alter the fit of the cast and therefore change the support provided to the affected area (see Chapter 4, Skin Care).

Preventing Cast Soiling   The cast can become soiled during mealtimes, snacks, and elimination. Soiling at mealtimes can be prevented with a covering on the cast, such as a towel. If the cast becomes dirty, it can be cleaned with any mild abrasive cleanser and a slightly damp cloth. The cleansing powder is rubbed into the cast to remove the soil, lightly rinsed, and the cast is allowed to dry (*Going home in a cast,* 1984).

Protecting the cast from soiling during elimination is more difficult. For example, the edges of a long leg cast must be protected from urine and stool. Plastic wrap can be temporarily tucked into the top edges of long leg casts immediately prior to elimination in order to protect the edges of the cast from soiling (Hilt & Schmitt, 1975). When the student has finished elimination or the plastic wrap becomes soiled, the plastic wrap is removed. The plastic wrap can be left in place if the student wears diapers. As soon as the plastic becomes wet, it should be removed, and after the skin is cleaned and dried, the plastic wrap should be replaced around the cast edge.

Protection from soiling during urination and stooling is more difficult when the student is in a hip spica cast because the cast surrounds the student's genital area. The cast areas around the student's genitals can be protected during elimination with plastic wrap gently tucked around the edges of the cast in this area. The student in a hip spica cast must use a bedpan for elimination (male students can use a urinal for urination). When the student in a hip spica cast is placed on a bedpan, the student's head must be higher than the hips to /prevent urine from flowing back under the cast.

If the student is unable to warn others of the need to eliminate or if the student has no control over the release of urine or stool, there must be continual protection of the cast. This can be done with plastic wrap constantly in place around the edges of the cast.   The plastic wrap should be changed as needed (when soiled with urine or stool) (Hilt &

Schmitt, 1975) or at least once daily (*Cast care protocol: Hip spica,* 1984).

Bathing the Student with a Cast   Bathing the student with a cast can be difficult because of the damaging effect moisture can have to both the cast and the skin underneath. The plaster cast must remain dry. A wet plaster cast can soften, weaken, break apart, and no longer support the casted area in the desired position. If the padding beneath the plaster cast becomes wet, prolonged contact with this moisture can result in skin irritation (Hilt & Schmitt, 1975).

The student must not bathe in a tub because of the possibility of getting the plaster cast wet, and covering a cast with a plastic bag does not make it water proof during a shower. A sponge bath, that is, bathing a student using soap and water from a basin, is the recommended alternative (*Cast care instructions,* 1978). Care should be taken, even with a sponge bath, to avoid water leaking underneath the cast. If the plaster becomes wet, the area should be allowed to dry thoroughly before the student resumes normal activity.

Managing the Activity of a Student with a Cast   Procedures involved in managing the activity of the student with a cast address monitoring the materials used by the student and the student's activity that affects the condition of the skin around and underneath the cast.

Small items and food must be monitored carefully to ensure that they do not fall in or remain underneath the cast. They can create a source of constant irritation for the skin with eventual breakdown of the skin and the development of pressure sores (see Chapter 4, Skin Care). If the student uses small toys/objects, the student must be carefully supervised and the top of the cast should be covered (Hilt & Schmitt, 1975). It has been recommended that an adult reach with the hand as far as possible beneath the cast to check for crumbs or small toys/objects (*Going home in a cast,* 1984). No other object, such as a hook or tongue depressor, should be inserted under the cast because this may cause additional skin irritations.

The tops of most casts are loose enough to allow at least partial observation of the skin with a flashlight. Besides looking beneath the cast and carefully observing the edges, listening to the student's complaints of pain at certain points on the cast can be helpful in identifying areas of irritation. If the student is unable to verbalize that there is discomfort at certain points on the cast, careful observations must be made when the student's position is changed (Hilt & Schmitt, 1975).

If the student is not capable of walking or moving around with some degree of independence, the staff must assist the student in repositioning at least every 2 hours (Hilt & Schmitt, 1975). This is done to promote adequate circulation and prevent excessive pressure on areas beneath the cast (see Chapter 7, Therapeutic Management).

Students, who are able, will move frequently even with the cast on. This movement can cause skin irritation as the skin rubs against the cast; reddening usually appears around the edges of the cast. The skin susceptible to this irritation can be toughened by being rubbed with alcohol. Isopropyl alcohol (70%) is recommended for the care of the skin around the cast edges. Lotions, oils, and powders should not be used on skin around cast edges or beneath the cast. Lotions and oils will soften the student's skin and increase the chance of skin breakdown. Powders tend to cake on the skin and cause additional skin irritation. The skin should be rubbed with alcohol at least four times a day. If the student is limited to lying down (as with a spica cast), rubbing the spine, heels, ankles, and elbows with alcohol at least four times a day can prevent these areas from becoming irritated. If alcohol causes drying and flaking of the skin, the use of alcohol on the skin should be stopped. Lotions and oils should not be used to stop the flaking because they make the skin too soft (Hilt & Schmitt, 1975) (see Chapter 4, Skin Care).

Cast Fit   Cast care procedures also include routine checks to ensure that the cast is not too tight. If the cast is too tight, circulation to the affected area can be impaired. Checking the student's circulation includes checking the fingers or toes of the casted limb for color, proper temperature, presence of any swelling, and capillary filling. These conditions on the casted limb are compared with the same conditions on the uncasted limb. Optimally, the fingers or toes will be pink in color and warm to the touch. There will be no swelling in comparison with those on the other limb. Capillary filling can be evaluated by pressing on the nail bed on the fingers or toes. The color should return to normal rapidly when the pressure is released from the nail bed (Figure 10.6) (Hilt & Schmitt, 1975).

Sensation to touch and movement must also be routinely evaluated to determine the fit of the cast. The sensation and movement can be examined by touching the toes, fingers, and so forth. If the student moves or wiggles the toe or fingers when they are touched, sensation is present. The student who responds to directions can be asked to move his or her toes as a method of assessing movement. However, it is not adequate to just ask a student (under 10 years of age) if movement and sensation are present. Actual viewing of the student's responses are necessary (Hilt & Schmitt, 1975).

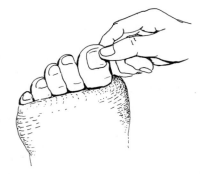

Figure 10.6.   An example of the procedure used to check proper blood circulation by evaluating capillary filling of the nail bed on the toes.

When the student has a new cast applied, checks for adequate circulation, sensation, and movement must be done often. The student should be checked every hour for the first 24 hours after the cast is applied, or until the circulation, movement, and sensation have returned to normal. When circulation, sensation, and movement have returned to normal (when compared with toes or fingers on the other side), the checks can be done every 4 hours. These checks should be carried out as long as the student is in a cast. Because students may not be able to identify a problem with the cast, careful observation is important (Hilt & Schmitt, 1975).

Procedures Following Cast Care

The condition of the student's cast and skin; the status of the circulation, sensation, and movement; and any problems or concerns must be documented daily in writing and reported to the school health personnel and parents and/or caregiver. If any sores are present, the clean-up procedures described in Chapter 4, Skin Care, should be followed.

WARNING SIGNS

A damaged cast needs attention to ensure that the student's body part that is to be immobilized is not injured. If an injury does occur, school staff need to report this occurrence immediately to the student's parents. The student's physician will need to be notified of the extent of the damage. The physician may need to examine the student and reinforce or replace the cast, depending on the extent of damage.

A plaster of Paris cast that becomes wet can present problems for the student. If the wet area is small, the cast may be allowed to air dry. If a large part of the cast becomes wet, the cast may need to be replaced. School staff should contact the health care worker in the school to assist in this determination. Parents and/or caregiver will need to be informed if urine and/or stool leak onto or underneath the cast. A cast soiled with urine or stool can lead to dermatitis, odor problems, and softening of the cast (Hilt & Schmitt, 1975).

If it is suspected that the student's cast is too tight, the health care worker and parents and/or caregiver must be informed. Signs that the cast may be too tight include: pale to white color of fingers or toes (depending on the area casted), fingers or toes cool or cold to the touch, sluggish capillary filling, swelling of the fingers or toes, numbness or tingling, a decrease or absence of sensation, or a decrease or absence of movement in the fingers or toes. If any one of the above occurs, the health care worker in the school must be notified immediately. The student's parents and/or caregiver and possibly the student's physician should be informed of the concern that the cast may be too tight. A change from normal to abnormal circulation, sensation, or movement may indicate a reduction in the blood flow to the affected limb. This may result in the beginning of degeneration of tissue, muscles, and nerves. A change in circulation requires immediate attention to return normal circulation.

Pressure areas may occur under a cast for a variety of reasons. They may result from improper molding of the cast during application or from constant pressure on a particular area, such as the skin over prominent bones and over joints. (When the cast is applied, extra padding generally is placed over prominent bones and joints for protection [Iversen & Clawson, 1987]). Sores may also result from the presence of food or small toys or objects in the cast. The presence of any of these materials beneath a cast can cause constant irritation and eventual skin breakdown (Hilt & Schmitt, 1975).

Repeated complaints of pain or gestures to the same area may indicate the presence of a pressure area. A student who complains for several days or a week of pain in one area and then suddenly stops complaining, could indicate a pressure area that has developed into a pressure sore. During the development of pressure sores, the sensation of pain stops when the skin sloughs off. A student who is unable to verbalize or communicate the presence of a problem may indicate that a problem exists by being irritable, fussy, or crying more than usual. If a change in temperament occurs with no apparent reason, it must be assumed that the problem may be with the cast (Hilt & Schmitt, 1975).

A pressure area under a cast should be detected before it becomes an open sore or a full thickness of skin sloughs off. If either problem does occur, however, the student will probably have an elevated temperature and/or an unfamiliar odor from the cast. If a pressure area is suspected, the health care worker in the school, the student's parents and/or caregivers, and the student's physician must be notified. A pressure area can result in sloughing of skin (separation of dead skin from healthy skin), which could require skin grafting (Hilt & Schmitt, 1975).

The presence of drainage on a cast could indicate an infection beneath the cast (*Cast care instructions,* 1978). This needs to be communicated to the student's physician immediately by the parents and/or the health care worker in the school. An infection can develop from either a pressure sore or from an infected incision beneath the cast.

SIGNS OF AN EMERGENCY

The presence of pain that is unusually greater than the pain expected for the student, decreased or absent movement, pain on stretching the toes or fingers, and decreased sensation to touch are indicators that there is pressure buildup beneath the cast. This pressure decreases circulation to the casted area. If the circulation to the area is not restored, damage can occur to the muscle tissue and nerves in the area (Rang, 1983). If a reduction in circulation because of pressure buildup occurs, the casted body part should be raised above the rest of the student's body. The physician needs to be notified immediately so the pressure can be released (Gartland, 1987).

ADDITIONAL RESOURCES

Information and direction on cast care can be obtained from the office of the student's orthopedic surgeon or the physician applying the student's cast. The physical therapist in the school system and the local community health nurse can also provide information on cast care.

LITERATURE CITED

Batshaw, M.L., & Perret, Y.M. (1981). *Children with handicaps: A medical primer.* Baltimore: Paul H. Brookes Publishing Co.

Batshaw, M.L., & Perret, Y.M. (1986). *Children with handicaps: A medical primer* (2nd ed.). Baltimore: Paul H. Brookes Publishing Co.

Cast care instructions. (1978). Kansas City: University of Kansas Medical Center Orthopedic Outpatient Department.

Cast-care protocol-hip spica. (1984). Kansas City: Department of Nursing Services, University of Kansas Medical Center, College of Health Sciences and Hospital.

Gartland, J.J. (1987). *Fundamentals of orthopaedics* (4th ed.). Philadelphia: W.B. Saunders.

Going home in a cast. (1984). Kansas City: University of Kansas Medical Center Department of Nursing Services.

Hilt, N.E., & Schmitt, E.W. (1975). *Pediatric orthopedic nursing.* St. Louis: C.V. Mosby.

Iversen, L.D., & Clawson, D.K. (1987). *Manual of acute orthopaedic therapeutics* (3rd ed.). Boston: Little, Brown.

Rang, M. (1983). *Children's fractures* (2nd ed.). Philadelphia: J.B. Lippincott.

Turek, S.L. (1984). *Orthopaedics: Principles and their application* (4th ed.). Philadelphia: J.B. Lippincott.

Whaley, L.F., & Wong, D.L. (1987). *Nursing care of infants and children.* St. Louis: C.V. Mosby.

11

GLUCOSE
MONITORING
FOR THE STUDENT
WITH DIABETES

An imbalance in the amount of glucose in a student's blood can result in a number of behaviors that interfere with the student's performance in the classroom. When these conditions remain unchecked the student's behavior worsens, resulting in a coma and possible death. Glucose monitoring is a procedure that identifies the amount of glucose, that is, sugar, present in the blood. Occasionally this monitoring must occur on a schedule that overlaps with the school day, for example, every 4–6 hours. In order for the student with a tendency towards an imbalance in glucose levels to remain in school, glucose levels must be monitored during the day, with the option of administering glucose or insulin as needed.

OVERVIEW

One form of imbalance in the amount of glucose in the blood is diabetes. Diabetes is a disorder in which carbohydrates are unable to be used by the body because of inadequate production or use of insulin. This results in excessive amounts of glucose in the person's blood and urine—hyperglycemia (Thomas, 1985). In this chapter, the term diabetes will be used to refer to diabetes mellitus. Diabetes mellitus affects approximately one out of 600 school age children (Balik, Haig, & Moynihan, 1986; Whaley & Wong, 1987).

Insulin is a hormone produced by the pancreas, a gland located near the stomach (Thomas, 1985). Insulin is needed for the body to use and store glucose normally. Glucose is normally stored in the liver and muscles or changed into fat in the body. Only a small amount of glucose remains in the blood stream. When there is inadequate insulin, too little glucose goes into the tissues where it can be used, and too much glucose stays in the blood. As glucose continues to be present in the blood, the glucose level in the blood rises. When this happens, some of the glucose leaves the body through the urine without being used by the body. The amount of glucose in the blood and urine can be measured (Jackson, Olson, Barnard, Jorgensen, & Olson, 1987).

Types of Diabetes

Diabetes can be classified as either Type I or Type II. Type I diabetes generally begins in childhood and adolescence. A person having Type I diabetes produces little or no insulin; therefore, an outside source of insulin is required to control glucose in the body. In addition to insulin, diet management and exercise are used to treat Type I diabetes (Haire-Joshu, Flavin, & Clutter, 1986). Persons with Type I diabetes can be either hyper- or hypo-glycemic. This means there can be either high levels or low levels of glucose in the blood.

The onset of Type II diabetes is usually in adulthood, usually after age 30 (Poole, 1986). The person with Type II diabetes produces insulin, yet tissues in the body are resistant to or less sensitive to insulin. Therefore more insulin is needed for these persons to reach the same glucose levels as persons without diabetes (Haire-Joshu et al., 1986). Treatment for Type II diabetes includes diet management, exercise, and, in some cases, oral medications. Some persons with Type II diabetes may be treated with insulin (Loman & Galgani, 1984). The oral medication taken for Type II diabetes stimulates the release of insulin from the pancreas and allows the person to become more sensitive to the insulin produced by the pancreas (Flavin & Haire-Joshu, 1986).

Testing Glucose Levels

Testing the urine for glucose has been a major part of managing diabetes in the past. Since the early 1970's, however, home measurement of glucose in the blood has become the test of choice for monitoring the person with diabetes. This has essentially replaced the measurement of glucose in the urine (Almond, 1986; Balik, Haig, Moynihan, 1986; Daneman et al., 1985; Hughes, 1987; Valenta, 1983). Self-monitoring of blood glucose in the home has increased as devices have become more readily available, easier to use, and less costly (Gifford-Jorgensen et al., 1986).

Urine testing for glucose has limitations. The amount of glucose in the urine may not accurately reflect the amount of glucose in the blood at the time the urine test was done. The blood glucose level usually reaches 150–180 milligrams per deciliter of blood (mg./dl.) before glucose spills into or can be identified in the urine (Bernstein, 1981). The lag time between the increase in blood glucose and the spilling of glucose in the urine can vary from 20 minutes to 2 hours (Valenta, 1983). Although there are limitations, urine testing for glucose may be recommended. Testing the urine for glucose may be carried out in young children whose glucose levels remain within control. This allows the young child to avoid having the fingers pricked for blood glucose level testing (Jackson et al., 1987).

Monitoring of glucose levels in the blood is being taught to children and their parents as a method of achieving optimal control of glucose levels. This means that efforts are made to identify abnormal glucose values and treat accordingly (Fow, 1983). Glucose levels vary, depending on the time the blood sample was obtained. Table 11.1 lists blood sugar goals that are ideal and acceptable (Jackson et al., 1987).

Table 11.1.   Blood sugar goals

	Ideal	Acceptable
Fasting	80–100 mg/dl	80–120 mg/dl
Before meals	80–105 mg/dl	80–130 mg/dl
After meals (1 hour)	90–160 mg/dl	90–180 mg/dl
After meals (2 hours)	100–120 mg/dl	100–150 mg/dl

Mg./dl. refers to milligrams per deciliter or the measure used to indicate the amount of glucose in milligrams per deciliter of blood. [Reprinted with permission from Jackson, R.L., Olson, J.M., Barnard, M.U., Jorgenson, R.G., & Olson, D., 1987. *The child with diabetes (manual for parents and child).* Kansas City: The University of Kansas Medical Center.]

Treatment

The child with diabetes mellitus has excessive amounts of glucose in the body that are unable to be used. Insulin is given to ensure that the glucose that is available is used by the body.

The current trend in diabetes management is keeping blood glucose levels between 60 and 150 mg/dl (milligrams per deciliter) of blood most of the time (Flavin & Haire-Joshu, 1986). The American Diabetes Association (1985) encourages the use of self-monitoring of blood glucose as part of routine management of persons requiring insulin. Self-monitoring of blood glucose is strongly recommended for persons receiving multiple insulin injections daily, for persons using insulin pumps, and for persons with Type I diabetes who are prone to hypo- glycemia (a lower than normal blood glucose) and do not experience the usual warning symptoms (see "Warning Signs" later in this chapter) (American Diabetes Association, 1985).

Many children are currently being taught to check their blood glucose level and take action depending on the results. The child's abil- ity to carry out this procedure depends on the cognitive, emotional, and psychomotor functioning of the child (Fow, 1983; Loman & Galgani, 1984). Generally, the 8- to 11-year-old child is physically capable of draw- ing up and injecting insulin and using the fingerstick method to test for blood glucose (Loman & Galgani, 1984). When the child does not have sufficient neuromuscular coordination of eyes and hands for fine motor tasks, the child's parents or other adults must carry out these proce- dures. Often the student with a disability depends on parents or others to perform the glucose monitoring and take action when the results are not acceptable.

The frequency of measuring blood glucose varies from student to student. The health care professional and family will decide how often and when the blood glucose levels should be checked. A common schedule for checking blood glucose is prior to meals and prior to the bedtime snack, about every 4 hours. Urine testing for glucose may be recommended at the same times (Loman & Gagani, 1984).

PROCEDURES

Procedures for monitoring blood glucose levels are described below. Since urine monitoring techniques are still used, these procedures are briefly presented in the Appendix to this chapter.

Preparing for Blood Glucose Monitoring

A schedule must be established identifying when the blood should be tested. Two or three staff persons should be instructed in the proper procedure. Ideally, however, the same person performs the test each day, at the same time of day, to avoid error. Equipment necessary for obtaining a blood glucose level is collected and placed near the student at the designated time. The equipment includes alcohol pads, a lancet (possibly a spring-activated lancet), a reagent strip, and possibly a glucose monitoring device. Samples of these materials are presented in Figure 11.1.

The reagent strip is a small plastic strip with a pad on one end of the strip that changes color after exposure to blood. The changed color of the pad indicates the level of glucose in the student's blood. The reagent strips should be fresh; they are usually effective for 2 months after the bottle is opened (Bergman, 1986). In order to determine the age of the reagent strips, the date the container was opened should be noted on the container. An expiration date written on the container by the manufacturer should be noted, and strips should not be used after the expiration date.

The device used for monitoring glucose levels must be calibrated to make certain the device is accurately measuring the glucose level. Some devices may need to be calibrated daily or weekly (Joyce, Kuzich, & Murphy, 1983). The methods for calibration vary with the glucose monitoring device. The method of calibration must be taught along with the procedure for obtaining blood glucose levels.

Performing Blood Glucose Monitoring

Blood glucose monitoring begins with removal of one reagent strip from the container. The reagent strip must be handled on the end away from the reagent pads (Figure 11.2). Oil from the skin can clog the coating on the reagent area of the strip (Jackson, 1985). The student's fingertip is cleansed with the alcohol, or soap and water, and allowed to dry. A clean cotton ball can be used to dry the skin (Jackson et al., 1987). After thorough cleansing of the fingertip, the side of the finger is pricked with the lancet or with a spring-activated lancet. A large drop of blood is allowed to form on the fingertip. When the drop of blood is large enough to cover the reagent area of the strip, the blood is carefully touched to the reagent area (Jackson, 1985).

After the fingertip is punctured to obtain a drop of blood, the drop

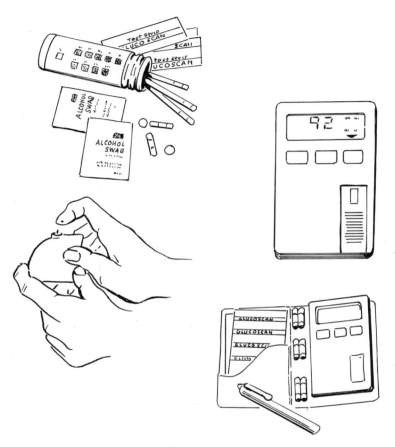

Figure 11.1.   Examples of equipment used to obtain and evaluate a student's blood for glucose levels.

of blood that forms on the fingertip may not be large enough to cover the reagent pad on the strip. This could result in falsely low results (Bergman, 1986). Attempting to smear the blood across the reagent pad will yield inaccurate results (Joyce et al., 1983). Techniques that may facilitate the formation of a large drop of blood include: washing the student's hands with warm water before the test, holding the student's hand down and gently shaking it after sticking, and squeezing the student's hand and finger moving toward the fingertip (Jackson et al., 1987). Pricking the side of the finger rather than the middle of the finger will increase blood flow (Joyce et al., 1983). Use of a spring-activated lancet will con-

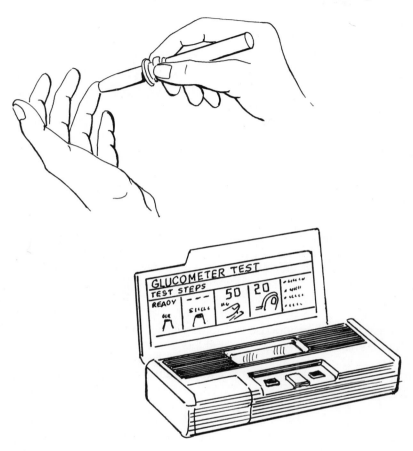

Figure 11.1.   (*continued*)

trol the depth of penetration and allow the formation of a blood droplet. When using a lancet alone, the depth of penetration cannot be controlled. Repeated sticks may be required before a drop of blood is obtained (Joyce et al., 1983).

Manufacturers vary their directions, depending on the type of reagent strip used. The directions for the specific reagent strip being used must be followed and will most likely include: beginning timing once the blood touches the reagent, wiping or washing the blood off the strip, and comparing the colors on the reagent strip to the color blocks on the reagent container to obtain results (Jackson, 1985; Joyce et al., 1983; Valenta, 1983).

Figure 11.2. Method for handling a reagent pad used in evaluating a student's blood glucose levels.

Using reagent strips that are discolored or from a container that has been open for more than 2 months can also give false results. A reagent strip that is not covered completely with blood can yield false low results. Removing the blood too soon from the reagent strip can yield false low results. Removing too little blood or removing the blood too late can yield false high results (Bergman, 1986). Directions for the use of reagent strips and the glucose monitoring devices must be followed carefully to ensure accuracy of results. If the glucose level is obtained using visual interpretation, the reagent strip is compared to a color chart. False results can be obtained due to poor lighting, poor eyesight, or by subjectively reading the value higher or lower than the actual value (Fow, 1983).

When a glucose monitoring device, instead of a reagent strip, is used to obtain the blood glucose level, the fingertip is cleansed as described above. The side of the fingertip is pricked and a large drop of blood is allowed to form. The drop of blood must be large enough to cover all of the reagent area. Once the blood touches the reagent strip, timing must begin. Most devices have a built-in timer that will alert the tester when a certain time period has passed. After this period has elapsed, the blood is removed from the reagent strip using a dry cotton ball, a special piece of paper, or water. The strip is then placed into the device. After the necessary time has passed, the glucose level is indicated on the device (Joyce et al., 1983; Valenta, 1983).

Procedures Following Blood Glucose Monitoring

After the reagent strip or monitoring device has been read, the value of the blood glucose is recorded in the student's record. Determination must be made as to whether the blood glucose level is low, acceptable, or high for the student. This information can be provided by the student's health care professional. The student may receive insulin, depending on the glucose level. The student's physician must specify the amount of insulin to be given, depending on the blood glucose level. Refer to Chapter 3, Medication Administration, for guidelines pertaining to the administration of prescription medications.

Blood glucose levels are reported to the parents and/or caregiver and physician according to a plan agreed upon by the parents, physician, and school staff. If school staff communicate daily in writing with the student's parents, the glucose level can be written in the daily notes to the parents. If the glucose measuring device is transported with the student to and from school, the most recent glucose level can be attached to the monitoring device by a parent when the student leaves home and by school staff when the student leaves school.

Warning Signs

Problem areas include trauma to the fingers continually used for the testing, the development of an insulin reaction (hypoglycemia), or the development of ketoacidosis (hyperglycemia).

The student's fingers may become tender after repeated pricks with the lancet. Rotating the fingers, pricking the sides rather than the center of the fingers, and using a spring-activated lancet can help diminish traumatic punctures (Loman & Galgani, 1984). Toes or ear lobes may also be used to obtain a drop of blood for glucose testing (Fow, 1983). Infection resulting from pricking the fingers could occur if clean technique is not used. Washing the hand thoroughly or cleaning the fingertip with alcohol, and using a new lancet each time can prevent infection (Loman & Galgani, 1984).

The student may experience an insulin reaction or a situation in which the insulin overbalances the glucose. The blood glucose level may drop too fast or too low. This will most likely occur before a meal or a snack (Jackson et al., 1987).

Signals that the student may be having an insulin reaction, or hypoglycemia, include: shaking, sweating, hunger, dizziness, paleness, irritability, confusion, poor coordination, headaches, double or blurred vision, and numbness or tingling of the lips. If any of the signals of an insulin reaction occur, the student should eat a snack containing fast-acting glucose, such as: one small box of raisins, one Fruit Roll-up, one half cup of soda pop (not diet), six or seven Lifesavers, ½ cup of fruit juice, or five small sugar cubes (Balik et al., 1986). Another recommendation for handling the first sign of an insulin reaction is to give the student 1 teaspoon (packet) of sugar in a small amount of water or give 1–2 teaspoons of honey. In 10–15 minutes, the student is given some food. The student should improve in 15–30 minutes (Jackson et al., 1987). Orange juice is also recommended (Fow, 1983). Glucose in the form of food and/or drink must always be available for the student with diabetes in the classroom. The student's parents can provide information on the most effective food to use for the individual student when any signs of an insulin reaction occur.

The presence of ketones in the student's urine indicates that the student is using fat as a source of fuel alternate to glucose. This occurs because insulin is absent (hyperglycemia), and with the absence of insulin, glucose cannot be used by the cells. Fat is used instead of glucose (Whaley & Wong, 1987). The ketones are strong acids that produce ketoacidosis or an acid condition of the body. Ketoacidosis usually occurs slowly. Signs of ketoacidosis include loss of appetite, abdominal pain, nausea and vomiting, and rapid and deep breathing (Jackson et al., 1987). Table 11.2 presents a comparison of hypoglycemia, and hyperglycemia.

If, for any reason, the student has persistent vomiting (more than two to three times per hour), severe nausea and inability to take fluids, or persistent diarrhea (more than two to three stools per hour), the health care worker in the school should call the student's parents or physician (as designated by the student's parents). If the student has one episode of vomiting or diarrhea, the student is allowed to rest and given frequent fluids. The health care worker can detemine when the student can return to class (Balik et al., 1986).

When the student is ill, the amount of physical activity and food intake should be decreased. The insulin dosage may also need to be adjusted. The student will probably be less hungry and will take in a smaller amount of calories than usual. When the student has an infection, the insulin required will usually increase. As with any student, attendance at school is not advisable when an infection is present (Jackson et al., 1987).

SIGNS OF AN EMERGENCY

The student in ketoacidosis (hyperglycemia) may experience coma, and death may occur if the condition is not reversed by insulin therapy (Whaley & Wong, 1987). Because the onset of ketoacidosis is slow, in-

Table 11.2.   Comparison of hypoglycemia and hyperglycemia

Feature	Hypoglycemia	Hyperglycemia
Onset	Rapid	Slow
Causes	Delayed or missed meal Excessive insulin Excessive exercise	Overeating Insufficient insulin Stress (e.g., illness, infection, surgery)
Manifestations	Weakness Sweating Blurred vision Mood change Hunger Pallor Rapid, labored respirations Seizures Shock Coma	Excessive urination Excessive thirst Nausea and vomiting Abdominal pain Drowsiness Sweet (acetone) breath Rapid pulse Coma
Laboratory values Urine		
Glucose	Usually absent	Positive
Acetone	Negative	Positive
Blood		
Sugar	Decreased	Increased
Acetone	Negative	Positive
Treatment	Administration of glucose	Administration of insulin
Response to treatment	Rapid	Slow

Extra clues	Urine test not accurate
	    at this time
	If ever in doubt, eat
	    sugar
		Urine test may show
		    ketone spilling
		Flu-like symptoms

Adapted from Scipien, G.M., Barnard, M.U., Chard, M.A., Howe, J., & Phillips, P.J. (1986). *Comprehensive pediatric nursing.* New York: McGraw-Hill.

sulin can be given as the elevated blood glucose and presence of ketones are identified. If insulin therapy is not effective in lowering the blood glucose and eliminating ketones from the urine, the student's parents and physician should be notified immediately. If the student moves into a coma, emergency measures must be followed as outlined by school protocol.

The student experiencing hypoglycemia may be uncooperative in eating the needed sugar. An injection of glucagon may be administered to provide necessary glucose. Untreated hypoglycemia can lead to seizures and unconsciousness. If this occurs, emergency measures must be followed as outlined by the school protocol.

Children with disabilities may not be able to communicate to others when symptoms of hyperglycemia (excessive glucose in the blood) or hypoglycemia (abnormally low glucose in the blood) are occurring. Parents are resources for school staff in identifying the student's behaviors that indicate hyperglycemia or hypoglycemia.

If staff suspect that a student is not receiving adequate insulin coverage, the school health care professional or physician must be notified. A blood test for glycosylated hemoglobin (HbA1) can provide information on the degree of hyperglycemia over a 4–8 week period. This test can also be used to evaluate the accuracy of the test results for the blood glucose levels taken at home and at school (Fow, 1983; Saucier, 1984).

ADDITIONAL RESOURCES

Additional information on diabetes, signs and symptoms, may be located by contacting diabetes educators and dieticians at local hospitals or medical centers.

Nurses in the physician's office, the diabetes educator, a local medical supply company, or the manufacturer may provide information on the use of the glucose monitoring device. The diabetes educator or nurses in the physician's office may provide assistance with urine testing for glucose and ketones.

The American Diabetes Association may have local affiliates that can be contacted for more information that can be helpful to parents and school staff.

Other information can be obtained from the following:

American Diabetes Association
2 Park Avenue
New York, NY 10016

Juvenile Diabetes Foundation, International
23 East 26th Street
New York, NY 10010
Telephone: (800) 223-1138

Medic Alert (Diabetes Identification)
P.O. Box 1009
Turlock, CA 95381-1009
Telephone: (800) 432-5378

National Diabetes Information Clearinghouse
Box NDIC
Bethesda, MD 20205
Telephone: (301) 496-7433

LITERATURE CITED

Almond, J. (1986). Measuring blood glucose levels. *Nursing Times, 82*(41), 51–54.

American Diabetes Association. (1985). Self-monitoring of blood glucose. *Diabetes Care, 8*(5), 51.

Balik, B., Haig, B., & Moynihan, P.M. (1986). Diabetes and the school-aged child. *The American Journal of Maternal/Child Nursing, 11*(5), 324–330.

Bergman, E. (1986). Blood glucose monitoring: Pointers for your patients. *The American Journal of Nursing, 86*(11), 1257.

Bernstein, R.K. (1981). *Diabetes—The Glucograf™ method for normalizing blood sugar.* New York: Crown Publishers.

Daneman, D., Siminerio, L., Transue, D., Betschart, J., Drash, A., & Becker, D. (1985). The role of self-monitoring of blood glucose in the routine management of children with insulin-dependent diabetes mellitus. *Diabetes Care, 8*(1), 1–4.

Flavin, K., & Haire-Joshu, D. (1986). The pharmacologic repertoire. *The American Journal of Nursing, 86*(11), 1244–1251.

Fow, S.M. (1983). Home blood glucose monitoring in children with insulin-dependent diabetes mellitus. *Pediatric Nursing, 9*(6), 439–442.

Gifford-Jorgensen, R.A., Borchert, J., Hassanein, R., Tilzer, L., Eaks, G.A., & Moore, W.V. (1986). Comparison of five glucose meters for self-monitoring of blood glucose by diabetic patients. *Diabetes Care, 9*(1), 70–76.

Haire-Joshu, D., Flavin, K., & Clutter, W. (1986). Contrasting Type I and Type II diabetes. *The American Journal of Nursing, 86*(11), 1240–1243.

Hughes, B. (1987). Diabetes management: The time is right for tight glucose control. *Nursing '87, 17*(5), 63–64.

Jackson, B. (1985). Testing your blood glucose levels. *Nursing Life, 5*(6), 42.

Jackson, R.L., Olson, J.M., Barnard, M.U., Jorgenson, R.G., & Olson, D. (1987). *The child with diabetes (manual for parents and child).* Kansas City: The University of Kansas Medical Center.

Joyce, M.A., Kuzich, C.M., & Murphy, D.M. (1983). Those new blood glucose tests. *Registered Nurse, 46*(4), 46–52.

Loman, D., & Galgani, C. (1984). Monitoring diabetic children's blood-glucose levels at home. *The American Journal of Maternal Child Nursing, 9*, 192–196.

Poole, D. (1986). Type II diabetes mellitus update: Diagnosis and management. *The Nurse Practitioner, 11*(8), 26–27, 32–34, 36, 41.

Saucier, C.P. (1984). Improvement in long-term control of children performing blood glucose self-monitoring. *The Diabetes Educator, 10*(3), 33–35.

Scipien, G.M., Barnard, M.U., Chard, M.A., Howe, J., & Phillips, P.J. (1986). *Comprehensive pediatric nursing.* New York: McGraw Hill.

Thomas, C.L. (Ed.). (1985). Taber's cyclopedic medical dictionary (15th ed.). Philadelphia: F.A. Davis.

Valenta, C.L. (1983). Urine testing and home blood-glucose monitoring. *Nursing Clinics of North America, 18*(4), 645–659.

Whaley, L.F., & Wong, D.L. (1987). *Nursing care of infants and children.* St. Louis: C.V. Mosby.

Appendix

PROCEDURE FOR MONITORING
GLUCOSE AND KETONES IN THE URINE

Preparation for Monitoring
Glucose and Ketones in the Urine

A sample of the student's urine is needed to test for glucose and ketones. If the student has control of urination and alerts the staff to the
need to urinate, a sample may be collected in a small, clean container. If
the student wears a diaper, a small amount of urine may be obtained by
pulling urine from the wet diaper using a clean syringe (Figure 11.3).
Materials used in testing for glucose or ketones are placed in the area
where soiled diapers are placed or urine is disposed of.

Materials needed for urine testing for glucose will depend on the
method used. The Clinitest method requires the use of a Clinitest tablet,
a test tube, eyedropper, and color chart (found in the Clinitest kit). The
Diastix, Clinistix, Ketostix, Keto-Diastix, and Chemstrip uG methods in-

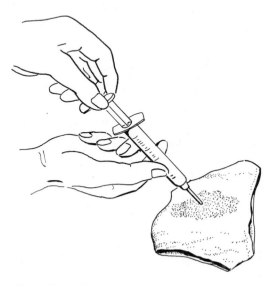

Figure 11.3.   Method used to obtain a sample of urine from a diaper in order
to test for glucose or ketones in the urine.

volve the use of a stick that is dipped into urine. Tes-tape involves the use of a piece of tape that is dipped into urine (Valenta, 1983).

The materials used in testing urine for ketones also vary. The Acetest method for testing for ketones is suggested for use with Clinitest since both methods require an eyedropper and a color chart (found in the Acetest kit). Ketostix, Keto-Diastix, and Chemstrip uK require the use of a stick that is dipped into urine (Valenta, 1983).

Performing a Test for Glucose or Ketones in the Urine

After the urine sample has been obtained, the test is conducted. The Clinitest method involves dissolving a Clinitest tablet in a precise mixture of urine and water in a test tube. After the dissolving boiling action has ceased, the color of the mixture is compared to a color chart. The chart identifies the glucose present in urine in a range from 0% to 10%. The Acetest method involves dropping one drop of urine on a tablet and waiting exactly 30 seconds. The color of the tablet is compared to a color chart. The Acetest results can indicate negative, trace, small, moderate, or large (Valenta, 1983).

When using any of the remaining methods (Diastix, Clinistix, Ketostix, Keto-Diastix, Chemstrip uG, Chemstrip uK), the strip is dipped into urine. After a precise period of time, the strip is compared to a color chart on the container of strips or accompanying the strips (Valenta, 1983).

The accuracy of methods of testing urine for glucose and ketones has been questioned. If the urine is discolored due to medication, all methods of urine testing are adversely affected. If tablets, sticks, or tape are exposed to moisture or inadequately stored, inaccurate readings may result. Certain medications can cause false results (Valenta, 1983).

12

COLOSTOMY OR ILEOSTOMY CARE

The purpose of a colostomy or an ileostomy is to provide an effective way for the student to eliminate feces from the bowel without passing it through the rectum. Since the student has no control over when this process will occur, it is highly likely that feces will be passed during the school day and that the school staff will be involved. Procedures for ostomy care should first and foremost center on maintaining the privacy and dignity of the student. Efforts should also be made to ensure that the method of collection of feces is safe and odor free and that the skin around the colostomy/ileostomy is healthy and free of breakdown.

OVERVIEW

A colostomy or ileostomy is characterized by the portion of the intestinal tract involved. Since feces have a different consistency in the different parts of the intestines, different ostomies will produce different types of elimination. A brief review of the intestinal system is presented as a preview to a discussion of the various types of colostomies or ileostomies.

Structure and Function of the Intestines

The intestine consists of the small and large intestines. The small intestine is composed of three sections: the duodenum, the jejunum, and the ileum (Figure 12.1). The duodenum is that part of the small intestine extending from the stomach to the jejunum. The duodenum receives food from the stomach, mixes enzymes with the food, and begins absorbing nutrients from the food. The next two portions of the small intestine are the jejunum and the ileum; both continue to absorb nutrients from food.

Muscles of the small intestine contract often, mixing the food and digestive juices. The movement forces this mixture to come in contact with the walls of the small intestine, allowing absorption to occur. As the mixture moves closer to the cecum, a portion of the large intestine, this movement slows down, allowing as much absorption of nutrients from the digested material as possible. It may take 2–4 hours for the food to move through the small intestine (Sordelett, 1982).

The large intestine is composed of the cecum, the ascending colon, the transverse colon, the descending colon, and the rectum (Figure 12.2). The partially digested food and enzymes leave the ileum and move into the cecum. The large intestine continues to absorb water from the partially digested mixture and stores feces until they are expelled through the anus. The mixture enters the colon as a liquid and becomes semisolid as it progresses through the colon (Sordelett, 1982).

Muscle contraction in the large intestine generally is slower than in the small intestine. Because of this slow movement, material entering the colon remains there for 18–24 hours. Three to four times a day, usually after meals, a marked increase in movement occurs. This increased movement may lead to mass movement during which large sections of the colon contract and push fecal material one third to three fourths the length of the colon in a few seconds (Vander, Sherman, & Luciano, 1975). Feces are moved into the rectum by this mass movement. Normally a person can make a choice about whether to allow the feces to pass through the anus or prevent passage of the feces from the rectum through the anus (Sordelett, 1982) (see Chapter 5, Bowel Care, for a further discussion).

Structure and Function of a Colostomy or Ileostomy

A colostomy or ileostomy is usually performed in infants and children because of a medical problem resulting in the obstruction or blockage of all or part of the intestine. Passage of intestinal contents is prevented,

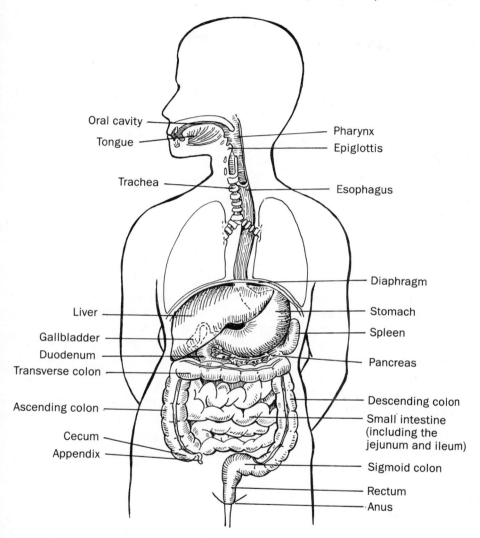

Figure 12.1.   The parts of the large and small intestines, with the small intestine consisting of the duodenum, the jejunum, and the ileum.

and surgery is required to relieve this problem. This surgical redirecting of flow of feces can be temporary or permanent (Adams & Selekof, 1986). The following discussion and procedures are the same for the student having a permanent ileostomy or colostomy as for the student having a temporary ileostomy or colostomy.

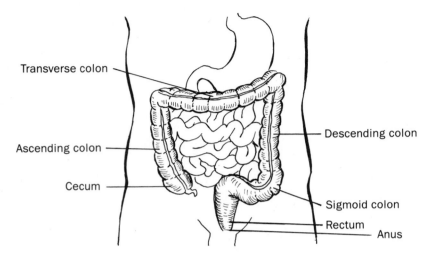

Figure 12.2.   The parts of the large intestine.

When a colostomy or ileostomy has been surgically created, the student no longer has the ability to retain feces in the rectum or allow feces to pass through the rectum and anus. Instead, feces are eliminated through an opening on the abdomen without the control of the student. This opening, called a stoma, is a portion of the inside of the intestine that is secured in place on the surface of the skin on the abdomen during surgery (Figure 12.3a). This inner surface of the intestine has no nerve fibers and has no sensation when touched (Boarini, 1985). The stoma is usually pink and moist like the inside of the cheek of the mouth. It usually protrudes 1.5–2.0 centimeters above the surface of the skin (Alterescu, 1987). A pouch or special plastic bag [attached to a skin barrier (Figure 12.3b)] is secured over the stoma for collection of fecal material as it is eliminated from the intestine.

Ileostomy   When the student has an ileostomy (the stoma is created from a portion of the ileum), the fecal material passing through the stoma is liquid or pasty in consistency and contains digestive enzymes. This fecal material can be very irritating to the skin (Adams & Selekof, 1986). Contact of the contents of the ileum with the skin will result in a breakdown of the skin. The pouch must be properly fitted around the stoma to prevent fecal material from touching the skin. A drainable pouch, as opposed to a replaceable pouch, is worn for two reasons: the feces, or contents of the ileum, are semiliquid, and material passes through the ileostomy frequently during the day and night (Erickson, 1987).

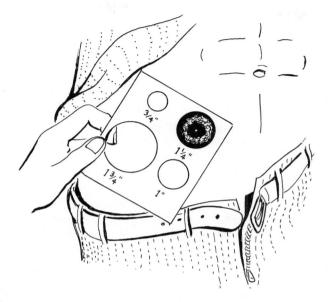

Figure 12.3a.   The stoma, an opening into the intestine.

Figure 12.3b.   The skin barrier, which is attached to the drainage pouch.

Colostomy   A colostomy can be created from any part of the colon: ascending, transverse, or descending (sigmoid) (Figure 12.2). When a colostomy is created from the ascending colon, the feces are liquid or semiliquid and may contain some digestive enzymes. The ascending colostomy is similar to the ileostomy in terms of the care required to protect the skin. A drainable pouch is recommended and fitted to prevent feces from touching and irritating the skin (Dudas, 1982).

When the student has a transverse colostomy, the fecal material eliminated from the stoma varies in consistency from thick liquid to pasty. A drainable pouch is also usually worn (Dudas, 1982) because of the frequency of eliminations.

When the student has a colostomy created from the sigmoid colon, feces eliminated through the stoma are similar in consistency to feces eliminated from the rectum. Feces are formed and will usually be eliminated from the stoma at regular intervals. Some students with sigmoid colostomies may be able to regulate fecal elimination by the procedure of irrigating the stoma or through attention to diet. If fecal elimination is regulated, a covering, rather than a bag, may be worn over the stoma for protection. Other students who do not have regulated eliminations may wear a pouch that is not drainable (i.e., is a closed end pouch) in the event that feces pass through the stoma at an unscheduled time (Dudas, 1982).

PROCEDURES

Preparing for Colostomy or Ileostomy Care

Preparing for colostomy or ileostomy care involves establishing a routine or pattern of elimination and acquiring the proper training in use of the necessary materials.

Establishing a Routine   When planning for colostomy or ileostomy care, consideration must be given to the variability of bowel functioning from individual to individual. Factors influencing the pattern of bowel functioning and elimination include culture, early family lifestyle, diet, activity, growth and development, and anxiety and stress (Brill & Kilts, 1980) (see Chapter 5, Bowel Care).

The frequency of pouch emptying is determined not only by the student's diet, level of activity, medications, and emotions (Smith, 1985), but also by the location of the colostomy or ileostomy in the intestine. The student's pattern of bowel functioning can also be determined by the predetermined times for stoma irrigation as well as the number of times the pouch is changed. The student with a sigmoid colostomy may also have an irrigation once daily to stimulate the passage of fecal material from the colon. This may be the only time that fecal material is passed from the stoma. Students with other types of colostomies or ileostomies require more frequent bag changes or emptying of the contents.

Training School staff working with the student's colostomy or ileostomy need to know how to change the pouch, empty it, or release gas that has accumulated in the pouch. School staff who know beforehand that a student will be having ostomy surgery can learn about colostomy or ileostomy care with the parents and/or caregiver. An enterostomal therapist from the hospital prepares the parents and the student for the surgery and the care of the colostomy or ileostomy afterward. Persons in the school system who will be working with the student could participate in training at this time.

If the student has a colostomy or ileostomy prior to enrollment in school, school staff can work with the health care worker in the school, the enterostomal therapist, the student's physician, and health professionals working with the physician to learn about ostomy care. School staff need to know the usual pattern of elimination of feces, the usual consistency of feces, special diet modifications, medications on the ostomy, signs and symptoms of complications, the procedure for changing the pouch, and supplies needed for the pouch change.

Materials The equipment necessary for colostomy or ileostomy care is collected prior to removal of the existing pouch. Items needed will most likely include: skin sealant or skin preparation wipe, skin barrier, colostomy or ileostomy pouch, washcloth, and warm water. It is recommended that extra supplies be available at school for unexpected leaks (Adams & Selekof, 1986). Additionally, an extra set of clothes needs to be kept at school in case of leakage from the pouch.

Skin sealants are used to protect the skin and are used under adhesive materials. They are available as sprays, wipes, gels, or liquids. Skin barriers are used to protect the skin from fecal material eliminated through the stoma. Skin barriers are available as solid wafers, pastes, powders, or rings. Colostomy or ileostomy pouches may be drainable or nondrainable (i.e., closed end). Drainable pouches are used with ostomies that eliminate fecal material and require frequent emptying. The pouches are odorproof or nonodorproof, and may or may not have a skin barrier attached. Closed end pouches may have a gas-release filter as part of the pouch. Reusable pouches are available for use when disposable pouches are ineffective because of frequency of elimination (Broadwell, 1984).

Performing Colostomy or Ileostomy Care

Colostomy or Ileostomy care procedures include when and how to change a student's pouch, when and how to empty the fecal material from an attached pouch, and when and how to release accumulated gas.

Changing a Pouch   Changing of the colostomy or ileostomy pouch usually occurs at home. The student may, however, require a pouch change at school if the pouch loosens or begins leaking. The pouch for an infant or young child may be changed every 1–2 days. As parents and the student become more comfortable with the routine and necessary care, it is hoped that the pouch will stay secure for 3–5 days between changing (Erickson, 1987).

When changing the pouch, a location is used that is private and allows for minimal distraction of the school staff person(s) and the student. The student needs to be in the position that best facilitates removal of and application of the pouch. Generally this is a reclining position. A deodorant spray can be used in the room prior to removing the old pouch. If the student is restless or tends to interfere with the process of applying a clean pouch, two persons may be needed. One person may be able to change the pouch alone by giving the student a toy to play with or distracting the student with music and visual stimuli. Thorough handwashing is performed prior to beginning the procedures. The necessary equipment is gathered at the side of the student.

Generally the student will be fitted with a drainable pouch with a separate adhesive skin barrier attached. The following procedures describe the use of these materials: If the opening in the pouch has not been pre-cut to fit around the stoma, it should be cut to be $\frac{1}{16}$ inch to $\frac{1}{8}$ inch larger than the stoma. The skin barrier is also cut to fit around the stoma with the opening being $\frac{1}{16}$ to $\frac{1}{8}$ inch larger than the stoma (Figure 12.3b). The nonadhesive side of the skin barrier is attached to the adhesive side of the pouch.

The old pouch is removed with soapy water or solvent. The skin around the stoma is cleaned with water. If soap is used, it should be a mild soap. The skin is rinsed thoroughly, and patted dry, and carefully checked for signs of redness or irritation. The stoma is also carefully examined. If a skin sealant is being used, it is applied to the skin and allowed to dry. The adhesive side of the skin barrier is applied to the skin fitting around the stoma. The person applying the pouch holds one hand in place over the pouch for a minute or more to ensure a leakproof seal. The pouch is closed with a rubber band or colostomy or ileostomy clip. Paper clips or other closures that the student could easily remove and swallow are not used (Adams & Selekof, 1986).

Emptying the Pouch   Emptying of the pouch can be done only with the drainable pouch. It is recommended that the pouch be emptied when it is about one third full, to prevent the pouch from being loosened by the heavy amounts of fecal material (Dudas, 1982). The student is positioned over the toilet seat (if possible). The end of the pouch is opened and drained into the toilet. The inside of the pouch is rinsed with clear warm water and dried carefully with a paper towel. The end of the pouch is secured with a colostomy or ileostomy clamp or a rubber band (whichever is recommended by the enterostomal therapist).

Releasing Gas   Releasing accumulated gas from the pouch can be done with the drainable pouch. The end of the pouch is opened and the excess gas is released as the pouch is compressed with the hand. Gas accumulation in a closed end pouch can be released when holes are punched in the pouch material with a pin. The gas is released when the pouch is compressed with the hand. A piece of tape is then placed over the pinholes (Adams & Selekof, 1986). This strategy may not be recommended because the odor can permeate the pouch material (Dudas, 1982; Smith, 1985). Erickson (1987) recommends that if a closed end (nondrainable) pouch is used, that the pouch should have a gas filter. The choice of pouches can be discussed with the enterostomal therapist.

Procedures Following Colostomy or Ileostomy Care

After the new pouch has been applied, the contents of the old pouch are emptied into the toilet. The old pouch is placed into a plastic bag, which is sealed closed. The old pouch is not flushed down the toilet; disposable does not mean that the pouch is to be flushed. Thorough handwashing at a sink, not used for food preparation, is necessary after the old pouch has been discarded. Remaining supplies are noted and replaced in the area for storing the student's supplies. School staff should ensure that adequate supplies are available for the next change.

The parents and/or caregiver need to be informed that the student's pouch was changed. Additional information might include the color, consistency, and amount of feces in the pouch. Any signs of redness or irritation of the stoma is also reported.

Warning Signs

Problems associated with a colostomy or ileostomy involve the condition of the stoma, the skin around the stoma, and the elimination of fecal material through the stoma.

Condition of the Stoma   The stoma is a portion of the inside of the intestine that is secured as an opening on the surface skin of the abdomen. The healthy stoma normally appears pink in color and glistening (Smith, 1985). Because it is a portion of the intestine the stoma tolerates contact with fecal material. Problems occur when there is a change in the color of the stoma or if the stoma pulls away from the surrounding skin.

All of the following problems must be reported to the student's parents and/or caregiver, and the student's physician must be aware of and/or deal with the condition.

1. The stoma may turn dusky, dark, or black. This is an indication that the tissue is dead or dying.
2. The stoma may no longer protrude from the abdomen. It may have drawn back inside the abdomen, resulting in difficulty in fitting the pouch on the student's abdomen (Boarini, 1985).
3. The stoma may separate from the skin and leave an open wound around the base of the stoma. This condition may begin when the skin around the base of the stoma turns red. The skin may eventually separate from the stoma. When this occurs, the student experiences pain or burning as the fecal material is eliminated through the stoma and touches the open wound (Boarini, 1985).

A laceration or cut on the surface of the stoma can occur at any time. A laceration is usually a minor complication, and bleeding often stops on its own or with direct pressure to the stoma (Boarini, 1985). The student usually does not feel anything, but blood may be noticed in the pouch or oozing from the stoma. It is important to identify the source of the bleeding and make certain the bleeding stops and that it is not coming from inside the abdomen.

Condition of the Skin Around the Stoma   Problems can develop with skin around the stoma. The skin can become irritated, develop an infection, or break down. These conditions can be caused by the fecal material from the stoma or products placed on the skin for colostomy or ileostomy care. It is important that the source of irritation be identified and eliminated or prevented.

Infection, either fungal or bacterial, can develop in the skin around the stoma. The most common infections, however, are yeast infections. The infection may appear as patchy, reddened, dry, or scaly itching skin; or skin that is reddened, weeping (moist), and stinging. Yeast infections are usually seen in the area covered by the adhesive or the skin barrier or by the belt tabs (if a belt is worn to help hold the pouch in place over the stoma). Treatment of a fungal infection is usually with nystatin (Mycostatin) powder and exposure of the skin to air before application of the powder (Watt, 1985). The health care worker in the school needs to be aware of the condition of the student's skin around the stoma and communicate any concerns to the enterostomal therapist and/or the student's physician. Injury to the skin can occur when the skin barrier or other adhesive material is removed from the skin or when pressure is applied to a certain area of skin (e.g., when a belt is worn to hold the pouch in place). This can occur when colostomy or ileostomy pouches are removed too frequently. The methods of cleaning used should allow the pouch to remain in place for a longer period of time. The skin under the belt can be padded to prevent pressure from the belt tabs (Watt, 1985).

The presence of redness of the skin around the stoma is a concern for actual or potential problems. Redness that is transient (disappears after adhesive is removed) is normal and needs no treatment (Boarini, 1985). Signs of redness, drainage, or increased sensitivity of the skin around the stoma should be reported immediately to the health care worker in the school and the student's parents and/or caregiver. The enterostomal therapist can provide much assistance in this area.

Elimination of Fecal Material   The student with an ileostomy can experience food blockage caused by inadequately digested food and a narrowed stoma. Methods of preventing food blockage include ensuring that the student chews food thoroughly and eats adequate amounts of high fiber foods (see Chapter 5, Bowel Care, for a list of foods high in fiber content). Certain foods have been noted as frequently identified with food blockage. These include popcorn, peanuts, coconut, Chinese vegetables, string beans, and olives (Dudas, 1982). Signs of food blockage include swelling of the stoma, cramping, abdominal pain, vomiting, and no elimination from the ileostomy. There may be a large amount of thick liquid output before complete blockage because water passes around the blocked food initially. Distention and vomiting are signs that appear later as the blockage becomes more severe and prolonged. The student needs to be referred to the physician for relief of the blockage (Dudas, 1982).

Other Problems and Considerations   The student with a colostomy or ileostomy may have additional problems that become complex issues as the result of the presence of a colostomy or ileostomy and bag. These may include problems associated with diarrhea, gas, odor from the pouch, and leakage of fecal material.

The student may develop diarrhea from a virus or as a reaction to a particular food. Diarrhea has been associated with ingestion of broccoli, beans, prunes, raw fruit, and fruit juices (Adams & Selekof, 1986).

This will result in frequent emptying of the pouch, increased watery drainage, and foul-smelling feces. The presence of diarrhea must be reported to the health care worker in the school.

The student may have problems with excessive gas, resulting in inflation of the pouch. Certain foods that have been connected with excessive gas or odor include: cabbage, onions, brussel sprouts, beans, broccoli, and carbonated beverages. Gas may be reduced by giving the student 2–3 tablespoons of applesauce at breakfast (Adams & Selekof, 1986), and cranberry juice and yogurt are helpful in controlling gas (Hutchinson & Shipes, 1981). Although a food causing diarrhea or gas may be eliminated from the diet, it is important for the student to eat a balanced diet and have adequate intake of fluid (Rideout, 1987).

Odor from the pouch may be a concern of parents and school staff. Most pouch material is odorproof, and deodorizing agents are available for odor control. Some persons have advised the use of aspirin as a deodorant in pouches. Most enterostomal therapists, however, do not advise that aspirin be used because of the danger of ulceration occurring from contact with the aspirin. Emptying the pouch at regular intervals and changing the pouch at established intervals can help prevent odor from the pouch and skin barrier itself. Parents and school staff will learn which foods cause odor and may choose to elminate these foods from the student's diet (Dudas, 1982).

Leakage of fecal material beneath the skin barrier and onto the skin can occur. This leakage can be due to improper application of the pouch or the skin barrier and the use of oily soaps, bath oils, ointments, or creams on the skin around the stoma. These materials can interfere with the adhesion of the pouch or skin barrier to the skin (Dudas, 1982). The pouch may loosen as a result of activity of the student, intentional pulling on the pouch by the student, or the heaviness of an unemptied pouch. Keeping the pouch covered with clothing can prevent easy access to the pouch; one piece garments, such as overalls, can discourage the student from pulling on the pouch. Emptying the pouch on schedule or when one third full can prevent the pouch from loosening and needing to be changed more often. This is especially true during activities and exercises directed by school staff and the physical therapist.

After an ileostomy or colostomy is performed, the diet is advanced from a clear liquid diet to a low fiber diet. It is important that the student chew foods well and that new foods be added only one food at a time to determine the tolerance to each new food. Foods high in fiber are approached cautiously; small quantities are eaten and chewed completely. If a food causes diarrhea or gas, that food may be omitted from the diet. It is important to eat a balanced diet and have adequate intake or fluid (Rideout, 1987). The pediatrician should specify the fluid requirements for the student during the school day.

SIGNS OF AN EMERGENCY

An obstruction or blockage of the intestine that is not relieved can present severe problems for the student. The student may experience abdominal cramping, distention of the abdomen, and vomiting. As fluid and gas accumulate in the abdomen, pressure can be placed on the intestine, resulting in decreased circulation and death of intestinal tissue. If this continues, a hole could open in the intestine, requiring emergency care and surgery (Dudas, 1982).

Infection of the skin around the stoma that is not treated properly can progress, causing severe breakdown of the surrounding skin. If untreated, this can lead to septicemia (blood poisoning). If septicemia develops, the student should have antibiotic therapy intravenously.

Diarrhea that continues can result in loss of fluid and dehydration that is moderate to severe. If severe dehydration develops, the student may experience a change in circulatory status and a drop in blood pressure. This results in shock (refer to Chapter 5, Bowel Care).

Bleeding from the stoma that does not cease within a few minutes also indicates an emergency. The health care worker in the school and the student's parents should be contacted to assess stomal bleeding and make a decision about referral to the student's physician.

ADDITIONAL RESOURCES

The United Ostomy Association and the American Cancer Society can provide literature and information on colostomy or ileostomy care. Local ostomy association chapters or the local supplier of ostomy products can provide support and information about local resources to parents and school staff. The International Association for Enterostomal Therapy (IAET) provides a Directory of Out-Patient Resources and Services that lists all clinics staffed by members of the IAET. These persons are board certified in enterostomal therapy. The list can be obtained by writing:

International Association for Enterostomal Therapy
5000 Birch Street, Suite 400
Newport Beach, CA 92660

LITERATURE CITED

Adams, D.A., & Selekof, J.L. (1986). Children with ostomies: Comprehensive care planning. *Pediatric Nursing, 12*(6), 429–433.

Alterescu, K.B. (1987). Colostomy. *Nursing Clinics of North America, 22*(2), 281–289.

Boarini, J. (1985). The ostomy: What can go wrong: *The American Journal of Nursing, 85*(2), 1358–1362.

Brill, E.L., & Kilts, D.F. (1980). *Foundations for nursing.* New York: Appleton-Century-Crofts.

Broadwell, D.C. (1984). Study guide for ostomy products. *Journal of Enterostomal Therapy, 11*(2), 74–76.

Dudas, S. (1982). Postoperative considerations. In D.C. Broadwell & B.S. Jackson (Eds.). *Principles of ostomy care* (pp. 340–368). St. Louis: C.V. Mosby.

Erickson, P.J. (1987). Ostomies: The art of pouching. *Nursing Clinics of North America, 22*(2), 311–320.

Hutchinson, S.J., & Shipes, E.A. (1981). *The physical and psychosocial care of children with stomas.* Springfield, IL: Charles C Thomas.

Rideout, B.W. (1987). The patient with an ileostomy: Nursing management and patient education. *Nursing Clincs of North American, 22*(2), 253–262.

Smith, D.B. (1985). The ostomy: How is it managed? *The American Journal of Nursing, 85*(11), 1246–1249.

Sordelett, S.S. (1982). Gastrointestinal system. In D.C. Broadwell & B.S. Jackson (Eds.). *Principles of ostomy care* (pp. 23–43). St. Louis: C.V. Mosby.

Vander, A.J., Sherman, J.H., & Luciano, D.S. (1975). *Human physiology: The mechanism of body function* (2nd ed.). New York: McGraw-Hill.

Watt, R. C. (1985). The ostomy: Why is it created? *The American Journal of Nursing, 85*(11), 1242–1245.

ADDITIONAL READINGS

Alterescu, V. (1985). The ostomy: What do you teach the patient? *The American Journal of Nursing, 85*(11), 1250–1253.

Broadwell, D.C. (1987). Peristomal skin integrity. *Nursing Clinics of North America, 22*(2), 321–332.

Broadwell, D.C., & Jackson, B.S. (1982). *Principles of ostomy care.* St.Louis: C.V. Mosby.

Kirkland, S. (1985). Ostomy dolls for pediatric patients. *Journal of Enterostomy Therapy, 12*(3), 104–105.

Motta, G.J. (1987). Life span changes: Implications for ostomy care. *Nursing Clinics of North America, 22*(2), 333–339.

Rolstad, B.S. (1987). Innovative surgical procedures and stoma care in the future. *Nursing Clinics of North America, 22*(2), 341–356.

Shipes, E. (1987). Psychosocial issues: The person with an ostomy. *Nursing Clinics of North America, 22*(2), 291–302.

Thielman, D.E. (1983). Patient teaching guidelines. *Journal of Enterostomal Therapy, 10*(5), 166–168.

Wong, D., & Whaley, L. (1986). *Clinical handbook of pediatric nursing* (2nd ed.). St. Louis: C.V. Mosby.

13

NASOGASTRIC TUBE FEEDING

$\mathbf{F}$or a variety of reasons a student may be unable to eat sufficient amounts of food for adequate weight gain or be unable to take
nourishment by mouth at all. One strategy used to provide nourishment, on a temporary basis, is a nasogastric (NG) tube. This is a tube
extending through the nose, down the esophagus, into the stomach.
The student receives nutrients, in a liquid form, through the NG tube.
The sole purpose of nasogastric tube feeding is to provide nourishment
to the student unable to take nourishment through the mouth or provide
additional nourishment to the student when intake through the mouth
is inadequate.

OVERVIEW

Students with disabling conditions are sometimes unable to take feedings by mouth because of an inadequate suck, extreme difficulty chew-

---

Chapters 13 and 14 both deal with methods of providing nourishment to the student
who is unable to take sufficient nourishment by mouth. Chapter 13 deals with a method of
providing nourishment on a temporary basis—nasogastric tube feeding. Chapter 14 deals
with a method of providing nourishment on a long-term basis—gastrostomy tube feeding. The two chapters are, therefore, very similar.

ing and swallowing, or frequent episodes of aspiration pneumonia (pneumonia resulting from stomach contents or formula being drawn into the lungs) (Batshaw & Perret, 1981). Because of the long-term effect of poor food consumption, the student may require higher than normal amounts of calories and protein, yet be unable to take these amounts by eating (Clinical Forum, 1984). In order to assist the student in meeting his or her nutritional needs, a nasogastric tube is passed through the nose and into the stomach (Figure 13.1) so that a liquid diet can be passed through the tube into the stomach. A nasogastric tube is used for feeding as a short-term intervention. Length of its use is not expected to be prolonged. If assisted feeding through a tube is expected for prolonged periods of time, a gastrostomy tube may be inserted (see Chapter 14, Gastrostomy Tube Feeding).

The liquid nutrients can be passed through the NG tube using several different strategies, each varying the rate at which the food enters the stomach. Using the *bolus method* (Figure 13.2) formula is allowed to flow through the nasogastric tube into the stomach within a few minutes (Jones, 1984). The *intermittent gravity drip method* (Figure 13.3)

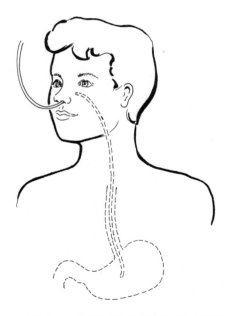

Figure 13.1.   The placement of the nasogastric tube through the nose into the stomach.

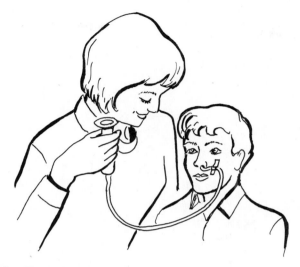

Figure 13.2.   The bolus method used to pass formula into the stomach.

allows formula to drip slowly over a 20- to 30-minute period from a hanging container. Both of these methods present nutrients during a short period of time, four to six times a day (at mealtimes and snack times) (Konstantinides & Shronts, 1983).

Two other methods present nutrients slowly, over a longer period of time. The *continuous gravity drip method* (Figure 13.3) presents the fluid into the nasogastric tube at a carefully controlled rate over a 16- to 24-hour period (Jones, 1984). The *continuous infusion by pump method* (Figure 13.4), presents the liquid into the nasogastric tube at a rate regulated by the infusion pump over a 16- to 24-hour period (Konstantinides & Shronts, 1983).

The method chosen usually depends on the student's ability to tolerate the feedings. The *bolus method* and the *intermittent gravity drip method* are used when the student can tolerate relatively large amounts over a short time. Using these methods the student receives the feeding over a short time and is then disconnected from the feeding bag and/or pump. When the student is unable to tolerate large amounts of formula at a time, the feeding is given by the *continuous gravity drip method* or the *continuous infusion by pump method.*

Nasogastric tubes left in place for long periods are usually made of polyurethane or silastic. These tubes are flexible, cause less local irritation (than tubes made from polyethylene), and are reusable. Once in

Figure 13.3.   The intermittent gravity drip and continuous gravity drip methods used to pass formula into the stomach.

place, nasogastric tubes require little care, other than ensuring that they are taped securely in place (Guest, Murray, & Antonson, 1982).

PROCEDURE

Preparation for Feeding Using a Nasogastric Tube

Preparation for using an NG tube involves collecting the needed equipment, establishing a routine for mealtime social activity, and identifying appropriate activities and positions following the mealtime. The needed equipment is collected and placed near the student. The equipment may include the feeding bag and tubing, formula, water, syringe, stethoscope, pole or hook to suspend feeding bag, and infusion pump when needed. The equipment must be safe from manipulation by other students. If an infusion pump is used, electrical outlets must be located conveniently near the meal area.

After proper handwashing, the exact amount of formula is measured out and placed in the feeding container 20–30 minutes prior to

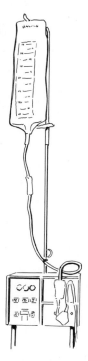

Figure 13.4.   An infusion pump used to regulate the flow of formula through a nasogastric tube into the stomach.

the mealtime. The liquid must reach room temperature prior to presentation. A sufficient amount of water is also collected to use to flush the tubing after the feeding is completed (not needed in the continuous feedings). An intravenous (IV) pole or plant hook can be used to suspend the feeding bag or syringe, allowing the formula to flow into the student.

Since eating is also a social activity, usually taking place with others, the NG tube feeding should take place during and with other mealtime activities. The location for the nasogastric feeding needs to be carefully chosen (except for the student receiving a continuous nasogastric tube feeding) and each student's individual needs must be considered. For example, one student may be easily distracted by other students and activities, turning toward the sounds and/or sights. This movement of the student may inhibit or slow the flow of formula into the stomach. Another student may not be distracted by activities in the environment and can be fed near other students and activities. Whenever possible students need to be fed in an environment as near to normal as possible to promote development. Generally the appropriate position for an NG tube feeding is an upright position, preferably in a chair. If necessary, however, the younger student may be held. If the feeding is continuous, the student might be held for brief periods during a scheduled mealtime. Activities planned to occur prior to the feeding should allow time for the student to relax and adjust more easily to the less active time during feeding.

Feeding Using a Nasogastric Tube

Feeding using an NG tube involves: 1) checking for the placement of the tube and any residual contents in the stomach, 2) presenting the liquid, 3) presenting any accompanying oral feeding, and 4) socialization typical to mealtime.

The position of the nasogastric tube is checked by aspirating (pulling out) stomach contents to ensure that the tube is in the stomach. A syringe is attached to the end of the nasogastric tube and the plunger of the syringe is pulled back to withdraw stomach contents (Figure 13.5). A second method of checking the positon of the nasogastric tube is to inject a small amount of air into the tube while listening for air entering the stomach through a stethoscope placed over the student's stomach (Figure 13.6) (Clinical Forum, 1984).

The student must also be checked for residual formula, that is, the amount of formula remaining in the student's stomach from the previous feeding. The syringe is attached to the nasogastric tube and the plunger is pulled back, withdrawing any/all residual formula. The amount of residual formula is usually subtracted from the amount of formula given at the next feeding to avoid overfeeding the student. For students receiving nasogastric feeding continuously, residual formula should be checked every 8 hours and re-fed to the student to prevent loss of important fluids and nutrients (Konstantinides & Shronts, 1983).

The formula must be administered as prescribed by the physician. The type and amount of formula as well as the method of presentation are determined by the physician. When the feeding is completed, the nasogastric tube is flushed with water to remove formula that may plug the tube. The tube is then clamped securely to prevent leakage.

Often a student may receive feedings by mouth in addition to the nasogastric feedings. The use of both strategies simultaneously is appropriate and allows the student to participate in the mealtime. Self-feeding should be encouraged at this time if it also is a goal for the

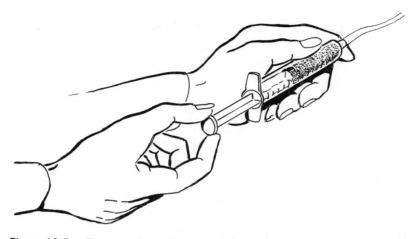

Figure 13.5.   The use of a syringe (without a needle) to withdraw a portion of stomach contents in order to check for the correct position of the nasogastric tube.

student and is developmentally appropriate (Perez, Beckom, Jebara, Lewis, & Patenaude, 1984). If the student (infant and toddler) is able to suck, but unable to perform other oral-motor activities, a pacifier can be provided during the nasogastric feeding. Sucking on a pacifier has been shown to increase weight gain and decrease crying in infants (Anderson, 1986). If the student is not eating by mouth, he or she should be encouraged to manipulate cups, spoons, and other utensils during this time (Guest et al., 1982). The time for nasogastric feeding is also an appropriate and functional time to carry out any required oral stimulation (c.f. Morris & Klein, 1987).

Time should be allowed to talk with the student during the feeding in order to provide an opportunity for face to face contact between the student and school staff. Younger children may be held and talked with, while older children can be touched. The nasogastric feeding is usually carried out with the student in an upright position. The student receiving continuous feeding usually is not restricted to an upright position and is allowed to be mobile during the feeding (Figure 13.7).

Procedures Following Feeding Using a Nasogastric Tube

The student should be placed on the right side or in an upright position (30 degrees or higher) for at least 1 hour after feeding (Whaley & Wong, 1987). The right-sided and upright positions allow the stomach to empty

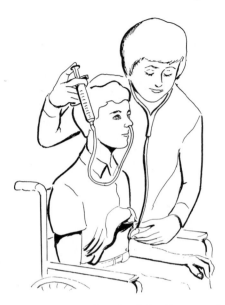

Figure 13.6.   The procedure used to check for the correct placement of the NG tube by injecting a small amount of air into the stomach.

more easily. Positioning on the abdomen may also be possible, preventing aspiration of any formula that the student may have regurgitated. (Regurgitation is the back flow of formula from the stomach to the mouth.)

The equipment used during the feeding is washed thoroughly in warm, soapy water. Washing of feeding equipment must be done in a sink area separate from the sink area used for handwashing and toileting. (Two sink areas need to be available: one area for food preparation/cleanup and one area for handwashing and care of toilet needs.) The equipment for nasogastric tube feeding is stored in a clean space designated for the one student only. Feeding tubing, feeding bags, and formula are not interchangeable among students.

Commercially prepared formulas stored at room temperature are sterile until opened. Once opened, the formula must be used immediately or refrigerated. Label, date, and refrigerate the remaining opened formula; formula not used within 24–48 hours is discarded. Formula should not hang in a feeding bag at room temperature for longer than 6–8 hours since it provides an environment for bacteria to grow (Bayer, Scholl, & Ford, 1983; Folk & Courtney, 1982).

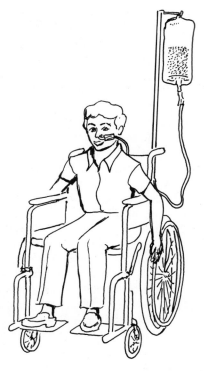

Figure 13.7.   A student receiving continuous feeding through an NG tube.

Warning Signs

Problems with NG tube feedings can occur with the formula, how it is given, and with the tubing itself.

Problems with the formula may occur from heating it, adding medications, or presenting cold formulas. Heating or adding medications to formula can change the chemical composition of formula (Jones, 1984). This may result in altered nutritional value for the student. The manufacturer's recommendations will identify specific medications appropriately given in the formula.

The flow of formula into the nasogastric tube may stop unexpectedly. This can occur because of the viscosity of formula, plugging of the tube with medications, a kink in the tube, or the student's movements. Liquid medications should be used whenever possible because poorly crushed medications can block the NG tube. Gently flushing the tube with water can remove the plug, allowing the feeding to resume. Cold formula is never given because it can cause severe cramps. Allowing the formula to reach room temperature is recommended. The rate of flow of formula into the stomach can be regulated by the control clamp on the feeding tubing and by raising or lowering of the feeding bag. If using an infusion pump, the flow of formula is regulated by the pump, which is regularly checked for accuracy of rate.

Even with an appropriately prescribed formula, the student may have difficulty tolerating the presentation. Problems may occur during the flow of formula into the stomach. Distention of the abdomen, nausea, vomiting, or diarrhea indicate that the student is having difficulty tolerating the formula or the rate at which the formula is being presented. The formula should be stopped or reduced until these signs disappear. If these signs have not disappeared within 1 hour, or within a time previously established with the health care worker, presentation of formula must not be resumed. The parent(s) and/or caregiver and health care worker in the school must be notified.

Problems may develop concerning the position of the NG tube or irritation to the skin caused by the tube or tape securing the tube. The nasogastric tube is taped securely in place on the student's face after it is inserted (Figure 13.8). The skin underneath and around the tape should be checked daily for signs of irritation such as redness, tenderness, or swelling, and tape should be changed every day or two. If irritation of the nostril around the nasogastric tube occurs, the tube should be changed to the other side of the nose.

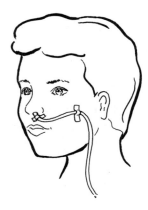

Figure 13.8. Correct taping of the NG tube to the student's nose and cheek.

A polyethylene nasogastric tube is used for an average length of 1–3 days. Polyurethane tubes can be in place up to 2–4 weeks. The student's parents(s) and/or caregivers are usually taught when and how to change the nasogastric tube (Guest et al., 1982). Cleaning and reuse of the feeding bag is carried out as recommended by the physician. If the nasogastric tube comes out, the health care worker in the school and/or the student's parent(s) must be notified and replace the tube. School staff may need to be trained to replace the nasogastric tube. This is especially true if the student is receiving a continuous feeding.

SIGNS OF AN EMERGENCY

If the feeding tube moves up from the stomach into the esophagus (back of the throat) formula could move into the student's lungs and cause pneumonia. It is also possible for formula to move from the stomach into the esophagus while the nasogastric tube is properly placed.

If there is choking, vomiting, or aspiration of the formula, the feeding is discontinued immediately. The student must be suctioned by a trained individual to remove secretions from the mouth and back of the throat. During suctioning, the student is placed on the left side with the head lower than the rest of the body. If suctioning is successful, the student is allowed to rest and is carefully observed. The feeding can be resumed after the student has recovered. If the suctioning is not successful and the student stops breathing, resuscitaiton efforts must be initiated (see Chapter 8, Cardiopulmonary Resuscitation) and the Emergency Medical Services (EMS) in the community must be notified immediately.

ADDITIONAL RESOURCES

Medical supply companies can provide information about, and training in the use of equipment (i.e., nasogastric tube, feeding bag and tubing, and infusion pump) used in nasogastric tube feeding.

Local representatives of companies supplying formulas also provide information about the formulas and the medications that can or cannot be mixed with the formula. Local hospital staff (nurses, pharmacists) may also provide assistance in this area.

Nurses in the local hospital, the pediatrician's office, or the public health office can provide information on the "how to's" of nasogastric tube feeding. Nutrition support staff in hospitals and the student's physician can also provide assistance when there is suspicion that the student is not tolerating the formula.

Training to respond to emergency situations such as choking and absence of breathing can be provided in courses offered by the American Heart Association or the American Red Cross.

LITERATURE CITED

Anderson, G.C. (1986). Pacifiers: the positive side. *American Journal of Maternal Child Nursing, 11*(2), 122–124.

Batshaw, M.L., & Perret, Y.M. (1981). *Children with handicaps: A medical primer.* Baltimore: Paul H. Brookes Publishing Co.

Bayer, L.M., Scholl, D.E., & Ford, E.G. (1983). Tube feeding at home. *American Journal of Nursing, 83*(9), 1321–1325.

Clinical forum: Procedures for nasogastric feeding. (1984). *Nursing Mirror, 158*(20), i–viii.

Folk, C.C., & Courtney, M.E. (1982). Home tube feedings: General guidelines and specific patient instructions. *Nutritional Support Services, 2*(6), 18–22.

Guest, J.E., Murray, N.D., & Antonson, D.L. (1982). Continuous nasogastric feeding in pediatric patients. *Nutritional Support Services, 2*(5), 34–41.

Jones, S. (1984). Simpler and safer tube-feeding techniques. *Registered Nurse, 47*(10), 40–47.

Konstantinides, N.N., & Shronts, E. (1983). Tube feeding: Managing the basics. *American Journal of Nursing, 83*(9), 1312–1320.

Morris, S.E., & Klein, M.D. (1987). *Pre-feeding skills.* Tucson: Communication Skill Builders.

Perez, R.C., Beckom, L., Jebara, L., Lewis, M.A., & Patenaude, Y. (1984). Care of the child with a gastrostomy tube: Common and practical concerns. *Issues in Comprehensive Pediatric Nursing, 7,* 107–119.

Whaley, L.F., & Wong, D.L. (1987). *Nursing of infants and children.* St. Louis: C.V. Mosby.

14

GASTROSTOMY TUBE FEEDING

$\mathbf{F}$or a variety of reasons a student may be unable to eat sufficient amounts of food for adequate weight gain or be unable to take
nourishment by mouth at all. One strategy used to provide nourishment, on a long-term basis, is a gastrostomy tube. This is a tube extending directly through the abdomen into the stomach. The student receives nutrients, in a liquid form, through this tube. The sole purpose of
the gastrostomy tube feeding is to provide nourishment to the student
unable to take nourishment through the mouth or provide additional
nourishment to the student when intake through the mouth is inadequate. The procedures and conditions dealing with gastrostomies are
very similar to those dealing with nasogastric tube feedings.

OVERVIEW

Students with disabling conditions are sometimes unable to take feedings by mouth because of an inadequate suck, extreme difficulty chew-

---

Chapters 13 and 14 both deal with methods of providing nourishment to the student
who is unable to take sufficient nourishment by mouth. Chapter 13 deals with a method of
providing nourishment on a temporary basis—nasogastric tube feeding. Chapter 14 deals
with a method of providing nourishment on a long-term basis—gastrostomy tube feeding. The two chapters are, therefore, very similar.

ing and swallowing, or frequent episodes of aspiration pneumonia (pneumonia resulting from stomach contents or formula being drawn into the lungs) (Batshaw & Perret, 1981). Because of the long-term effect of poor food consumption, the student may require higher than normal amounts of calories and protein, yet be unable to take these amounts by eating (Clinical Forum, 1984). In order to assist the student in meeting his or her nutritional needs, a gastrostomy tube is passed directly into the stomach, so that a liquid diet can be passed through the tube into the stomach. A gastrostomy tube is used for feeding over prolonged periods or on a permanent basis. A nasogastric tube is used as a short-term intervention (see Chapter 13, Nasogastric Tube Feeding).

The liquid nutrients can be passed through the gastrostomy tube using several different strategies, each varying the rate at which the food enters the stomach. Using the *bolus method* (Figure 14.1) formula is allowed to flow through the gastrostomy tube into the stomach within a few minutes (Jones, 1984). *The intermittent gravity drip method* (Figure 14.2) allows formula to drip slowly over a 20- to 30-minute period from a hanging container. Both of these methods present nutrients during a

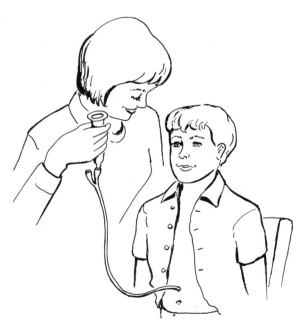

Figure 14.1.   The bolus method used to pass formula into the stomach.

short period of time, four to six times a day (at mealtimes and snack times) (Konstantinides & Shronts, 1983).

Two other methods present nutrients slowly, over a longer period of time. The *continuous gravity drip method* (Figure 14.2) presents the fluid into the gastrostomy tube at a carefully controlled rate over a 16- to 24-hour period (Jones, 1984). The *continuous infusion by pump method* (see Figure 14.3) presents the liquid into the gastrostomy tube at a rate regulated by the infusion pump over a 16- to 24-hour period (Konstantinides & Shronts, 1983).

The method chosen usually depends on the student's ability to tolerate the feedings. The *bolus method* and the *intermittent gravity drip method* are used when the student can tolerate relatively large amounts

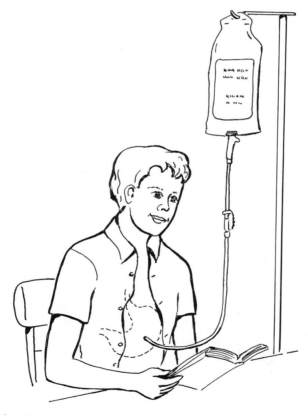

Figure 14.2.   The intermittent gravity drip and continuous gravity drip methods used to pass formula into the stomach.

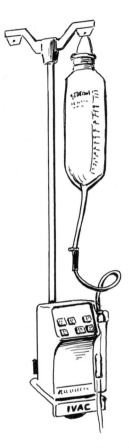

Figure 14.3.   An infusion pump used to regulate the flow of formula through a gastrostomy tube into the stomach.

over a short time. Using these methods the student receives the feeding over a short time and is then disconnected from the feeding bag and/or pump. When the student is unable to tolerate large amounts of formula at a time, the feeding is given by the *continuous gravity drip method* or the *continuous infusion by pump method.*

The actual gastrostomy tube (Figure 14.4) is a polyurethane or silicone tube that is soft and flexible and about 8–12 inches long. The tube is inserted through the abdominal wall into the stomach and may be secured into place by a suture. The stomach is sutured to the lining of the abdominal cavity to prevent leakage of the formula from this open-

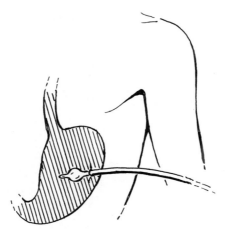

Figure 14.4.   The placement of a gastrostomy tube.

ing into the abdominal cavity. Often a clean gauze dressing is taped in place around the gastrostomy tube to protect the opening and absorb any leakage. This, however, may be omitted to reduce the chances of irritation to the skin.

For a button gastrostomy a short tube is inserted into an established opening in the stomach (Figure 14.5). The button fits snugly against the skin on the abdomen and has a small plug that is removed for feedings (Gauderer & Stellato, 1986). Tubing from the feeding bag can be placed into the button allowing formula to flow into the stomach. As soon as the feeding is completed, the tubing is disconnected from the button and the button is plugged. The button fits flat against the skin, which helps prevent leaking around the tube and accidental pulling out of the tube. The fact that the tube fits flat against the skin can provide a psychological benefit to the student and parent because this tube is not as noticeable as the traditional gastrostomy tube (Figure 14.4) (Gauderer & Stellato, 1986).

PROCEDURES

Preparation for Feeding Using a Gastrostomy Tube

Preparation for using a gastrostomy tube involves collecting the needed equipment, establishing a routine for mealtime social activity, and iden-

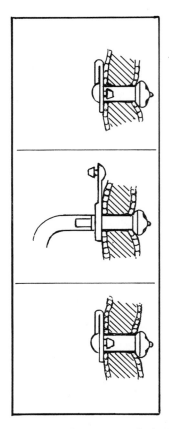

Figure 14.5.   The appearance and structure of a button gastrostomy.

tifying appropriate activities and positions following the mealtime. The needed equipment is collected and placed near the student. The equipment may include the feeding bag and tubing, formula, water, syringe, pole or hook to suspend the feeding bag, and infusion pump when needed. The equipment must be safe from manipulation by other students. If an infusion pump is used, electrical outlets must be located conveniently near the meal area.

After proper handwashing, the exact amount of formula is measured out and placed in the feeding container 20–30 minutes prior to the mealtime. The liquid must reach room temperature prior to presentation. A sufficient amount of water is also collected to use to flush the tubing after the feeding is completed (not needed in the continuous feedings). An intravenous (IV) pole or plant hook can be used to suspend the feeding bag or syringe, allowing the formula to flow into the student.

Since eating is also a social activity, usually taking place with others, the gastrostomy tube feeding should take place during and with other mealtime activities. The location for the gastrostomy feeding needs to be carefully chosen (except for the student receiving a continuous gastrostomy tube feeding), and each student's individual needs must be considered. For example, one student may be easily distracted by other students and activities, turning toward the sounds and/or sights. This movement of the student may inhibit or slow the flow of formula into the stomach. Another student may not be distracted by activities in the environment and can be fed near other students and activities. Whenever possible, students need to be fed in an environment as near to normal as possible to promote development. Generally the appropriate position for an gastrostomy tube feeding is in an upright position, preferably in a chair. If necessary, however, the younger student may be held. If the feeding is continuous, the student might be held for brief periods. Activities planned to occur prior to the feeding should allow time for the student to relax and adjust more easily to the less active time during feeding.

Feeding Using a Gastrostomy Tube

Feeding using a gastrostomy tube involves: 1) checking for any residual contents in the stomach, 2) presenting the liquid, 3) presenting any accompanying oral feeding, and 4) socialization typical to mealtime.

The student must be checked for residual formula, that is, the amount of formula remaining in the student's stomach from the pevious feeding. A syringe is attached to the end of the gastrostomy tube and the plunger of the syringe is pulled back to withdraw stomach contents (Figure 14.6). A second method of checking for residual formula is to attach a syringe to the end of the gastrostomy tube and lower the syringe and tubing until stomach contents move freely into the syringe. The amount of any residual formula is usually subtracted from the amount of formula given at the next feeding to avoid overfeeding the student. For students receiving continuous feedings, the amount of residual formula should be checked every 8 hours. Residual formula is re-fed to the student to prevent loss of important fluids and nutrients (Konstantinides & Shronts, 1983).

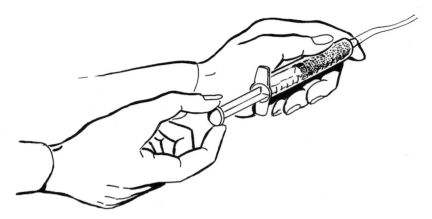

Figure 14.6.   The use of a syringe (without the needle) to withdraw a portion of stomach contents in order to check for the correct position of the gastrostomy tube.

The formula must be administered as prescribed by the physician. The type and amount of formula as well as the method of presentation are determined by the physician. When the feeding is completed, the gastrostomy tube is flushed with water to remove formula that may plug the tube. The tube is then clamped securely to prevent leakage (Metheny, 1985).

Often a student may receive feedings by mouth in addition to the gastrostomy tube feedings. The use of both strategies simultaneously is appropriate and allows the student to participate in the mealtime. If the student (infant or toddler) is able to suck, but unable to perform other oral-motor activities, a pacifier can be provided to approximate eating during the gastrostomy feeding. Sucking on a pacifier has been shown to increase weight gain and decrease crying (Anderson, 1986). The time used for gastrostomy feeding is also an appropriate and functional time to carry out any required oral stimulation (c.f. Morris & Klein, 1987). But, if possible, self-feeding should be encouraged during any tube feeding process (Perez, Beckom, Jebara, Lewis, & Patenaude, 1984). If the student is not eating by mouth, whether using a pacifier or not, he or she should be encouraged to manipulate cups, spoons, and other utensils during this time (Guest, Murray, & Antonson, 1982).

The gastrostomy feeding is usually carried out with the student in an upright position. The student receiving continuous feeding, however, usually is not restricted to an upright position and is allowed to be mobile during the feeding.

Procedures Following Feeding Using a Gastrostomy Tube

The student should be placed on the right side or in an upright position (30 degrees or higher) for at least 1 hour after feeding (Whaley & Wong, 1987). The right-sided and upright positions allow the stomach to empty more easily. Positioning on the abdomen may also be possible, preventing aspiration of any formula that the student may have regurgitated. (Regurgitation is the back flow of formula from the stomach to the mouth.)

The equipment used during the feeding is washed thoroughly in warm, soapy water. Washing of feeding equipment must be done in a sink area separate from the sink area used for handwashing and toileting. (Two sink areas need to be available: one area for food preparation/ cleanup and one area for handwashing and care of toilet needs.) The equipment for gastrostomy tube feeding is stored in a clean space designated for the one student only. Feeding tubing, feeding bags, and formula are not interchangeable among students.

Commercially prepared formulas stored at room temperature are sterile until opened. Once opened, the formula must be used immediately or refrigerated. Label, date, and refrigerate the remaining opened formula; formula not used within 24–48 hours is discarded. Formula should not hang in a feeding bag at room temperature for longer than 6–8 hours since it provides an environment for bacteria to grow (Bayer, Scholl, & Ford, 1983; Folk & Courtney, 1982).

Warning Signs

Problems with gastrostomy tube feedings can occur with the formula, how it is given, and with the tubing itself.

Problems with the formula may occur from heating it, adding medications, or presenting cold formula. Heating or adding medications to formula can change the chemical composition of formula (Jones, 1984). This may result in altered nutritional value for the student. The manufacturer's recommendations will identify specific medications appropriately given in the formula.

The flow of formula into the gastrostomy tube may stop unexpectedly. This can occur because of the viscosity of formula, plugging of the tube with medications, a kink in the tube, or the student's movements. Liquid medications should be used whenever possible because poorly crushed medications can block the gastrostomy tube. Gently flushing the tube with water can remove the plug, allowing the feeding to resume. The rate of flow of formula into the stomach can be regulated by the control clamp on the feeding tubing and by raising or lowering of the feeding bag. If using an infusion pump, the flow of formula is regulated by the pump, which is regularly checked for accuracy of rate.

Even with an appropriately prescribed formula, the student may have difficulty tolerating the presentation. Cold formula is never given because it can cause severe cramps. Allowing the formula to reach room temperature is recommended. Problems may occur during the flow of formula into the stomach. Distention of the abdomen, nausea, vomiting, or diarrhea indicate that the student is having difficulty tolerating the formula or the rate at which the formula is being presented. The formula should be stopped or reduced until these signs disappear. If these signs have not disappeared within 1 hour, or within a time previously established with the health care worker, presentation of the formula must not be resumed. The parent(s) and/or caregiver and health care worker in the school must be notified.

Redness, drainage, foul odor, tenderness, or bleeding may occur around the gastrostomy tube. To guard against irritation, infection, and leakage of formula, the gastrostomy tube must be kept firmly fixed and free of tension. This position of the tube minimizes movement of the tube and subsequent widening of the skin opening around the tube. The skin around the gastrostomy tube must be kept clean and dry. The dressing must be checked before and after the feedings (Perez et al., 1984). The student's physician may recommend keeping the skin around the gastrostomy tube clean and dry and eliminating the dressing. Keeping the gastrostomy tube covered with the student's clothing can lessen the likelihood that the child will play with the tube.

The gastrostomy tube may shorten as peristalsis (wave-like movements of the digestive tract) slowly pulls the tube in and along the digestive tract. The gastrostomy tube may lengthen as the tube is pulled and tugged on by forces on the outside of the student. Any decrease or increase in visible length of the tube must be reported to the health care worker in the school and the student's parents and/or caregiver. The tube can be marked at the level of the dressing to identify changes in the length easily.

SIGNS OF AN EMERGENCY

If there is choking, vomiting, or aspiration of the formula, the feeding is discontinued immediately. The student must be suctioned by a trained individual to remove secretions from the mouth and back of the throat. During suctioning, the student is placed on the left side with the head lower than the rest of the body. If suctioning is successful, the student is allowed to rest and is carefully observed. The feeding can be resumed after the student has recovered. If the suctioning is not successful and the student stops breathing, resuscitation efforts must be initiated (see Chapter 8, Cardiopulmonary Resuscitation) and the Emergency Medical Services (EMS) in the community must be notified immediately.

The gastrostomy tube may come out occasionally. If this occurs, a clean, dry dressing must be taped securely over the opening. The health care worker in the school, the parent, or a previously identified person in the community must be notified immediately. If there is a delay in replacing the gastrostomy tube, the opening can close in a few hours (Gauderer & Stellato, 1986). A surgical procedure may be required to replace the tube.

ADDITIONAL RESOURCES

Medical supply companies can provide information and training in the use of equipment (i.e., gastrostomy tube, feeding bag and tubing, and infusion pump) needed in gastrostomy tube feeding.

Local representatives of companies supplying formulas also provide information about the formulas and the medications that can or cannot be mixed with the formula. Local hospital staff (nurses, pharmacists) may also provide assistance in this area.

Nurses in the local hospital, the pediatrician's office, or the public health office can provide information on the "how to's" of gastrostomy tube feeding. Nutrition support staff in hospitals and the student's physician can also provide assistance when there is suspicion that the student is not tolerating the formula.

Training to respond to emergency situations such as choking and absence of breathing can be provided in courses offered by the American Heart Association or the American Red Cross.

LITERATURE CITED

Anderson, G.C. (1986). Pacifiers: the positive side. *American Journal of Maternal Child Nursing, 11*(2), 122–124.
Batshaw, M.L., & Perret, Y.M. (1981). *Children with handicaps: A medical primer.* Baltimore: Paul H. Brookes Publishing Co.

Bayer, L.M., Scholl, D.E., & Ford, E.G. (1983). Tube feeding at home. *American Journal of Nursing, 83*(9), 1321–1325.

Carroll, P.F. (1986). Aspirated feeding solution. *Nursing 86, 16*(1), 33.

Clinical forum: Procedures for nasogastric feeding. (1984). *Nursing Mirror, 158*(20), i–viii.

Folk, C.C., & Courtney, M.E. (1982). Home tube feedings: General guidelines and specific patient instructions. *Nutritional Support Services, 2*(6), 18–22.

Gauderer, W.L., & Stellato, T.A. (1986). Gastrostomies: Evolution, techniques, indications, and complications. *Current Problems in Surgery, 23*(9), 661–719.

Guest, J.E., Murray, N.D., & Antonson, D.L. (1982). Continuous nasogastric feeding in pediatric patients. *Nutritional Support Services, 2*(5), 34–41.

Jones, S. (1984). Simpler and safer tube-feeding techniques. *Registered Nurse, 47*(10), 40–47.

Konstantinides, N.N., & Shronts, E. (1983). Tube feeding: Managing the basics. *American Journal of Nursing, 83*(9), 1312–1320.

Metheny, N.M. (1985). Twenty ways to prevent tube-feeding complications. *Nursing 85, 15*(1), 47–50.

Morris, S.E., & Klein, M.D. (1987). *Pre-feeding skills.* Tucson: Communication Skill Builders.

Perez, R.C., Beckom, L., Jebara, L., Lewis, M.A., & Patenaude, Y. (1984). Care of the child with a gastrostomy tube: common and practical concerns. *Issues in Comprehensive Pediatric Nursing, 7,* 107–119.

Whaley, L.F., & Wong, D.L. (1987). *Nursing of infants and children.* St. Louis: C.V. Mosby.

15

CLEAN INTERMITTENT CATHETERIZATION

Marianne Taylor

Students with some types of spina bifida, myelomeningocele, and other defects of the spinal cord experience neurologically impaired bladder function. This is referred to as a neurogenic bladder and results in urinary incontinence. The student with a neurogenic bladder does not sense bladder fullness, cannot voluntarily control bladder emptying, and has limited if any sensation of wetness when the bladder overflows or automatically empties. Clean intermittent catheterization (CIC) is a technique for regularly emptying the urinary bladder to prevent urinary tract infection, preserve kidney function, promote dryness, and enhance social acceptability.

Given the increasing number of students with a variety of disabilities receiving service in the schools, it is likely that a teacher may have a student with a neurogenic bladder. Since this student has no control over the process of emptying the bladder, the student will need as-

Marianne Taylor is a Clinical Nurse Specialist at the Child Development and Rehabilitation Center, Oregon Health Sciences University, Eugene, Oregon.

sistance in controlling the release of urine, and school staff generally will be involved. Procedures for CIC should, first and foremost, center on maintaining the privacy and dignity of the student and should ensure that the method of urine collection is safe.

OVERVIEW

Information relevant to clean intermittent catheterization includes an understanding of impaired bladder function, the basics of CIC, and any medications associated with maintaining a healthy bladder.

Normal and Impaired Bladder Function

The ease and coordination of the elimination of urine differ significantly between an intact and a neurogenic bladder. Clean intermittent catheterization is used to avoid many of the negative complications associated with incomplete emptying of the bladder.

A bladder functioning normally gradually stretches as it fills with urine. When the bladder is full, nerve signals from the bladder cause it to contract and empty. When normal sensation and motor function are present, the individual can inhibit bladder emptying by voluntarily contracting the urinary sphincter and muscles of the pelvic floor (Figure 15.1). The individual with a normal bladder, therefore, can control the occurrence of urination.

The individual with a neurogenic bladder has limited or no control over bladder emptying. The muscles related to the elimination of urine function irregularly or inconsistently. A neurogenic bladder may overstretch (overdistend), or it may contract reflexively either frequently or irregularly. The sphincter muscle at the bladder outlet to the urethra often does not work in cooperation with the bladder contractions. There may be too little or too much sphincter tone, allowing urine to constantly dribble or prevent complete bladder emptying.

All of these conditions—overdistention of the bladder, frequent, irregular bladder contractions, and high sphincter tone—may contribute to increased bladder pressure and possible subsequent bladder and kidney disorders. Increased pressure in the bladder may lead to a back flow (reflux) of urine toward the kidneys causing infection or malfunction. A bladder that fails to empty completely provides a warm, moist environment in which bacteria may grow and cause infection in the bladder. The overdistention makes the bladder more susceptible to in-

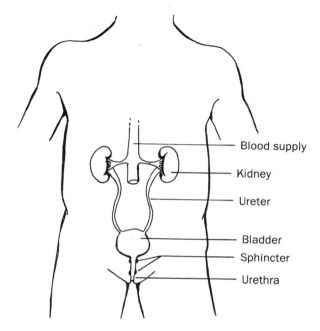

Figure 15.1.   Parts of the urinary tract, including particularly the bladder, urethra, and urinary sphincter.

fection and the high bladder pressure may lead to kidney infection or damage. Over time, recurrent kidney infections or exposure to increased pressure eventually cause kidney damage and impaired kidney function.

What Clean Intermittent Catheterization Involves

Clean intermittent catheterization involves inserting a plastic or rubber tube (a catheter) through the urethra (Figure 15.1) into the bladder. The tube bypasses the problem of the abnormal functioning of the sphincters and uretha, allowing the bladder to empty. The procedure is usually done every 3–4 hours during the day, or as prescribed by the student's physician. Regular, complete emptying of the bladder and prevention of overdistention of the bladder are the most critical elements in preventing urinary tract infections (Lapides, 1974).

Clean, rather than sterile, technique is used because (generally) there is not a high risk of infection with regular, intermittent catheterization. Urine is normally bacteria free, therefore sterile catheterization is not necessary to prevent infection. Infection is avoided when the bladder is emptied completely, at regular intervals, and overdistention is avoided. The materials used for catheterization can be washed with soap and water and used multiple times before discarding.

Before a program of clean intermittent catheterization is instituted, a urologist (a physician specializing in disorders of the urinary tract) carefully evaluates the student's urinary system. This includes testing kidney functioning, bladder pressure, and sphincter tone to determine if the student can benefit from intermittent catheterization in managing urinary incontinence. Intermittent catheterization is not appropriate for every student with a neurogenic bladder. Some students may learn to facilitate emptying the bladder using other techniques, such as external palpation.

A number of other students can participate in their own urinary management programs by learning to catheterize themselves. It has been suggested that, in order to be independent in self-catheterization, the student should be able to do problem solving at an approximate 5-year level, have adequate fine motor control to manipulate the catheter and his or her clothing, be motivated to learn self-catheterization, and have the support of his or her parents and other significant adults (University of Colorado School of Nursing, 1986). The student is taught to follow the same steps presented below, with particular emphasis on washing his or her hands, the catheter, and the genitalia. As with any learning task, individual students will require varying degrees of prompting and supervision before becoming independent in self-catheterization. Students who do not possess the prerequisite skills for self-catheterization should be encouraged to partially participate by washing their hands, holding equipment (e.g., cotton balls, urine container), lubricating the catheter, and so forth.

Medications

Several different medications may be prescribed by the student's physician to facilitate prevention of infection and promotion of dryness. A single dose of antibiotics may be given daily to prevent urinary tract infections in some students. Other medications act to relax the bladder, minimize irregular bladder contractions, or tighten the bladder sphincter. When the bladder is relaxed or the bladder sphincter tightened, larger quantities of urine are held in the bladder and clean intermittent catheterization is more successful in assisting students to remain dry for longer intervals. When medications are required during school hours they are administered within established school health guidelines. Table 15.1 lists some medications commonly used in urinary management (University of Colorado School of Nursing, 1986).

Table 15.1.   Medications commonly prescribed to manage urinary incontinence

Type	Comments	Side effects (Most frequent)
Propantheline bromide (brand name: Pro-Banthine)	Decreases motility of urinary tract Helps prevent wetness from bladder spasms by blocking nerve impulses to the bladder	Dry mouth, constipation, urinary retention, flushing, drowsiness, blurred vision, dizziness
Pseudoephedrine hydrochloride (brand names: Actifed; Dristan)	Acts on the neck of the bladder; causes tightening of the sphincter	Dryness of mouth, nose and throat, constipation, drowsiness, dizziness, headache
Oxybutynin chloride (brand name: Ditropan)	Blocks nerve impulses to bladder—thus preventing bladder spasms; also causes direct relaxation of the bladder muscle, anticholinergic (drying) effects	Dry mouth, decreased sweating, flushing, tachycardia, drowsiness, blurred vision
Phenylpropanolamine hydrochloride, Chlorpheniramine (brand name: Ornade)	Vaso-constriction, antihistamine; Promotes urine retention and helps prevent wetness	Drowsiness; excessive drying of the mouth, nose, and throat; nervousness and insomnia
Imipramine hydrochloride (brand name: Tofranil)	Anticholinergic, antihistaminic effects; Promotes urine retention and helps prevent wetness	Blurred vision, constipation, dry mouth

Clean intermittent catheterization. (1986). University of Colorado Health Sciences Center, School of Nursing. Distributed by Learner Managed Designs, Lawrence, KS; reprinted with permission.

PROCEDURES

Preparation for Clean Intermittent Catheterization

Preparation for CIC involves establishing a schedule, preparing an appropriate area, collecting the necessary materials, and providing the necessary clothing (if needed).

Catheterization Schedule, Area, and Materials Designated times for catheterization need to be established so that they take into account the times during which meals and snacks occur, and so that they cause the least disruption of the student's overall day. Generally a routine of catheterization every 3–4 hours is sufficient to maintain a healthy bladder. The area selected for catheterization must be a location that ensures the student's privacy. The area must also have a sink for proper cleansing during the preparation for and follow up of the procedure.

The materials needed for CIC should be available to the student, or teacher, in a small container, such as a small cosmetics bag or a plastic baggie, in order to facilitate privacy and convenience. The materials include a catheter (sometimes stored in a toothbrush holder) cotton balls and soap or several towelettes, a syringe, a urine collection container (usually the toilet), and antibacterial solution. Male students also require a water soluble lubricant. Equipment may be kept at school if storage facilities are available.

Incontinent Wear Even with careful management of the neurogenic bladder by clean intermittent catheterization and appropriate medications, complete dryness cannot be achieved for some students. Students who achieve good urinary control with these management techniques may also experience leakage or stress incontinence when laughing, sneezing, or coughing. Various types of specially designed underpants or absorbent liners used with regular underwear prevent wetness from becoming a source of social embarrassment. A variety of sources now exist for these products (see Appendix to this chapter) at varying cost to the student and family. Before a single product is selected, it is often helpful to request product samples to avoid undue expense.

Performing Clean Intermittent Catheterization

Catheterization procedures, as would be expected, differ for males and females. The procedures include positioning, cleansing the area, insertion of the catheter, draining the bladder, removing the catheter, and cleanup.

The student may use a position that is most comfortable and that encourages independent catheterization or partial participation. The student may be seated on the toilet, standing, or reclining, depending on his or her motor abilities. If a student has spasticity of the lower extremities or orthopedic deformities, consultation with the physical therapist will be helpful in selecting a comfortable position for catheterization. When the student is catheterized in a reclining position, it is helpful to place a towel, absorbent pad, or diaper underneath the hips to absorb any leakage or spilling. A container to collect the urine from the catheter is necessary if the urine will not be drained directly into the toilet. The catheterization equipment is laid out within easy reach of the student on a clean surface. Both the student and anyone assisting the student wash their hands with soap and water.

The genitalia are cleansed with a towelette or soap and water. If the student is a male then cleansing with soap is done in a circular motion starting at the opening at the tip of the penis and moving outward. The soap is rinsed off using the same motion with a clean cotton ball and water (Figure 15.2). If the student is a female then the labia are gently separated and the perineal area is cleansed with soap in a downward direction toward the rectum. This motion prevents bacteria at the rectum from being drawn toward the urethra. A separate clean cotton ball or towelette is used for each downward cleansing motion. Soap is rinsed off using the same downward motion with a clean cotton ball and water.

When the catheter is inserted for the *male student,* the catheter tip is first lubricated with water-soluble jelly (not vaseline). The penis is held erect to straighten the urethra and the catheter is gently inserted (Figure 15.3). Resistance is often felt during the insertion of the catheter. The insertion is continued with gentle pressure, changing the angle of the penis, or having the student take a deep breath to relax the muscles near the bladder sphincter. The catheter is inserted an additional 1–2 inches once urine begins to flow. When the urine flow stops the student is asked to cough, bear down, or come to a more upright position to be sure that the bladder is empty (Chapman, Hill, & Shurtleff, 1979).

Lubrication of the catheter tip generally is not necessary for *female students.* The catheter is gently inserted into the urethra approximately 2–3 inches or until urine flows (Figure 15.4). When the urine flow stops the student may be asked to cough, bear down, or come to a more upright position to ensure that the bladder is empty (Mapel, 1985). If the catheter is inadvertently dropped or inserted into the vagina, it is washed, rinsed, or wiped off. The catheterization procedure is then completed. Once the urine stops flowing, the catheter is gently re-

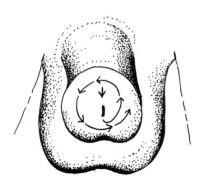

Figure 15.2.   The progression of cleansing for a male student.

moved. If more urine begins to drain as the catheter is withdrawn, removal is stopped and then continued when no more urine flows. When
the catheter has been removed, the genitalia are again washed with
soap and water or a towelette to remove any urine and to prevent odors.

Occasionally the physician may ask that an antibacterial solution
be instilled into the bladder as part of the catheterization procedure
(Wolraich, Hawtrey, Mapel, & Henderson, 1983). The implementation of
this procedure generally requires a trained and licensed health care
professional. The procedure involves first preparing a syringe with the
desired amount of antibacterial solution. When the urine flow stops, the
syringe is attached to the end of the catheter and the solution is gently
pushed into the bladder when the syringe plunger is depressed. When
the solution has been instilled, the catheter is gently removed with the
syringe attached and the catheter pinched to allow the solution to stay
in the bladder. Some antibacterial solutions stain readily (e.g., silver ni-
trate), so care must be taken that the solution does not soil the student's
clothing (Mapel, 1985). School health guidelines for administration of
medications during school hours are followed if a bladder instillation is
required.

After use the catheter is washed with soap and water between the
hands. A syringe may be used to push soapy water and rinse water
through the catheter. Once clean and air dried, the catheter is returned
to its carrying case.

When catheterization is required and handwashing facilities are
unavailable, the catheterization should proceed as scheduled since regular bladder emptying is more critical in preventing urinary tract infections than maintaining absolute cleanliness (Lapides, 1974). Sanitary

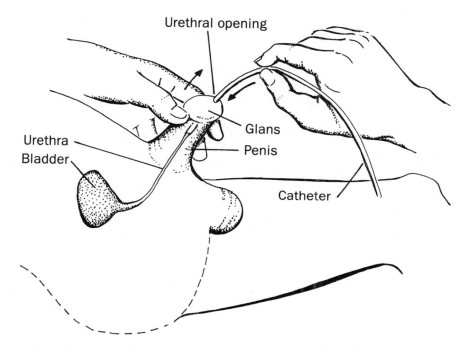

Figure 15.3.   The procedure used to insert the catheter through the urethra in the penis into the bladder.

wipes or moistened towelettes, although not sufficient for cleansing in routine catheterization, may be used for cleansing when soap and water are unavailable. Using separate dry catheters for each bladder emptying may be recommended at times for students with recurrent urinary tract infections.

Procedures Following Clean Intermittent Catheterization

The physician or health care worker in the school may require a recording of the amount or frequency of urination throughout the school day. These amounts should be recorded and reported to the health care worker or the student's family.

All catheters are washed at the end of the day, rinsed with a solution of equal parts of water and vinegar, and allowed to air dry through the night. Catheters that are regularly washed may be used for a period of 6–8 weeks before being discarded (Stauffer, 1984).

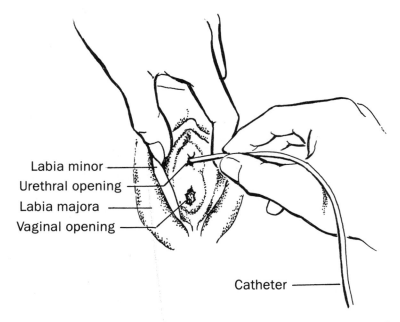

Labia minor
Urethral opening
Labia majora
Vaginal opening

Catheter

Figure 15.4.   The procedure used to insert the catheter through the urethra into the bladder for the female student.

Warning Signs

Although prevention of urinary tract infection is one goal of clean intermittent catheterization, infection may still occur for some students. A foul or strong urine odor is a common initial sign of bladder infection. Cloudiness or unusual urine color, bloody urine, nausea, fever, and increased dampness between catheterizations may also be signs of a urinary tract infection. Students with impaired sensation rarely report burning, urgency, or a sensation of bladder spasms. Any of these signs should be reported to the student's parents, school health care worker, and physician.

Infrequently, a small amount of bleeding may occur during catheterization of some students. Although not a cause for alarm, the parents should be notified so that this information can be conveyed to the student's physician. Inadequate lubrication of the catheter prior to insertion may contribute to small amounts of bleeding. Recurrent or excessive bleeding is extremely unusual and requires prompt reporting to the parents, school health care worker, and the student's physician.

Clean intermittent catheterization is a relatively simple procedure to perform. For the novice, however, meeting resistance when inserting the catheter can be disconcerting. This resistance occurs when the catheter reaches the bladder sphincter but subsides with continued, gentle pressure.

ADDITIONAL RESOURCES

School personnel will find the videotape *Clean Intermittent Catheterization,* developed by the University of Colorado, and other sources listed at the end of this chapter useful for additional information regarding clean intermittent catheterization. School nurses, nurse specialists in health clinics serving children and adults with myelomeningocele, or the student's urological specialist can provide assistance in adapting the information presented here to individual students needs. Discussion with school administration will be necessary to determine or develop policies related to performance of clean intermittent catheterization by school personnel other than school nurses and to make provisions for training and supervision of nonnursing personnel.

LITERATURE CITED

Action Committee on Myelodysplasia, Section on Urology, American Academy of Pediatrics.(1979). Current approaches to evaluation and management of children with myelomeningocele, *Pediatrics, 63*(4), 663–667.

Chapman, W., Hill, M., & Shurtleff, D.B. (1979). *Management of the neurogenic bowel and bladder.* Oak Brook, Illinois: Eterna Press.

Clarkson, J.D. (1982). Self catheterization training of a child with myelomeningocele. *American Journal of Occupational Therapy, 36*(2), 95–98.

Lapides, T. (1974). Neurogenic bladder, Principles of treatment. *Urologic Clinics of North America, 1*(1), 81–97.

Mapel, J. (1985). Introduction to Intermittent Catheterization. In M.L. Wolraich & M.H. Lozes (Eds.), *What you should know about your child with spina bifida.* Iowa City: Division of Developmental Disabilities, University Hospital School, University of Iowa.

Stauffer, D.T. (1984). Catheterization—a health procedure schools must be prepared to provide. *Journal of School Health, 554*(1), 37–38.

University of Colorado School of Nursing (1986). *Clean intermittent catheterization.* (Videotape and user's manual). Lawrence, KS: Learner Managed Designs, Inc.

Wolraich, M.L., Hawtrey, C., Mapel, J., & Henderson, M. (1983). Results of clean intermittent catheterization for children with neurogenic bladder. *Urology, 22*(5), 479–482.

Appendix

INCONTINENT WEAR DISTRIBUTORS

Diagnostic Medical Equipment Corp. (DIMEDCO)
63 Commercial Ave.
Garden City, NY 11530
Distributors of Hygienecare Incontinent Products

DriPride Division of Weyerhaueser
1159 Brynmawr
Itasca, IL 60143

Hospital Marketing & Management Services, Inc.
10 Southern Place
Lake Wylie, SC 29170
Distributors of Kanga Incontinent Pants

Humanacare International, Inc.
P.O. Box 838
East Brunswick, NJ 08816
Distributors of Dignity Incontinent Wear

Principle Business Enterprises, Inc.
P.O. Box 129
Dunbridge, OH 43414
Distributors of Tranquility Incontinent Wear

Undercover Products International U.S.A., Inc.
Suite F, 1980 Parker Court
Stone Mountain, GA 30087
Distributors of Hygi Incontinent Pants

Local medical supply companies may carry incontinent wear. Some large pharmaceutical chains and discount department stores also carry their own brands of incontinent products.

16

TRACHEOSTOMY CARE

The likelihood that schools will provide services to students with intact tracheostomies is increasing. This is true because, while the overall number of tracheostomies being performed for children is decreasing, the length of time tracheostomies remain in place is increasing (Carter & Benjamin, 1983; Line, Hawkins, Kahlstrom, MacLaughlin, & Ensley, 1986; Wetmore, Handler, & Potsic, 1982). The trend toward the long-term placement of tracheostomies has resulted primarily from the prolonged survival of children with multiple disabilities (Line et al., 1986). Since tracheostomies are remaining in children for longer periods, it is not uncommon for a child to be discharged from a hospital with a tracheostomy tube in place. For the student to then safely attend school, staff must be prepared to perform tracheostomy care during the school day.

Tracheostomy care is performed for the student with a tracheostomy to ensure that air moves easily in and out of the student's airway, to prevent the development of infection around the trachea or in the lungs, and to prevent irritation around the opening into the trachea.

OVERVIEW

A tracheostomy is an opening that is made by cutting the skin over the trachea and creating an opening (the stoma) into the trachea to permit air movement in and out of the lungs (Thomas, 1985). A hollow tube is placed into this opening. The tube, called a tracheostomy tube, is secured into place by cotton ties around the neck (Figure 16.1). The tube allows the student to breathe through the trachea rather than through the mouth and/or nose.

Tracheostomies are performed on children as a result of a variety of problems. These may include: obstruction of the upper airway, central nervous system disorders, congenital heart disease, respiratory distress syndrome, and craniofacial disorders (Wetmore et al., 1982). Tracheostomies can also be performed as an emergency procedure in the hospital.

The tracheostomy tube generally consists of three parts: the outer cannula (a), the inner cannula (b), and the obturator (c) (Figure 16.2). Or the tracheostomy tube may be a single tube with an obturator but no inner cannula (Figure 16.3). The tubes may be composed of silver or a silicone material. The silicone tubes are preferred for use with children because they conform to the student's airway. The smooth surface of these silicone tubes reduces the build-up of secretions on the inside of the tracheostomy tube (Tepas, 1983; Whaley & Wong, 1987). Students may have a tracheostomy open to the air, have humidified air passing

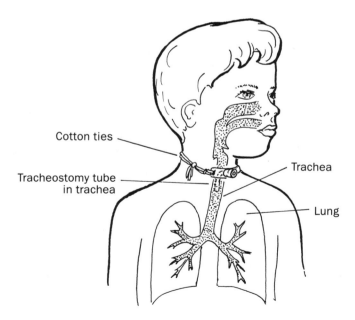

Figure 16.1.   Position of the tracheostomy tube.

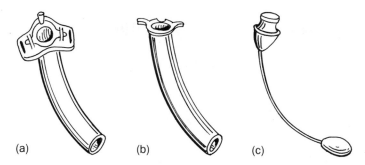

Figure 16.2.   Parts of the tracheostomy tube: the outer cannula (a), the inner cannula (b), and the obturator (c).

over the tracheostomy (Figure 16.4a), or be connected to a mechanical ventilator for control of, or assistance with breathing (Figure 16.4b).

Release from the hospital with the tracheostomy in place decreases the financial burden of prolonged hospitalization and helps avoid the negative effects of prolonged separation of the child from the family. The personal attention and care given to the child by properly trained parents can compensate for the sophistication of the hospital. The continuity of care from hospital to home, and the decreased risk of becoming infected with organisms present in the hospital, are advantages of home care for the person with a tracheostomy. Parents, therefore, are routinely trained to care for the child with the tracheostomy in the home. It has been recommended that at least two family members (usually parents) be taught tracheostomy care, and when possible, a third person with whom the child is familiar also should be instructed (Ruben et al., 1982). If school staff are informed prior to the time that a

Figure 16.3.   A tracheostomy tube with a single tube and obturator.

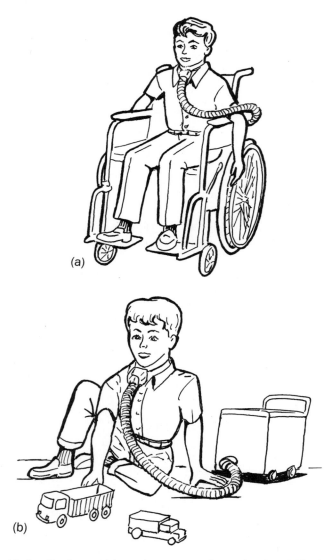

Figure 16.4.   Students with tracheostomy tubes using humidified air (a) or a mechanical ventilator (b).

student is to receive a tracheostomy, one or more staff persons should also be trained with the parents in the procedures involved in tracheostomy care. Training should also include preparation for cardiopulmonary resuscitation of the student with a tracheostomy, as well as routine tracheostomy care.

Tracheostomy care includes removal (suctioning) of secretions from the student's trachea, cleaning the inner cannula of the tracheostomy tube, care of the skin around the stoma, changing the tracheostomy ties, and changing the tracheostomy tube.

PROCEDURES

Preparation for Tracheostomy Care

Supplies and necessary equipment must be available for tracheostomy care during hours when the student is in school. It is generally advised that the home, and school, have supplies available for a 2-week period. The necessary supplies for removing secretions from the trachea include: suction catheter (sterile or clean), gloves (sterile or clean), saline (sterile), water (sterile or clean), container (sterile or clean), and a suction machine (Kennedy, Johnson, & Sturdevant, 1982; Persons, 1987). The supplies necessary for cleaning the inner cannula include: hydrogen peroxide; saline or water (sterile or clean); pipe cleaners or a small tube brush; and two containers (sterile or clean), one for the hydrogen peroxide and one for saline (King, Wieck, & Dyer, 1983; Persons, 1987). For caring for the skin around the stoma, necessary supplies include: cotton tipped applicators, tracheostomy bib or dressing (sterile or clean), hydrogen peroxide, and paper cups (clean) (Kennedy et al., 1982; Persons, 1987). The supplies necessary for changing the ties include: twill (cotton) tape, scissors, and a roll for the shoulders (rolled towel) (Kennedy et al., 1982). For changing the tube the necessary supplies include: a spare tracheostomy tube with ties in place, scissors, and a roll for the shoulders (rolled towel) (Kennedy et al., 1982).

Certain supplies used may be either sterile or clean, depending on the protocol being followed for the student's care. Tracheostomy care using clean technique has been shown to be associated with less infection than care using sterile technique in the period following the surgical creation of the tracheostomy (Harris & Hyman, 1984). Clean techniques involve thorough handwashing, the use of disinfectants and warm water to clean the materials, and air drying. Sterile techniques generally require either boiling or steam cleaning. Because the controversy of clean versus sterile technique has not been resolved, procedures established by the hospital or the physician performing the tracheostomy should be followed.

A suction machine, usually used in cleaning the trachea, needs to be available in the classroom. A humidifier may also need to be available for the student during school hours to prevent the drying out of secretions in the trachea and lungs. The suction machine and humidifier must be plugged in at all times and placed in the area where the student spends most of the school day. One suction machine is used for one student. This implies that a suction machine should be available for each student with a tracheostomy. A DeLee suction catheter with mucus trap is necessary equipment for the student needing suctioning during travel to and from school (Figure 16.5). Gentle suction is created by sucking on one end of the tubing after the other end has been placed into the student's tracheostomy to remove secretions (Figure 16.6). A portable, battery operated suction machine may also be used for suctioning the student during travel (Kennedy et al., 1982).

The staff person performing the tracheostomy care for the student initially prepares the student for the procedure by informing the student of what to expect. This explanation is given to the student even though the cognitive ability of the student might be limited. Efforts should be made to relax and calm the student. If the student is unable to lie quietly during the care procedure, the student may need to be restrained during the procedure by another person. Unexpected movements by the student can result in ineffective suctioning or potential damage to the stu-

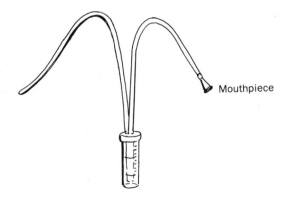

Mouthpiece

Figure 16.5.   A DeLee suction catheter with a mucus trap.

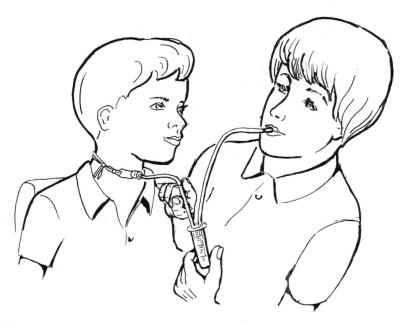

Figure 16.6. A DeLee suction catheter being used to remove mucus through a tracheostomy tube.

dent's trachea. Tracheostomy care, particularly suctioning, should be done before the student is fed (Kennedy et al., 1982; Ruben et al., 1982).

Performing Tracheostomy Care

Performing tracheostomy care involves suctioning to remove secretions, cleaning the inner cannula of the tracheostomy, care of the skin around the stoma, changing the ties, and changing the tracheostomy tube. In order to reduce the risk of infection it is critical that all materials be prepared using clean or sterile techniques and that staff carry out thorough handwashing. The sink used for these procedures must be separate from the sink used for food preparation.

Removal of Secretions from the Trachea Signs indicating the student's need for suctioning include: restlessness and an inability to be calmed, difficulty breathing and/or faster breathing, a frightened look, flaring of the student's nostrils, pale or bluish color around the student's mouth, or bubbles of mucus that are seen or heard at the opening of the tracheostomy tube (Perry, 1982).

To facilitate suctioning, the student is placed flat on the back with the head elevated (Persons, 1987). The suction catheter is connected to the suction machine and the suction machine is turned on (Figure 16.7). Sterile water is poured into the container. Gloves are worn if they are recommended for the specific procedure established for the student. Two to three drops of sterile saline may be placed into the student's trachea before suctioning in order to stimulate the student to cough (Kennedy et al., 1982). The saline also helps loosen secretions and crusts inside the trachea to allow them to be removed more easily by the suction catheter (Whaley & Wong, 1987).

The suction catheter is inserted to the depth recommended by the student's established procedure. The catheter must be inserted deep enough to remove secretions that can be heard. Suction is applied to the catheter after it reaches the maximum depth and as the catheter is withdrawn. Actual suction is created by placing a finger over an opening in the catheter and is terminated by removing the finger (Figure 16.8). As the catheter is withdrawn, it is gently rotated.

Because the student's airway is obstructed during suctioning, each insertion and withdrawal of the suction catheter should take no longer

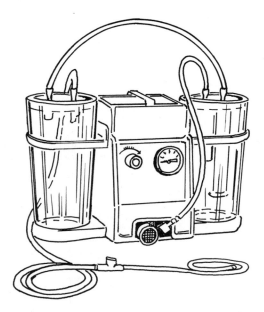

Figure 16.7.   A suction machine used to remove mucus through a tracheostomy tube.

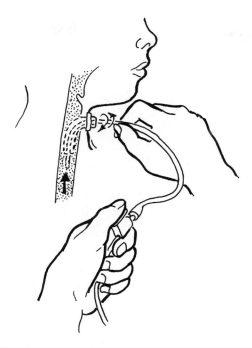

Figure 16.8.   The placement of the finger on a catheter to create suction when using a suction machine to remove mucus through a tracheostomy tube.

than 10–15 seconds (no longer than 5 seconds in an infant). A 30- to 60-second rest period should be allowed between insertions of the catheter for suctioning to allow the student to briefly recover (Whaley & Wong, 1987). If the student is on a ventilator, two staff persons are needed to perform suctioning of the tracheostomy. One person detaches the ventilator while the other suctions the tracheostomy tube. The student may require ventilations between insertions of the suction catheter. These ventilations may be provided with an Ambu bag if needed (Figure 16.9).

The suction catheter is rinsed between insertions into the trachea by suctioning sterile water to flush the inside of the catheter (tap water may be used depending on the established procedure). Suctioning is stopped when no more secretions are seen or heard from the tracheostomy tube.

The student may spontaneously cough up secretions to the top of the tracheostomy tube. A bulb syringe (Figure 16.10) may be used to

Figure 16.9.   An Ambu bag used to provide ventilation between episodes of suctioning.

retrieve the secretions and prevent them from going back down the trachea. The bulb syringe is used for surface suctioning (Kennedy et al., 1982) and should never be placed into the tracheostomy tube.

Cleaning the Inner Cannula of the Tracheostomy   The inner cannula needs to be cleaned when secretions stick to its sides and are unable to be suctioned out. The inner cannula is removed from the outer cannula to be cleaned two to three times a day or as often as needed (Kennedy et al., 1982). The inner cannula may be removed prior to suctioning and may be cleaned at this time (Ruben et al., 1982). Gloves may be worn when removing the inner cannula. The inner cannula is removed and placed into a container with hydrogen peroxide. After soaking, pipe cleaners or a small tube brush can be used to clean the inside of the inner cannula. The inner cannula is rinsed with water or saline and replaced into the tracheostomy tube in the student's throat (Persons, 1987).

Care of the Skin Around the Stoma   The skin around the stoma must be cleaned daily (Kennedy et al., 1982) or more often as secretions collect on the tracheostomy bib or dressing (Figure 16.11). The old tracheostomy bib is removed from beneath the student's tracheostomy tube. The skin around the stoma is cleansed with an applicator wet with one-half strength hydrogen peroxide and water. This is followed by

Figure 16.10.   A bulb syringe used to assist in removing mucus from the surface of the tracheostomy.

cleansing the skin with water or saline soaked applicators. Dried or crusted secretions are removed. The skin around the stoma is dried with a dry applicator. The clean tracheostomy bib is then slid beneath the tracheostomy tube (Kennedy et al., 1982; Persons, 1987; Rouses, 1984). The student having a tracheostomy for a long period might not use a bib or dressing.

   Changing Tracheostomy Ties   Tracheostomy ties are changed when they become soiled, when the tracheostomy tube is changed, or when the bib or dressing around the stoma is changed. The ties should be changed at least daily (Perry, 1982) and this is usually done at home. The ties, however, may become soiled at school and require changing. Soiled ties left on the student's skin can result in irritation.

   A roll is placed under the student's shoulders to allow the neck to bend back and the tracheostomy area to be exposed. The old tracheostomy ties are slid to the bottom of the slots and the new ties are threaded into the upper half of one slot. Both ends are brought around behind the patient's neck and one end is threaded through the other slot. The ties are tied into a square knot so that one or two fingers can fit between the ties and the student's neck (Figure 16.12). Only then are the old ties cut and removed. A folded gauze pad or piece of foam can be placed between the patient's neck and the square knot to prevent skin irritation from the ties (Dunleap, 1987; Kennedy et al., 1982).

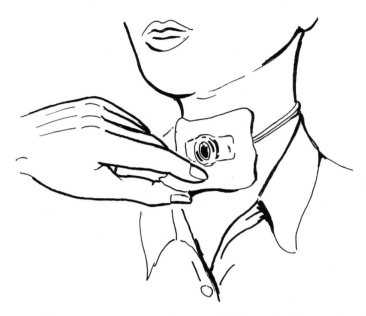

Figure 16.11.   The dressing used to assist in keeping the tracheostomy clean.

Changing the Tracheostomy Tube   The amount of secretions produced by the student will determine how often the tube will need to be changed (Ruben et al., 1982). Although weekly tube changes have been recommended (Kennedy et al., 1982), the student's own established procedure for tracheostomy care must be followed. These changes usually take place in the home.

The student may need to be restrained to prevent movement of the head or neck. The active or resisting student will require restraint to prevent movement and allow easy removal and replacement of the tracheostomy tube. The roll is placed under the student's shoulders to allow the neck to bend back and the tracheostomy area to be exposed. The old ties are cut and the tube is removed from the student's neck. The new tube is gently inserted into the stoma in the neck as one piece, with the ties and the obturator in place. The obturator is then removed (Kennedy et al., 1982; Perry, 1982) (Figure 16.13). The ties are tied at the side of the neck as described under the "Changing Tracheostomy Ties" section of this chapter. It has been suggested that the tube change occur in the early morning before breakfast and before the student is fully awake because the process can cause some distress. This may make the pro-

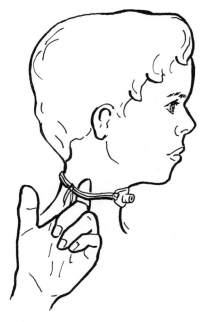

Figure 16.12.   Placement of ties for the tracheostomy tube.

cedure easier for the student and the persons changing the tube (Kennedy et al., 1982).

Procedures Following Tracheostomy Care

School staff should wash their hands and the cleaning equipment thoroughly after performing tracheostomy care for the student. Hands are washed and equipment cleaned at a sink that is not used for food preparation. School staff should make certain that adequate supplies are available for the next time tracheostomy care is given.

Supplies that are used only once for tracheostomy care are disposed of in a plastic bag that can be sealed airtight. If supplies are reused, they must be cleaned by following the procedure established for the student's care. Cleaning suction catheters for reuse has been described in the literature (Foster & Hoskins, 1981; Kennedy et al., 1982; Ruben et al., 1982; Shabino, Erlandson, & Kopta, 1986). The tracheostomy tube that is reused must be sterilized after being thoroughly cleaned (Kennedy et al., 1982; Ruben et al., 1982).

Figure 16.13.   Replacement of the tracheostomy tube.

Sterile water and sterile saline need not be purchased; they can be made easily (Kennedy et al., 1982; Ruben et al., 1982; Scipien, Barnard, Chard, Howe, & Phillips, 1986). The suction bottle and humidifier should be cleaned at the end of the school day to prevent the growth and spread of organisms to the student (Kennedy et al., 1982).

The care given the student should be documented in the student's records and the student's behaviors during a specific aspect of tracheostomy care should be noted. The amount, consistency, color, and odor of secretions removed from the trachea and the condition of the skin around the stoma are also described. Placing this information in the student's records facilitates communication between the person giving the care and the student's parents and other school staff working with the student.

Warning Signs

The student with a tracheostomy can develop problems related to the tracheostomy tube, the skin around the stoma, the trachea, the lungs, and the equipment needed to provide care. The most common complication is partial or complete blockage of the tracheostomy tube (Ruben et al., 1982). The tube can be blocked by a mucus plug or other object;

this can be life-threatening for the student. This problem is described under the "Signs of an Emergency" section of this chapter.

The tracheostomy tube can also become completely or partially dislodged. If the tube comes completely out of the stoma, a new, sterile tube should be inserted. If a sterile tube is not available, the old tube must be reinserted (Ruben et al., 1982) and the health care worker notified. If the tube cannot be reinserted, one person should stay with the student while another person calls the ambulance. To ensure that the tube does not come out of the stoma, the ties should be checked periodically to ensure that the tube is secure. The student should never be left unattended with the ties of the tracheostomy tube untied or removed. In addition, a spare sterile tracheostomy tube should be available at all times (Persons, 1987). It may be helpful for school staff to prepare for this situation by role playing what they would do if the student's tracheostomy tube became dislodged.

Respiratory distress can occur for many reasons. School staff need to watch for difficulty breathing or abnormally rapid respirations. Therefore the student's temperature, pulse, and respirations should be routinely checked to identify what is normal for the student. Abnormally rapid respirations or difficulty breathing should be responded to by the health care worker in the school and may require immediate attention by the student's physician (Ruben et al., 1982).

Respiratory tract infections continue to be a major complication of a tracheostomy (Harris & Hyman, 1984). When the student has a respiratory infection, the secretions may become thicker, change color, and develop an odor. The student may also require suctioning more often than usual (Ruben et al., 1982). If odor or change in color of the secretions lasts for 12–24 hours, the student's physician must be notified (Kennedy et al., 1982). If the student develops a temperature of 101° Fahrenheit, the health care worker in the school and possibly the student's physician are to be notified (Ruben et al., 1982).

Respiratory infections may be avoided by following the clean or sterile procedure for tracheostomy care. Careful handwashing is also necessary before and after performance of the tracheostomy care. The tracheostomy must be protected from objects such as dust, animal hair, bugs, toys, or food entering the tracheostomy and causing irritation. Substances such as hair sprays, perfumes, smoke, or cleaning agents with ammonia, can cause irritation to the student's trachea and lungs and should be avoided (Kennedy et al., 1982). On days when the outdoor temperatures are below freezing, cold air should be kept out of the tracheostomy with a handkerchief loosely tied around the student's neck. This may also be done on dusty days to prevent dust particles from causing dry, crusting mucus to develop (Kennedy et al., 1982). The student may also be given more fluids to help maintain loose and thin secretions (Perry, 1982).

Blood tinged mucus may indicate that the student is being suctioned too frequently, that the pressure of the suction machine is too great, or that there is not enough humidity (Kennedy et al., 1982; Perry, 1982; Ruben et al., 1982). If the student has bright red mucus or prolonged bleeding, the health care worker in the school and the student's physician must be notified immediately (Ruben et al., 1982).

Skin irritation may develop around the stoma. If excessive redness or pimples develop, only water should be used to clean around the stoma. The concentration of humidity over the stoma may need to be reduced (Kennedy et al., 1982). If a rash, drainage, or unusual odor develops around the stoma, the health care worker in the school should be notified. The student's physician may also be contacted for advice (Perry, 1982). Unnecessary movement of the tracheostomy tube should be avoided to reduce irritation to the trachea and the skin around the stoma (Persons, 1987).

The ability to speak is a concern for the student with a tracheostomy. Air from the lungs is not passing through the vocal cords, as occurs when speech is normally produced. The student may be able to only make some noises as some air passes through the vocal cords. Because of this inability to speak, the student may not be able to alert others to a need for help. The student in respiratory distress will need another method to call for assistance. A bell, attached to a student's limb, has been suggested as a method to use to call for help. The student in respiratory distress most likely will not lie quietly, but will become restless and ring for help (Ruben et al., 1982). Alternate modes of communication must be developed by the language therapist to enable the student to ask for help.

Equipment, such as the suction machine, may malfunction. A back-up suction machine or alternate method of suctioning should be available until the malfunctioning machine can be replaced. The utility company should be notified that the student with life-sustaining equipment is in the school so that procedures can be established in the event of a power failure (Ruben et al., 1982).

SIGNS OF AN EMERGENCY

The most critical complication for the student with a tracheostomy tube is blockage of the tube. When the tube is blocked, the student will not be able to move air in and out of the lungs. An attempt should be made to suction the tube (Kennedy et al., 1982). If the student has a mucus plug that is not removable by suctioning, dropping one ml. (milliliter) of sterile water into the tracheostomy tube may stimulate a cough that can dislodge the mucus plug (Ruben et al., 1982).

If the student does not start breathing or if the suction catheter cannot be easily inserted, the tracheostomy tube should be removed and a new one inserted. If the student does not breathe, the student's mouth and nose should be covered. The trained professional then places his or her mouth over the stoma to form a seal and delivers two quick puffs of air. Another staff person should call the emergency medical services and make arrangements for transportation to the hospital. If the student has not responded, the pulse is located. If no pulse is felt, the staff person begins compressions of the chest as recommended in Chapter 8, Cardiopulmonary Resuscitation (*Heartsaver Manual,* 1987; Kennedy et al., 1982).

ADDITIONAL RESOURCES

A support team for tracheostomy care includes a health care professional in the school, an equipment company, and local emergency medical services (EMS) or a local rescue unit. Tracheostomy care can be taught by qualified persons such as nurses and respiratory therapists who have taught the student's parents. The health care professional in the school can provide immediate information about tracheostomy care and about the need to contact persons outside the school for assistance. An equipment company can provide assistance when equipment malfunctions and can provide information about the equipment being used. The local emergency medical services can provide assistance in emergency situations and can transport the student to a hospital for further care. Plans must be made for the possibility of power failure and alternate methods of providing care for the student. Telephone numbers for the emergency medical services, the equipment company, the student's physician, and the local hospital should be placed near the telephone.

A support system is necessary for the school staff working with a student with a tracheostomy. This support system could include the nursing specialist from the hospital where the student receives care, the community health nurse, the student's physician, a social worker, and the health care worker in the school. Frequent and open communications among school staff, health care professionals in the community, and the student's parents are vital to ensuring proper ongoing care for the student.

LITERATURE CITED

Carroll, P.F. (1985). Changing the suction catheter each time you enter a tracheostomy—Con. *Nursing Life, 5*(3), 45.

Carter, P., & Benjamin, B. (1983). Ten-year review of pediatric tracheotomy. *Annals of Otology, Rhinology, & Laryngology, 92*(4), 398–400

Dunleap, E. (1987). Safe and easy ways to secure breathing tubes. *Registered Nurse, 50*(8), 26–27.

Foster, S., & Hoskins, D. (1981). Home care of the child with a tracheostomy tube. *Pediatric Clinics of North America, 28*(4), 855–857.

Harris, R.B., & Hyman, R.B. (1984). Clean vs. sterile tracheostomy care and level of pulmonary infection. *Nursing Research, 33*(2), 80–85.

Heartsaver manual: A student handbook for cardiopulmonary resuscitation and first aid for choking. (1987). Dallas: American Heart Association.

Kennedy, A.H., Johnson, W.G., & Sturdevant, E.W. (1982). An educational program for families of children with tracheostomies. *The American Journal of Maternal Child Nursing, 7*(1), 42–49.

King, E.M., Wieck, L., & Dyer, M. (1983). *Quick reference to pediatric nursing procedures.* Philadelphia: J.B. Lippincott.

Line, W.S., Hawkins, D.B., Kahlstrom, E.J., MacLaughlin, E.F., & Ensley, J.L. (1986). Tracheostomy in infants and young children: The changing perspective 1970–1985. *Laryngoscope, 96*(5), 510–515.

Perry, K. (1982). *Care of the tracheostomy.* Kansas City, MO.: The Children's Mercy Hospital.

Persons, C.B. (1987). *Critical care procedures and protocols: A nursing process approach.* Philadelphia: J.B. Lippincott.

Rouses, S. (1984). An illustrated guide to trach care. *Registered Nurse, 47*(5), 48–50.

Ruben, R.J., Newton, J., Jornsay, D., Stein, R., Chambers, H., Liquori, J., & Lawrence, C. (1982). Home care of the pediatric patient with a tracheostomy. *Annals of Otology, Rhinology, & Laryngology, 91*(6), 633–640.

Scipien, G.M., Barnard, M.U., Chard, M.A., Howe, J., & Phillips, P.J. (1986). *Comprehensive pediatric nursing.* New York: McGraw-Hill.

Shabino, C.L., Erlandson, A.L., & Kopta, L.A. (1986). Home cleaning-disinfection procedure for tracheal suction catheters. *Pediatric Infectious Disease, 5*(1), 54–58.

Tepas, J.J. (1983). Tracheostomy in infants and children. *Ear, Nose, Throat Journal, 62*, 60–67.

Thomas, C.L. (1985). *Taber's cyclopedic medical dictionary.* Philadelphia: F.A. Davis.

Wetmore, R.F., Handler, S.D., & Potsic, W.P. (1982). Pediatric tracheostomy experience during the past decade. *Annals of Otology, Rhinology, & Laryngology, 91*(6), 628–632.

Whaley, L.F., & Wong, D.L. (1987). *Nursing care of infants and children.* St. Louis: C.V. Mosby.

INDEX

1/1997
DVD 2014

DUE DA